Routledge Guides to the Great Books

The Routledge Guidebook to Machiavelli's *The Prince*

Niccolò Machiavelli's *The Prince* is one of the most influential works in the history of political thought, and to this day we wonder whether his "Machiavellian" advice on how to acquire and maintain power is an education in evil or clear-eyed realism. How are we to grasp the meaning of Machiavelli's text, in both his time and our own? And how does a contemporary reader get to grips with a book full of references to the politics of the early sixteenth century?

The Routledge Guidebook to Machiavelli's The Prince provides readers with the historical background, textual analysis, and other relevant information needed for a greater understanding and appreciation of this classic text. This guidebook introduces:

- the historical, political, and intellectual context in which Machiavelli was working;
- the key ideas developed by Machiavelli throughout the text and the examples he uses to illustrate them;
- the relationship of *The Prince* to the *Discourses on Livy* and Machiavelli's other works.

Featuring a chronology, map, and suggestions for further reading throughout, this book is an invaluable guide for anyone who wants to be able to engage more fully with *The Prince*.

John T. Scott is Professor of Political Science at the University of California, Davis.

THE ROUTLEDGE GUIDES TO THE GREAT BOOKS
Series Editor: Anthony Gottlieb

The Routledge Guides to the Great Books provide ideal introductions to the texts which have shaped Western Civilization. The Guidebooks explore the arguments and ideas contained in the most influential works from some of the most brilliant thinkers who have ever lived, from Aristotle to Marx and Newton to Wollstonecraft. Each Guidebook opens with a short introduction to the author of the great book and the context within which they were working and concludes with an examination of the lasting significance of the book. *The Routledge Guides to the Great Books* will therefore provide students everywhere with complete introductions to the most significant books of all time.

Available:

Augustine's Confessions
Catherine Conybeare

Aquinas' Summa Theologiae
Jason T. Eberl

Kierkegaard's Fear and Trembling
John A. Lippett

Mill's On Liberty
Jonathan Riley

Einstein's Relativity
James Trefil

Gramsci's Prison Notebooks
John Schwarzmantel

Thoreau's Civil Disobedience
Bob Pepperman Taylor

Descartes' Meditations
Gary Hatfield

Hobbes' Leviathan
Glen Newey

Galileo's Dialogue
Maurice A. Finocchiaro

Wittgenstein's Philosophical Investigations
Marie McGinn

Aristotle's Nicomachean Ethics
Gerard J. Hughes

Heidegger's Being and Time
Stephen Mulhall

Hegel's Phenomenology of Spirit
Robert Stern

Locke's Essay Concerning Human Understanding
E. J. Lowe

Plato's Republic
Nickolas Pappas

Wollstonecraft's A Vindication of the Rights of Woman
Sandrine Bergès

The Routledge Guidebook to Machiavelli's *The Prince*

John T. Scott

Routledge
Taylor & Francis Group

LONDON AND NEW YORK

First published 2016
by Routledge
2 Park Square, Milton Park, Abingdon, Oxon OX14 4RN

and by Routledge
711 Third Avenue, New York, NY 10017

Routledge is an imprint of the Taylor & Francis Group, an informa business

British Library Cataloguing in Publication Data
A catalogue record for this book is available from the British Library

Library of Congress Cataloging in Publication Data
Names: Scott, John T., 1963– author.
Title: The routledge guidebook to Machiavelli's The prince / John T. Scott.
Description: Abingdon, Oxon ; New York, NY : Routledge, 2016. |
Series: The Routledge guides to the great books | Includes
bibliographical references and index.
Identifiers: LCCN 2015039802| ISBN 9780415707237 (hardback : alk. paper) |
ISBN 9780415707268 (pbk. : alk. paper) | ISBN 9781315726373 (e-book)
Subjects: LCSH: Machiavelli, Niccoláo, 1469-1527. Principe.
Classification: LCC JC143.M3946 S38 2016 | DDC 320.1–dc23
LC record available at http://lccn.loc.gov/2015039802

ISBN: 978-0-415-70723-7 (hbk)
ISBN: 978-0-415-70726-8 (pbk)
ISBN: 978-1-315-72637-3 (ebk)

Typeset in Times New Roman
by Taylor & Francis Books

CONTENTS

Series Editor's Preface   vii
Acknowledgments   viii
Introduction   ix
Map of Italy   xvii
Chronology   xviii

1 Machiavelli's Life and Times   1

2 The Composition of *The Prince*   17

3 The Title and Dedicatory Letter   22

4 Acquisition and the Emergence of the New Prince   40

5 The New Prince   73

6 Criminals, Citizens, Popes, and Other Types of Princes   101

7 Arms   128

8 Virtue and Vice   148

9 Prudence   205

10 Virtue, Fortune, and the Redemption of Italy   219

11 Machiavelli's Political Thought and His Legacy   239

References   261
Index   266

SERIES EDITOR'S PREFACE

"The past is a foreign country," wrote a British novelist, L. P. Hartley: "they do things differently there."

The greatest books in the canon of the humanities and sciences can be foreign territory, too. This series of guidebooks is a set of excursions written by expert guides who know how to make such places become more familiar.

All the books covered in this series, however long ago they were written, have much to say to us now, or help to explain the ways in which we have come to think about the world. Each volume is designed not only to describe a set of ideas, and how they developed, but also to evaluate them. This requires what one might call a bifocal approach. To engage fully with an author, one has to pretend that he or she is speaking to us; but to understand a text's meaning, it is often necessary to remember its original audience, too. It is all too easy to mistake the intentions of an old argument by treating it as a contemporary one.

The *Routledge Guides to the Great Books* are aimed at students in the broadest sense, not only those engaged in formal study. The intended audience of the series is all those who want to understand the books that have had the largest effects.

AJG
October 2012

ACKNOWLEDGMENTS

I would like to acknowledge a number of individuals who have assisted me. First, I would like to thank the students who took my graduate seminars devoted to Machiavelli's *The Prince* and then the *Discourses on Livy*, and especially Rex Stem, my friend and colleague who made these seminars a very enjoyable teaching collaboration, and who then read the manuscript of this book and offered useful suggestions. Christine Henderson also read the manuscript and offered helpful suggestions, as did William Connell, who also indulged me when I dared to offer recommendations concerning his translation. Alison Gushue read and edited the manuscript with great care and good judgment, and prepared the index. Finally, it is customary most of the time for an author who desires to acquire grace with his spouse to dedicate their books to him or her, and in this matter I gladly follow custom and dedicate this book to my wife, Adrienne.

INTRODUCTION

The Prince is surely one of the most infamous books ever written. Perhaps even more infamous than the shocking little book is its author, Niccolò Machiavelli. What other author is so widely known for inspiring an adjective? To call someone "Machiavellian" instantly and universally evokes a whole host of associations: the end justifies the means, playing the fox and the lion, manipulation, power politics, realism, etc. The author of *The Prince* as a supposed "teacher of evil" has long been associated with the devil, Old Nick. Yet when we call someone Machiavellian, we usually do so by tempering our moral condemnation with a certain begrudging admiration. For to be Machiavellian means to perceive the world as it actually is and not how we would like it to be, to see through appearances and posturing, to be brutally honest with oneself even while being dishonest with others. To be Machiavellian is to be nobody's fool. Christopher Marlowe captured our ambivalence when he brought Machiavelli on stage to introduce his play *The Jew of Malta* (1589/90), testimony to the fact that the author of *The Prince* has provoked similar reactions over the past 500 years:

> To some perhaps my name is odious;
> But such as love me, guard me from their tongues,

And let them know that I am Machiavel,
And weigh not men, and therefore not men's words.
Admir'd I am of those that hate me most:
Though some speak openly against my books,
Yet will they read me ... .

To read *The Prince* is to risk temptation. If Satan promises that eating the forbidden fruit will give us the knowledge of good and evil, our tempter is once again captured by Marlowe: "I hold there is no sin but ignorance." In short, to be a Machiavellian is to maneuver through politics, society, business, or whatever sphere in which we act, but above all politics, with the courage of the lack of our convictions.

Such is the nearly universal reputation of Machiavelli and of his supposedly Machiavellian treatise *The Prince*. But how accurate or adequate is it? Almost since its publication, readers of *The Prince* have sensed something afoul in the common view of Machiavelli as an unscrupulous teacher of princes. Oddly enough, they sensed something afoul because they knew that the author of *The Prince* was not foul, an immoral person, but was in fact a Florentine patriot and republican. How could such a man be the author of *The Prince*? After all, in his other major political work, the *Discourses on Livy*, Machiavelli avows his preference for republics over princes, and he also does not hesitate to call some of the very same rulers he politely terms "princes" in *The Prince* by their true name: "tyrants." Perhaps *The Prince* is not what it seems. Maybe his little treatise is actually a kind of satire on princes, a book meant to reveal the reality of princely rule in order to teach us how to prevent it or to avoid its temptations. Such was the view of one of the greatest political thinkers to come after Machiavelli, Jean-Jacques Rousseau, who wrote in his *Social Contract* (1762) that the author of *The Prince* hid his true intentions while living under Medici rule, that Machiavelli was a republican and his book a satire. Yet this view cannot be so simple, for if we turn to Machiavelli's book on republics, the *Discourses on Livy*, we find him giving some of the very same unscrupulous advice he gives in *The Prince* to republics and princes alike. What were Machiavelli's intentions in writing *The Prince*?

Machiavelli's portrait shows a man not so much smiling as smirking. Is he smirking at us? Or are we imagining that his slight smile is a sneer because of his longtime reputation? Such is the problem we encounter in trying to read *The Prince*, for almost no one picks up Machiavelli's work without some preconception about the author and his work. The reader predisposed to find a teacher of evil or at least amoral instruction on how to acquire and maintain political power will not be disappointed. Such a reader might point to chapter 7 and Machiavelli's evident relish in relating the theatrical executions and other acts performed by his example there of Cesare Borgia. Other readers looking for Machiavelli the republican might, like Jean-Jacques Rousseau, see his choice of this "execrable hero" as proof that *The Prince* is a satire. Such readers might point to chapter 9 on "civil principalities" as an indication of the work's republican thrust, or perhaps turn away from *The Prince* entirely and instead look to the *Discourses on Livy*. Still other readers see the concluding chapter of *The Prince* calling for a prince to liberate Italy from the "barbarian" outsiders and to unify Italy as the key to Machiavelli's intention, a project that would justify the less than savory means necessary for achieving this end. All of these readings of *The Prince* and many others have been put forward, and all of them can find support in the text. Perhaps *The Prince* is less a book in the "mirror-of-princes" genre than a mirror that reflects back to the observer what she or he expects or hopes to find in the book.

This guidebook offers a reading of *The Prince* that attempts to approach the work with as few preconceptions as possible. Rather than providing what I would claim is a single, definitive interpretation of *The Prince*, I have tried to honor the various interpretations of Machiavelli's little treatise which have been advanced almost since the work first appeared and which have endured for centuries, on the assumption that these different interpretations each have something—if not everything—to say about *The Prince*. In this way, then, I have not felt the need to "answer" all of the questions posed by the text, and while I sometimes offer what I find a satisfying solution to some of these puzzles, on other occasions I sketch some alternative solutions, and occasionally I leave the puzzle as a puzzle.

Two further remarks are necessary about the interpretative strategy I follow in this guidebook. First, I proceed in my analysis of *The Prince* on the assumption that Machiavelli is offering a consistent and coherent teaching in his book, which is not the same thing as saying that there is a single, univocal teaching in *The Prince*, since Machiavelli may in fact have had more than one purpose and more than one audience in mind when writing his book. This assumption of consistency and coherence is, of course, always susceptible of being proved wrong when we find that Niccolò too nods. However, I believe that such an interpretative assumption is both more charitable to the author, and especially to an author of Machiavelli's stature, and more profitable for understanding the work since it demands that we puzzle over the text more carefully. Second, despite the interpretative assumption of the consistency and coherence of the text, the manifest ambiguities and challenges we encounter in *The Prince* mean that reading the work does not simply generate any clear, single interpretation. That said, I do not believe that *The Prince* is susceptible to any interpretation whatsoever; some interpretations are more satisfying than others because they explain more of the text than others or offer more comprehensive and unified readings of the work by tying together its various strands more persuasively. It would be more accurate to say that there is a range of more or less persuasive interpretations of *The Prince*, and I have tried to give attention to the readings of the work within this plausible range. I have also occasionally entertained or pointed the reader to more speculative readings outside of this range.

Interpretations of *The Prince* tend to depart from one another on the question of where they come down on Machiavelli's ultimate intentions. In trying to assess his intentions we have access only to the text of *The Prince*, and to Machiavelli's other writings. But we do not have access to the author himself to ask about his intentions, even assuming the man with the enigmatic smile would give us an honest answer. Interpretation always requires some degree of inference from the text in order to grasp the author's intention. Machiavelli states in chapter 15 of *The Prince* that his intention is "to write a thing that is useful for whoever understands it." His statement of intention nonetheless throws us back to where we started: trying to understand his short treatise. The intention of this guide is to make some progress in understanding *The Prince*.

THE STRUCTURE OF THIS GUIDE

This main body of this guidebook proceeds chapter by chapter through Machiavelli's *The Prince*, so in addition to reading this book straight through (after first wrestling with the text of *The Prince* itself of course!), the reader can consult the discussion of any given chapter. In order to give a sense of the structure and development of Machiavelli's work, I have grouped the chapters of *The Prince* into separate chapters of this guide. For example, I have grouped my discussion of chapters 1–5 of *The Prince* into Chapter 4 under the heading "Acquisition and the Emergence of the New Prince," thus indicating Machiavelli's focus in these early chapters on the acquisition of political power and the emerging theme of the new prince as his primary interest. Similarly, I have grouped chapters 6–7 of *The Prince* into Chapter 5 and given this chapter the title "The New Prince," given that the titles to both chapters refer to new princes, with chapter 6 on the new prince who acquires his state with his own arms and virtue and chapter 7 on the new prince who does so with the fortune and arms of others, a pairing that also brings to the fore the major theme in *The Prince* of virtue and fortune. Since Machiavelli gives at best hints about the relationship between the chapters of *The Prince* and how they might connect together to form an overarching argument, this grouping of his chapters into separate chapters of the guide is already an interpretative decision on my part about what I believe are the central themes of *The Prince* as Machiavelli takes them during the course of the work. Indeed, it is instructive to compare how I have grouped these chapters in this guide with other interpreters of *The Prince*. Two examples of other recent works on Machiavelli's masterpiece will suffice to illustrate the point. In her *Machiavelli's "Prince": A New Reading*, Erica Benner also considers chapters 1–5 of *The Prince* together in a section of her book on types of states, but then groups chapters 6–9 in a section devoted to discussing modes of the acquisition of power.[1]

By contrast, in his *Machiavelli's "The Prince,"* Miguel Vatter discusses chapters 1–6 of *The Prince* together in a single chapter on acquiring states, and then treats chapters 7–10 as devoted to the security of society, in keeping with his argument that one of Machiavelli's discoveries is the concept of "society," including social class conflict, and the importance of these social classes for rule.[2] In reading this guide, therefore, the reader should consider the grouping of chapters I have chosen as a provisional interpretation of *The Prince* largely intended to help make the work more digestible by breaking the analysis into smaller bites.

In addition to the main body containing a chapter-by-chapter consideration of *The Prince*, this guide begins with a chapter on Machiavelli's life and times to orient the reader (Chapter 1) and then a brief chapter on the dating of the composition of *The Prince* (Chapter 2). The guide then concludes with a chapter on Machiavelli's political thought as a whole and his legacy as a thinker (Chapter 11). In this concluding chapter I outline a number of prominent lines of interpretation of *The Prince* by way of a discussion of how scholars have attempted to understand Machiavelli's little treatise in relation to his other political writings, and especially the *Discourses on Livy*. To put the matter simply, *The Prince* appears on its face to be a book devoted to princes whereas the *Discourses on Livy* seems to be a book on republics. How, then, could the author of a book on republics and a loyal servant of the Florentine Republic have written his short treatise on princes? Various answers have been offered to this question, and I sketch some of them in this concluding chapter. Since the spirit in which I have written this guide to *The Prince* is to offer myself more as a companion who is exploring Machiavelli's work alongside the reader, rather than as an expert staking out the definitive interpretation of the work, I have saved this sketch of major scholarly approaches until after going through *The Prince* itself and approaching it as best as possible on its own terms as it presents itself to us. A reader of this guide who would like to begin with a discussion of the different scholarly approaches to *The Prince* might therefore very well begin with the concluding chapter of this guide. Finally, this concluding chapter also gives some attention to Machiavelli's complex legacy as a thinker as an extension of my discussion of the scholarly debates over how *The Prince* relates to his other political writings, since the ways in which his work has been seen and appropriated over the centuries have depended decisively on whether we view him as a teacher of princes, of unscrupulous power politics, or as a republican writer reviving a lost or eclipsed tradition of civic republicanism or inaugurating a new brand of republicanism with princely teeth.

Since most of the twenty-six chapters of *The Prince* are fairly short, and since I generally follow the text as it develops through each chapter, I have not included page numbers for quotations or references for the chapter under analysis. However, I do include page references when referring to any portions of *The Prince* outside of the chapter being discussed. In other words, for example, when analyzing chapter 6, I do not provide page references for any quotations drawn from chapter 6, but I do include page references for any evidence cited from outside of chapter 6.

Since Machiavelli's other major political work, the *Discourses on Livy*, is often useful for understanding *The Prince*, I make frequent reference to it. All references to the *Discourses on Livy* are to the translation and edition by Harvey C. Mansfield and Nathan Tarcov (Machiavelli 1996), and references are to book, chapter, and then page number from that edition (e.g., I.12, 36).

I have throughout used William J. Connell's excellent translation of *The Prince* (Machiavelli 2005a), occasionally making changes in his translation without noting those changes. I have also consistently consulted Harvey C. Mansfield's also very fine translation of *The Prince* (Machiavelli 2005b). For the Italian, I have followed Giorgio Inglese's edition (Machiavelli 2013) and consulted the Sansoni edition of Machiavelli's collected works (Machiavelli 1971).

A final note on gendered language. It is tempting to want to avoid using "he," "him," etc., when referring to a prince or anyone else Machiavelli writes about or to whom he writes, for in principle what he writes could apply to women, and sometimes does (e.g., the Countess of Forlì in chapter 20), and in principle he could be speaking to women as well. Nonetheless, Machiavelli's prince does generally seem to be male, even emphatically so, and so I have reluctantly employed "he," "him," etc., throughout.

NOTES

1 Benner 2013.
2 Vatter 2013.

MAP OF ITALY

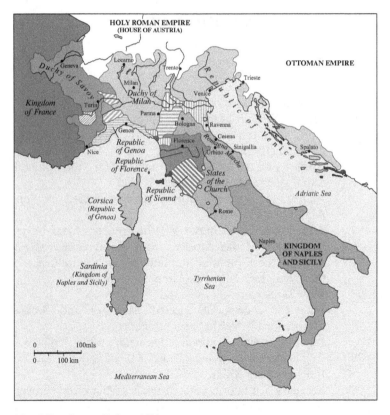

HOLY ROMAN EMPIRE
(HOUSE OF AUSTRIA)

OTTOMAN EMPIRE

Geneva

Locarno

Trento

Trieste

Duchy of Savoy

Milan

Duchy of Milan

Venice

Republic of Venice

Kingdom of France

Turin

Parma

Genoa

Bologna

Ravenna

Republic of Genoa

Florence

Cesena

Nice

Romagna

Sinigallia

Spalato

Republic of Florence

Urbino Marche

Corsica
(Republic of Genoa)

Republic of Sienna

States of the Church

Adriatic Sea

Rome

Sardinia
(Kingdom of
Naples and Sicily)

Naples

KINGDOM
OF NAPLES
AND SICILY

Tyrrhenian
Sea

0   100mls

0   100 km

Mediterranean Sea

Map 1 Renaissance Italy *c.* 1500

CHRONOLOGY

1434   Beginning of Medici dominance in Florence

1469   May 3: Niccolò Machiavelli born in Florence

1478   April 26: Pazzi conspiracy against Medici rule, Giulio de' Medici killed

1492   April 8: Death of Lorenzo de' Medici "the Magnificent"; succeeded by Piero de' Medici

August 11: Rodrigo Borgia (Borja) elected as Pope Alexander VI

1494   September: King Charles VIII of France invades Italy

November: Medici expelled from Florence; reestablishment of the Florentine Republic under the influence of the Dominican friar Girolamo Savonarola

1498   May 23: Savonarola executed

June 15: Machiavelli elected Secretary and Second Chancellor to the Florentine Republic

July 14: Machiavelli appointed Secretary to the Ten of War

1499   August–October: King Louis XII of France invades Italy, captures Milan

1500   February 5: Ludovico Sforza retakes Milan from French

April 10: French retake Milan, imprison Ludovico Sforza

August–December: Machiavelli on mission to French court

1501   August: Machiavelli marries Marietta Corsini

1502   June–December: Machiavelli on several missions to Cesare Borgia in the Romagna

September 22: Piero Soderini elected *Gonfaloniere* (Chief Magistrate) of Florence

December 26: Cesare Borgia has his minister Remirro de Orco executed in Cesena

December 31: Cesare Borgia assassinates mercenary captains at Sinigallia

1503   August 18: Death of Pope Alexander VI

October–December: Machiavelli on mission to Papal Court in Rome

November 1: Giuliano della Rovere elected as Pope Julius II

1504   January: Machiavelli on mission to French court

1506   February: Publication of Machavelli's *Decennale* (a verse history of Florence of 1494–1504)

March: Machiavelli's writes proposal to form a Florentine militia

August–October: Machiavelli follows Pope Julius II's army in the Romagna and Marche

1507   January: Creation of Florentine militia at Machiavelli's urging; Machiavelli appointed Chancellor to the newly created Nine of the Militia

1507   December (to June 1508): Machiavelli on mission to the court of Emperor Maximilian I

1508   February: Machiavelli at the siege of Pisa

1509   June 8: Fall of Pisa to the Florentines

1511   September–October: Machiavelli on mission to French court

October 4: Pope Julius II forms the Holy League to expel France from Italy

1512   April 11: French loss to Holy League at Battle of Ravenna

August 31: Piero Soderini forced to resign, flees Florence

September 16: Pro-Medici coup in Florence

November 7: Machiavelli dismissed from his government positions

1513   February 19: Machiavelli arrested on suspicion of conspiracy, imprisoned, tortured
February 21: Pope Julius II dies
March 9: Giovanni de' Medici elected as Pope Leo X
March 13–14: Machiavelli released from prison as part of a general amnesty
December 10: Machiavelli's letter to Francesco Vettori first mentioning *The Prince*

1515   May–June: Probable presentation of *The Prince* to Lorenzo de' Medici
Machiavelli probably begins writing the *Discourses on Livy*

1518   Machiavelli writes his comedy *Mandragola*

1519   May 4: Death of Lorenzo de' Medici, the dedicatee of *The Prince*

1520   September: Machiavelli commissioned by Cardinal Giulio de' Medici to write the *Florentine Histories*

1521   August: Publication of Machiavelli's *Art of War*

1522   November 19: Giulio de' Medici elected Pope Clement VII

1525   May: Machiavelli presents the *Florentine Histories* to Pope Clement VII

1526   May: Machiavelli named Chancellor to the magistracy overseeing Florence's fortifications

1527   May 6: Rome sacked by Emperor Charles V
May 17: Medici regime in Florence toppled, reinstitution of the Florentine Republic
June 21: Machiavelli dies in Florence

1531   *Discourses on Livy* published

1532   *The Prince* published

1559   Machiavelli's works, including *The Prince*, placed on the Index of Forbidden Books

1

MACHIAVELLI'S LIFE AND TIMES

A story about Machiavelli when he was on his deathbed gives some idea of his character and his concerns, whether or not the account is authentic. Awakening from a dream, Machiavelli told those gathered around his bed that he had dreamt that, given the choice of going to heaven or to hell, he chose to go to hell so that he could converse with the ancient authors whom he so relished reading while alive rather than associate with the blessed souls of paradise.[1] On a related note, not long before he died on June 21, 1527, Machiavelli wrote a friend that he loved his fatherland more than his soul.[2] His correspondence throughout his life with friends and political associates bursts with discussions of politics, of the partisan maneuverings at home in Florence and the military and diplomatic scene across Europe and beyond, and is peppered with ribald stories and irreverent remarks on Machiavelli's part and teasing from his friends concerning his less than regular Church attendance and his unorthodox views on matters religious, political, and otherwise. In short, the deathbed scene rings true even if it is not true—a fittingly ironic paradox for the author of *The Prince*.

Niccolò Machiavelli was born on May 3, 1469, in Florence. Machiavelli's family had a long and sometimes distinguished record of public service to the Florentine Republic, with several of his ancestors and relatives having been elected to the most important offices of the state, although the family was never among the small elite that dominated Florentine politics. While some of his relatives enjoyed financial success and some political influence during his youth, Machiavelli's own immediate family lived in modest circumstances and was not involved in political affairs. His father, Bernardo, obtained a doctorate in law, but he preferred a retired life devoted to humanistic studies to practicing his profession. His father owned a fairly large library for the time, with both a considerable number of manuscripts as well as bound books, which were still fairly rare at the time and quite expensive. The library contained classical authors of history, philosophy, and literature in Latin and perhaps Greek, although probably largely in Latin translation. Among other works, the library boasted a full edition of Livy's history of Rome, which included an index of place names which Bernardo himself was commissioned to do in 1476, although he only got around to having the loose sheets of the edition along with his index bound as a set of books a decade later, when the future author of the *Discourses on Livy* would have been old enough to study the work. Bernardo was active in intellectual circles in Florence, and among his friends was Bartolomeo Scala, a humanist scholar and First Chancellor of Florence (the state's highest administrative post). Scala made Bernardo a speaker in a dialogue he wrote on law, evidently as a tribute both to their friendship and to Bernardo's expertise in the subject.

The education Niccolò received was the typical course of studies for a boy of his social standing and his father's intellectual ambitions. The curriculum focused on learning to read and write Latin, the language of scholarship, law, political administration and diplomacy, and the Church. The training also included arithmetic and applications to accounting, an important subject in Florence given its power and wealth were based on banking, the wool trade, and other trading and manufacturing enterprises, although after he had lost his political posts Machiavelli admitted that he had no taste or talent for such trades. These studies would have occupied Machiavelli through his mid-teens, and he may have extended his education at the university in Florence, although there is no clear evidence that he did. A less conventional and more intriguing part of his training was the fact that he copied the entirety of Lucretius' *On the Nature of Things* (*De rerum natura*), the notorious materialist poem whose rediscovery in 1417 introduced an unapologetic Epicureanism into the intellectual discourse of the time and challenged philosophical and theological orthodoxies. The handwritten copy, with Machiavelli's marginal comments on philological issues, manuscript variations, and sometimes the philosophical topics raised in the text, was discovered in the Vatican Library, of all places, about fifty years ago. The marginalia suggest that Machiavelli was enlisted in a project, probably in the early 1490s, to produce a more critically informed edition of Lucretius' poem than yet existed. In addition to his Latin studies, which included translating Latin texts into Italian and vice versa, Machiavelli read works in the vernacular, and was particularly fond of the poetry of Dante and Petrarch. If Machiavelli's education was of the kind that would prepare him for the law or some other profession, we have no evidence of his entering upon a career until he suddenly comes on the political scene in 1498 with his election as Second Chancellor of the Florentine Republic.

Florentine politics in Machiavelli's youth and early adult life were tumultuous and dramatic. The Medici family had come to dominate Florence from 1434 onward, with the heads of the family being princes in all but name. Their rule was not uncontested, however. Most notably, on April 26, 1478, when Machiavelli was days away from his ninth birthday, a conspiracy led by the Pazzi family attempted to assassinate the heads of the Medici family, Lorenzo the Magnificent and his brother Giuliano. The brothers were attacked in the Duomo during mass, and while Giuliano lie bleeding to death on the floor of the cathedral after being stabbed some twenty times, the wounded Lorenzo managed to escape. Meanwhile, the conspirators were trapped and the leaders of the coup were killed, with the leader of the Pazzi family thrown out a window of the Palazzo Vecchio, the governmental palace where Machiavelli would later work, and then his body being dragged through the streets by a mob and thrown into the River Arno. Another conspirator, an archbishop of the Salviati family, was hung from the same building clothed in his ecclesiastical robes. Lorenzo de' Medici managed to regain control of the city and ruled until his death in 1492. Power passed from Lorenzo to his much less able son Piero, who lost control of the state after two years with the sudden turn in events that would throw Italy, and Florence with it, into turmoil for the next three decades.

In September 1494 word arrived in Florence that King Charles VIII of France had crossed the Alps into northern Italy with a formidable army, including the first siege train to include artillery. Charles marched toward Florence on his way to claim the throne of the Kingdom of Naples. The indecisive Piero de' Medici refused to support the king's expedition and so the French army began to sack and plunder towns in Tuscany within the Florentine dominion and threatened the city itself. A popular uprising in the city caused Piero to flee Florence, and Charles VIII entered Florence on November 17th without facing any resistance. As Machiavelli later wrote in *The Prince*, the French king took Italy "with a piece of chalk," referring to the fact that the French troops were billeted in selected houses marked with chalk.

With the Medici exiled, the Florentine Republic was reestablished under the influence of the Dominican friar Girolamo Savonarola, whose fiery sermons had prophesied that Italy would be punished for her sins by a redeeming prince who would come from the north. Savonarola, who would become Machiavelli's exemplar of an "unarmed prophet" in *The Prince*, called for political renewal, notably by proposing the expansion of the Great Council, in which supreme power was vested, to about 3,000 citizens to make it (relatively) more democratic. He also preached moral reform and urged the Florentines to burn lace, wigs, decks of cards, and other frivolous worldly possessions in what were called "bonfires of the vanities."

The four years during which Savonarola dominated Florentine politics were times of complex partisan strife, including both the reemergence of traditional conflict between the elite families which had traditionally controlled Florentine politics and the more popular faction that had been given increased power under the newly reorganized republic, as well as conflict between the followers and opponents of Savonarola. The friar did not limit his call for religious reform to the Florentines, but became increasingly bold in his criticism of the sinful ways of the Church. An exasperated Pope Alexander VI finally excommunicated Savonarola in 1497 and threatened Florence if it continued to protect the friar. Under pressure from both the Church and the Florentines, Savonarola agreed to stop preaching on March 18, 1498, but not before Machiavelli was able to hear a few sermons in order to report on the friar's activities to the Florentine ambassador to Rome. In the first extant letter we have from Machiavelli, dated March 9, 1498, he gives a lively summary of Savonarola's sermons. He relates how the friar attacked his opponents as partisans of the devil, warned the city of the rise of a tyrant in their midst, and for good measure spoke of the wickedness of the pontiff. More interestingly, Machiavelli then offers his own judgment of Savonarola: "Thus, in my judgment, he acts in accordance with the times and colors his lies accordingly."[3] Shortly after these last sermons Savonarola was arrested and then tried and convicted of heresy. On the morning of May 23, 1498, Savonarola and two of his Dominican adherents were led into the square below the Palazzo Vecchio and hung and then burned, with the ashes carefully carted away and dumped into the Arno in order to prevent his followers from collecting any relics.

The fall of Savonarola set the stage for the rise of Machiavelli. The future author of *The Prince* began his position as Second Chancellor of the Florentine Republic on June 19, 1498, entering his office in the government palace less than a month after Savonarola's execution and burning in the square below, and remained in his position and the other government positions he acquired until November 7, 1512. Machiavelli first stood for election for the chancery office in February 1498, but was defeated in the election in the Great Council by a pro-Savonarolan candidate. With the fall of Savonarola a little more than a year later, however, the Second Chancellor was dismissed, a new election was held, and Machiavelli prevailed over his anti-Savonarolan opponent. Since there was a desire to restore the chancery to its traditionally non-partisan role in administering the state bureaucracy, Machiavelli's success in the election may have been due to the fact he was not strongly identified with any faction.

Political power in Florence resided in the elected council drawn from a citizenry that was restricted to families who had enjoyed citizenship for a century or more, while the highest magistracies and political posts were effectively controlled by a small group of wealthy and powerful families. Since elected officials tended to rotate office after short terms, the republic created an administrative body, the chancery, whose officials and staff were continued in office for long periods of time so that they could gain the necessary expertise. The chancery was therefore effectively the republic's civil service. The chancellors and their staff drafted memoranda and diplomatic correspondence at the direction of the elected officials, but often enjoyed considerable influence over policy through their role as experienced administrators and as advisers to their superiors. The First Chancellor of the Florentine Republic was responsible for overseeing the entire chancery, including departments administering both internal and external affairs, but with particular responsibility for Florence's relations with foreign states. In turn, as Second Chancellor Machiavelli was primarily responsible for supervising Florence's relations with its subject cities and dominions, although he became increasingly involved with foreign relations and diplomacy as well. Less than a month after assuming his duties as Second Chancellor, Machiavelli was also appointed to serve as the secretary to the Ten of War, a body of officials overseeing Florentine military affairs. Later, in 1507, he was given the further responsibility of serving as chancellor of the Nine of the Militia, which administered the newly created militia, a project conceived and promoted by Machiavelli himself. In these various roles, Machiavelli would gain the "long experience" with political affairs of which he would later speak in the Dedicatory Letter of *The Prince*.

Machiavelli was an extraordinarily active and influential chancery official during his fourteen years in office. During that time, he went on over forty missions for his city, more than twenty of which were particularly significant, including diplomatic missions that involved delicate negotiations. His primary duties as Second Chancellor of administering affairs concerning Florence's subject cities and dominions often intersected with his role as secretary to the Ten of War since these cities and dominions were either in rebellion, such as Pisa, or suffered bloody partisan conflict, such as Pistoia, or were captured by other states and regained by Florence through negotiation, such as Arezzo. Particularly significant in his role as Second Chancellor was the long struggle to recapture Pisa, which had broken away from Florentine control in the tumultuous times of the French invasion of 1494. Machiavelli personally directed or was heavily involved with the military operations against Pisa, including a failed attempt in 1504 to divert the course of the Arno away from Pisa in order to deprive the city of access to the sea and thereby to starve the Pisans into submission, an operation for which Florence hired Leonardo da Vinci as its military architect. Pisa was finally retaken in June 1509, in part through using the militia Machiavelli had finally persuaded the city to establish in 1506, a militia for which Machiavelli himself recruited the troops, directed their training, and oversaw in his third official role as secretary to the Nine of the Militia.

Soon after he assumed office Florence made use of Machiavelli for diplomatic missions, and came to rely on him for such important tasks to an unusual degree given that foreign affairs were not part of his official portfolio. Although he was never named as an ambassador on any of these missions, since such appointments were reserved for members of the elite, he played a major role as a negotiator as well as an intelligence gatherer who was experienced at sizing up the ever-changing political scene and its leading players. His first important missions involved negotiating terms with the mercenary captains, or *condottieri*, Florence hired, thus giving him direct experience with the subject of mercenary and auxiliary arms that would preoccupy him when he later wrote *The Prince*. His first important diplomatic mission was a seven-month-long stay at the French court in 1500–1, and he would return to France several more times during his career. In 1502 he was sent by the republic to observe and report back on the activities of Cesare Borgia, who was then conquering large portions of the Romagna and Marche, regions to the east and northeast of Florence, and fomenting rebellion among Florence's subject cities. His eyewitness reports back to Florence on this mission, and another one he undertook from October 1502 to February 1503, include vivid assessments of Cesare Borgia's personality and actions and contain eyewitness accounts of events such as Cesare's grisly execution of his minister Remirro de Orco and his slaughter of his unreliable mercenary captains at Senigallia that would later make their way into *The Prince*. Similarly, Machiavelli was sent by his government to witness the papal conclave after the death of Cesare Borgia's father, Pope Alexander VI, in August 1503, and reported back on the election of Pope Julius II and the new pope's treacherous turn against Cesare Borgia, a dramatic series of events he also discusses in *The Prince*. Over the next few years Machiavelli was sent several times to negotiate with Julius II, particularly in the summer of 1506 as the so-called "Warrior Pope" led his troops, dressed in full armor, to conquer many of the same cities and provinces Cesare Borgia had earlier captured. Once again, Machiavelli's direct experience with the impetuous pope would make it into the pages of *The Prince*. One of Machiavelli's lengthiest diplomatic commissions occurred the following year when he was sent to the court of Maximilian I, the king of the Germans and would-be Holy Roman Emperor, with his mission lasting from December 1507 to June 1508. It was on that mission that he befriended Francesco Vettori, the man to whom he would first report writing *The Prince* six years later. Machiavelli was sent several more times over the next few years to negotiate with Maximilian as he attempted to extend his influence in Italy. His last diplomatic mission was a return to the French court in September to October 1511.

Machiavelli's diplomatic missions and other official duties kept him away from Florence and his family for extended periods. In August 1501 Machiavelli married Marietta Corsini, whose family was also long involved in Florentine politics and whose brother-in-law, Piero del Nero, was elected to the Ten of War, the administrative body for which Machiavelli served as secretary. We have an affectionate letter from Marietta to Machiavelli, then in Rome, from November 24, 1503, in which she describes their new-born son: "For now the baby is well, he looks like you: he is white as snow, but his head looks like black velvet, and he is hairy like you. Since he looks like you, he seems beautiful to me. And he is so lively he seems to have been in this world for a year; he opened his eyes when he was scarcely born and filled the whole house with noise."[4] Machiavelli and his wife would have six children together, two girls and four boys, and despite his many absences he would prove a devoted father (if also a sometimes wayward husband).

In addition to exercising influence on Florentine military and foreign affairs in his official capacities, Machiavelli played some role in influencing Florentine politics as a close adviser to Piero Soderini, who was elected *Gonfaloniere* (the chief magistrate of the republic) for life in 1502. Soderini evidently respected Machiavelli's abilities and trusted him as an adviser, and therefore gave him a greater role than was customary for someone in his administrative post. Notably, he supported Machiavelli's proposal to form a militia, a proposal opposed by most of the city's elites. Opponents of Soderini's regime noticed and resented Machiavelli's influence and worked to check him, for example rejecting Soderini's attempt to appoint him as ambassador on a mission to the Emperor Maximilian in 1507–8, and apparently even trying to have him dismissed as Second Chancellor. Nonetheless, Machiavelli was not simply Soderini's agent, and maintained good relations with powerful members of the elite who were outside the regime. Be that as it may, Machiavelli's close association with Soderini ensured that he himself would lose his offices when Soderini fell from power, which is precisely what happened in 1512.

One of Machiavelli's chief concerns in *The Prince* and his other political writings, a concern also evident in his diplomatic and personal correspondence during his time in office, was the vulnerability of Italy to foreign invasion due to its disunity and the shifting alliances between the chief states in Italy and with the emerging nation-states outside of Italy such as France, Germany, and Spain. This fragile and complex political struggle led to Machiavelli's own undoing. As noted above, Machiavelli's last important diplomatic mission was a two-month stay at the French court from September to October 1511 with the intention of cementing Florence's alliance with France against the so-called Holy League, an alliance formed by Pope Julius II with the intent of driving the French from Italy. After the French defeat at the battle of Ravenna on April 11, 1512, and their subsequent retreat from Italy, Julius was determined to force Florence into submission and had a

Spanish army march toward Florence to crush the city's resistance. Machiavelli's employer, Piero Soderini, ignominiously fled Florence on August 31, and then a pro-Medici coup occurred on September 16. After a pro-Medici government was elected six weeks later, Machiavelli was summarily dismissed from his official positions on November 7. In addition, he was ordered confined to Florentine territory and was forbidden from entering the government palace for a year. (Contrary to accounts that he was exiled from Florence, Machiavelli was actually condemned to what might be called "internal exile.") Machiavelli spent the next few months facing insulting inquiries into his handling of the chancery's finances.

Yet worse was to come for Machiavelli. On February 19, 1513, he was arrested after his name was found on a list of potential conspirators against the Medici regime and was thrown into prison. Over the next few days he was interrogated under torture. The method of torture was the *strappado*, which involved having his hands bound behind his back with a rope, raising him toward the ceiling, and then dropping him short of the floor, thereby painfully dislocating his shoulders. By Machiavelli's account, he endured six painful drops and proudly declared that he never confessed to anything. There is no evidence that Machiavelli was involved in the conspiracy, but clearly the new Medici rulers did not trust the former chancellor. He remained in prison as the known conspirators were executed, and he was only released as part of a general amnesty when Giovanni de' Medici's election as Pope Leo X was announced on March 11. For the following months Machiavelli largely lived at his little farm at Sant' Andrea in Percussina, about 10 miles south of Florence, only making occasional visits to the city. In a letter to Francesco Vettori a month after his release from prison Machiavelli quotes some verses from Petrarch that summarize his situation:

> Therefore, if at times I laugh or sing,
> I do so because I have no other way than this
> To give vent to my bitter tears.

After quoting these lines, Machiavelli tells Vettori, who was then serving as Florence's ambassador to the Papal Court, that he still hoped to be employed by the Medici, "being put to some use, if not on Florence's behalf, at least on behalf of Rome and the papacy; in which case I should be less mistrusted."[5]

For the next two years or so Machiavelli still hoped to obtain some employment with the new rulers of Florence, and it is in this context that he wrote *The Prince*. He first mentions his project in a letter to Francesco Vettori dated December 10, 1513. The letter to Vettori is typical of Machiavelli's writing as a mixture of comic irony and seriousness, and also provides a vivid portrait of his daily life on his farm and of the interior life of his mind. Responding to a letter in which Vettori complains at length about the tedious duties of his ambassadorial position, Machiavelli playfully retaliates by regaling his friend with a description of a typical day spent on his farm outside of Florence. He rises and sets traps for thrushes and other little birds, tends to the cutting of some woods he owns to earn some money, reads some poetry and wistfully recalls his past love affairs, and then dines at the local inn, chatting and playing backgammon and other games for small stakes with his rustic neighbors. "Thus, having been cooped up among these lice," he concludes his description of his daytime pastimes, "I get the mold out of my brain and let out the malice of my fate, content to be ridden over roughshod in this fashion if only to discover whether or not my fate is ashamed of treating me so." Machiavelli's mention of "the malice of my fate" is a not-so-gentle reminder to the grouchy ambassador that he himself has within the past year been removed from all of his political offices, imprisoned, tortured, and is living in near poverty.

If his daytime is filled with mundane tasks and bittersweet memories of the past, however, the evening reveals another Machiavelli. Continuing his account to Vettori, who had related how he relieved the tedium of his daily duties by his nighttime reading of Roman history, Machiavelli describes returning home and entering his study:

> When evening comes, I return home and enter my study; on the threshold I take off my workday clothes, covered with mud and dirt, and put on the garments of court and palace. Fitted out appropriately, I step inside the venerable courts of the ancients, where, solicitously

> received by them, I nourish myself on that food that *alone* is mine and for which I was born; where I am unashamed to converse with them and to question them about the motives for their actions, and they, out of their human kindness, answer me. And for four hours at a time I feel no boredom, I forget all my troubles, I do not dread poverty, and I am not terrified by death. I absorb myself into them completely.

The fruit of his conversations with the ancient authors, he now tells Vettori, is "a short study, *De Principatibus*."[6]

This is the first mention we have of *The Prince*. Machiavelli states that his little book should be welcome to a prince, "and especially by a new prince," and he therefore tells Vettori that he intends to address it to the new ruler of Florence, Giuliano de' Medici. Aware of the lowly position to which he has been reduced, Machiavelli voices some hesitation about whether to present his book to Giuliano himself or whether instead to send it to Vettori, clearly hinting that he hoped his friend would volunteer to act as an intermediary with his Medici employers. Machiavelli concludes his letter by stating that he has no other choice and is "wasting away" in poverty, adding: "Besides, there is my desire that these Medici princes should begin to engage my services, even if they should start out by having me roll along a stone. For then, if I could not win them over, I should have only myself to blame. And through this study of mine, were it to be read, it would be evident that during the fifteen years I have been studying the art of the state I have neither slept nor fooled around, and anybody ought to be happy to utilize someone who has had so much experience at the expense of other."[7] In his reply later that month, Vettori expressed interest in seeing his book,[8] and we know that Machiavelli did send a draft of part of his book since the ambassador declares himself delighted with the "chapters" he has been sent and explains he will defer offering a more definitive judgment until he sees the work as a whole.[9] Nonetheless, Vettori's silence about the work in further correspondence seems to indicate that he was unwilling to intercede with the Medici on the author's behalf. We will return to issues concerning the dating of the composition of *The Prince* in Chapter 2.

Out of political power, Machiavelli turned to writing about politics. During his years in the chancery, he did write and publish some poetry, notably a verse history of Italy from the French invasion of 1494 up to 1504, titled the *Decennale* and written in 1504 and published two years later, but all of his major political and other works were written only after his dismissal from office. In addition to *The Prince*, which as we have seen he began in 1513 and as we shall see completed by mid-1515, Machiavelli drew on his reading of the ancient historians to write the *Discourses on the First Decade of Titus Livy*. Machiavelli's work takes the form of a loose commentary on Livy's history of the rise of the Roman Republic, and although the title of the work suggests that his analysis focuses on the first ten books (or "decade") of Livy's history, Machiavelli in fact discusses the entirety of Roman history from its founding to the fall of the republic, and even the imperial period, as well as other ancient republics and kingdoms, and he does so by making frequent comparisons to modern states. The impetus for writing the *Discourses on Livy* were the conversations with friends he had in the Orti Oricellari, the gardens of the wealthy Rucellai family, probably beginning in 1515. He must have begun the *Discourses on Livy* at about that time, especially given that he seems to refer to his work on republics in chapter 2 of *The Prince* and since he refers twice in the *Discourses on Livy* to his treatise on principalities. He seems to have completed the work sometime between 1517 and 1519, and he dedicated it to two of the young men who urged him to write the work, Zanobi Buondelmonti and Cosimo Rucellai. Machiavelli would also honor his friends by setting the dialogue in his later *Art of War* in the Rucellai gardens. Machiavelli wrote the *Art of War* in 1519–20 and published it in 1521, the only major work on politics he published in his lifetime. In addition, he wrote his famous comedy *Mandragola* during this period, probably in 1518, with its first performance probably in 1520 and its publication in 1524. I will discuss the relationship between *The Prince* and the *Discourses on Livy* and Machiavelli's other political writings in Chapter 11.

During these busy years writing, Machiavelli still yearned to return to public service. Various overtures were made to the Medici on his behalf, but Cardinal Giulio, the head of the family, put a definitive end to any such idea of employing Machiavelli (unbeknownst to him) in January 1515 by instructing his nephew back in Florence not to have anything to do with "Niccolò."[10] In 1519, after the death of the dedicatee to *The Prince*, Lorenzo de' Medici, Machiavelli was among those asked by Cardinal Giulio de' Medici to advise him on the proposed constitutional reform of Florence. In his short work, the *Discourse on Florentine Affairs after the Death of the Younger Lorenzo de' Medici*, Machiavelli argued that Florence's regime had for more than a century proved to be unstable because it was neither a true principate nor a true republic, and he advised the Medici to establish a genuine republican government though only after continuing to rule it effectively as a monarchy during the lifetimes of the Medici pope Leo X and Cardinal Giulio. The proposed reforms came to naught, especially since the Medici suppressed political opposition after the death of Leo X on December 1, 1521. Machiavelli's memorandum must have impressed Cardinal Giulio, or at least not offended him, however, since the powerful cardinal commissioned Machiavelli with the prestigious task of writing a history of Florence, which had the additional benefit of giving him an income since he was to be employed as Florence's official historian. Machiavelli's predecessors in the chancery had often written histories of Florence, and so the commission effectively recognized not only his credentials as a scholar for undertaking the work, but also his long service to the state. The commission was negotiated in September 1520, with Machiavelli being given the choice to write the history in either Latin or Italian, and, having chosen to compose in the vernacular, Machiavelli began writing. The *Florentine Histories* covers the history of Machiavelli's native city from the decline of the Roman empire through the death of Lorenzo de' Medici in 1492. Writing about the period from 1434 to 1492 when the Medici effectively ruled Florence as princes would, he recognized, be a delicate matter given that he was writing the book for a Medici prince. Machiavelli presented his finished work to his patron, now Pope Clement VII, in Rome in June 1525, receiving an additional reward of 120 gold ducats for his work.

The favor shown to Machiavelli by the Medici pope raised his hopes of regaining some sort of government position. In June

1525 he was finally entrusted with a commission by the pope, namely a mission to aid Francesco Guicciardini, a friend and correspondent of Machiavelli's who was serving as governor of the Papal States in northern Italy, to establish a militia in the Romagna drawn from the native inhabitants. Guicciardini was skeptical about the project and it came to nothing, but the pope and his governor did employ Machiavelli on several other military and diplomatic missions over the next year. With the sack of Rome by the Colonna party at the encouragement of Emperor Charles V in September 1526 (a prelude to the more savage sack of the city by imperial forces the following May), Machiavelli accompanied the papal troops from Guicciardini's headquarters southward toward Rome, but this promising opportunity was cut short and Machiavelli stopped short in Florence. The nervous Florentine government employed him in November of the same year on a mission to Guicciardini to jointly assess the threat to both Florence and the Papal States posed by the Emperor Charles V. Machiavelli was again entrusted by the Medici in February 1527 on a nearly three-month-long mission, again to Guicciardini, to assist in military and diplomatic affairs. His attempts to negotiate with the emperor failed, and Rome was sacked by imperial troops on May 6th, the pope retreating behind the walls of the Castel Sant'Angelo. When news of the sack reached Florence a week later, the Medici regime collapsed and the republic was reinstated. Machiavelli returned to Florence shortly thereafter and worked for the new republican regime in his final government position as chancellor to the magistracy responsible for supervising Florence's fortifications, to which he had been appointed in May 1526. This position became increasingly important as the bellicose Emperor Charles V trained his sights northward toward Florence. Machiavelli worked on strengthening the fortifications of his native city, then a walled city. This task was taken up two years after his death by Michelangelo, who was hired as a military architect by the city and whose innovative and influential new design held off imperial troops during the siege of 1529–30, only to have the defeated Florentine troops surrender in October 1530 and the Medici return for good.

As for Machiavelli, upon returning to Florence in May 1527 he grew ill from a gastric disorder, probably peritonitis and possibly aggravated by the medicine he was given to treat it. He took to his bed, where he was surrounded by his friends, including one of the young men to whom he had dedicated the *Discourses on Livy*, Zanobi Buondelmonti, just returned from exile for having conspired against the Medici regime in 1522. He died on June 21st and his body was interred the next day in the family chapel in Santa Croce. The tomb that today sits in the church, nearby the tombs of Michelangelo, Galileo, and others, dates from 250 years after Machiavelli's death, after his reputation as a teacher of evil waned and his repute as an Italian patriot waxed.

The only major work Machiavelli published during his lifetime was the *Art of War* (1521), and although his other works, including *The Prince*, circulated in manuscript, they were only published after his death. The *Discourses on Livy* was published in 1531 and *The Prince* in 1532, in two simultaneous editions published in Florence and Rome. Both of these works were issued with the approval of papal privilege, but the growing challenge to Rome by the Protestant Reformation led to reactionary measures on the part of the Church including the establishment in 1559 of the Index of Forbidden Books (*Index Librorum Prohibitorum*), which condemned and prohibited all of Machiavelli's writings, including *The Prince*.

NOTES

1 Atkinson 2010, 28. The following account of Machiavelli's life draws on Atkinson 2010, Black 2013, and Vivante 2013.
2 Machiavelli to Francesco Vettori, April 16, 1527, in Machiavelli 2004, 416.
3 Machiavelli to Ricciardo Becchi, March 9, 1498, in Machiavelli 2004, 8–10.
4 Marietta Corsini to Niccolò Machiavelli, November 24, 1501, in Machiavelli 2004, 93.
5 Machiavelli to Francesco Vettori, April 16, 1513, in Machiavelli 2004, 228.
6 Machiavelli to Francesco Vettori, December 10, 1513, in Machiavelli 2004, 262–65. For an interesting analysis of the letter to Vettori, see Connell 2011.
7 Machiavelli to Francesco Vettori, December 10, 1513, in Machiavelli 2004, 264–65.
8 Francesco Vettori to Machiavelli, December 24, 1513, in Machiavelli 2004, 269.
9 Francesco Vettori to Machiavelli, January 18, 1514, in Machiavelli 2004, 277.
10 See Connell's edition of *The Prince* (Machiavelli 2005a), editor's note 31 to the introduction.

2

THE COMPOSITION OF *THE PRINCE*

As noted in the previous chapter, Machiavelli first refers to the writing of *The Prince* in a famous letter he wrote to his friend Francesco Vettori dated December 10, 1513. After describing how he enters his study at night, dressed in his "regal and courtly garments," and spends the next four hours conversing with the ancient authors, Machiavelli tells Vettori: "And because Dante says that no one understands anything unless he retains what he has understood, I have jotted down what I have profited from in their conversation and composed a short study, *De Principatibus*, in which I delve as deeply as I can into the ideas concerning this topic, discussing the definition of a principality, of what kinds they are, how they are acquired, how they are retained, and why they are lost."[1] Also as noted above, Machiavelli goes on to tell Vettori that he intends to address it to the new ruler of Florence, Giuliano de' Medici. Machiavelli's book will exhibit the understanding he has gained of through his long experience of politics and his nighttime conversations with the ancients.

The letter to Vettori reveals important information about when Machiavelli composed *The Prince* and something of his intentions in doing so. First, as for the composition, he must have begun writing the book sometime after his release from prison in March 1513. How far along he was in writing it by the time he wrote Vettori in December is not clear. He states in the letter that he has already shown a draft to a mutual friend and that he is still "fattening and currying it."[2] This characterization of the draft, along with the fact that he had already turned his mind to presenting it to Giuliano de' Medici, suggests that *The Prince* was drawing toward completion in December 1513. On the other hand, the letter from Vettori of January 1514 cited in the previous chapter thanking Machiavelli for the "chapters" he has sent suggests that the work was not fully complete at that point.

Even if the book was nearly complete in terms of the work he set out to write, how "complete" was it relative to the work we now know as *The Prince*? Two further considerations indicate that Machiavelli continued to revise the work after late 1513 and early 1514 when he was corresponding with Vettori about it, the question being how much. The first consideration derives from his summary of its contents in the letter to Vettori. Namely, as suggested by the title *De Principatibus*, what Machiavelli had drafted up to the point he wrote Vettori concerned principalities: what they are and how they are acquired, maintained, and lost. Some scholars have inferred from this summary that Machiavelli may have composed only the first eleven chapters of the work, which they argue fits this description of its contents, but not the remainder of the full work we now have, in which he takes up additional subjects. These scholars have therefore hypothesized that the original version of the work to which Machiavelli refers as *De Principatibus* in the letter to Vettori was a much shorter work than we now possess.[3] Other scholars counter that Machiavelli's description of the contents of the work could easily refer to the entire work as we now have it, and not just the first eleven chapters, and therefore suggest that the work may have reached more or less the full version not long after he wrote Vettori. Finally, a third group of scholars, generally holding that the original version of the work contained the first twenty-five chapters, argue that Machiavelli added the Dedicatory Letter to Lorenzo de' Medici and, more importantly, the concluding chapter, chapter 26, exhorting the Medici to free Italy from external powers, at a later date when he decided to present the work to the Medici in hopes of regaining a government position, perhaps between 1515 and 1517. Many of these scholars rely for this hypothesis on their view that the rhetorically heated tone of chapter 26 does not match the cold analysis throughout the rest of the work.[4] Since there is no further manuscript or other documentary evidence, these conjectures about the state of the composition of the work when he wrote the ambassador necessarily remain irresolvable on this evidence.

The second set of considerations for dating the composition of the work is more concrete since the reasons are derived from the text of *The Prince* itself. First, within *The Prince* Machiavelli makes mention of a number of political events that occurred after his letter to Vettori of December 1513, the last of which seems to be from early 1515. Machiavelli therefore obviously made at least some changes to the text sometime after the beginning of 1515 and probably not much later. Second, and most obviously, although he informed Vettori that he intended to dedicate the book to Giuliano de' Medici, the final version of the work as we now have it is dedicated to Lorenzo de' Medici. We do not know for certain whether *The Prince*, in some version, was presented to Giuliano, although it seems unlikely since we have a letter from January 1515 conveying instructions from the head of the Medici family, Cardinal Giulio, to his brother Giuliano warning him not to employ Machiavelli in any way. Machiavelli may have therefore turned his hopes at that point to Giuliano's nephew, Lorenzo, who returned to Florence in May 1515 with the mission of organizing the Florentine militia, a mission for which Machiavelli would have considered himself particularly qualified to advise upon, and who then assumed leadership in Florence in March 1516 when Giuliano died. From this evidence, we can fairly confidently narrow the window for the final form of *The Prince*, including the Dedicatory Letter, to May 1515 to March 1516, with the fact that the last events mentioned in the work occurred in early 1515 suggesting probable completion on the earlier side. Finally, we can further narrow this window by supplementing this information by the findings of ingenious detective work by a scholar with regard to Machiavelli's own personal affairs during this period, and particularly his dramatically declining financial position and need for employment. This evidence, in combination with the other facts discussed, persuasively suggests that Machiavelli took up writing again April or May of 1515, and completed his book at that time in order to present it to Lorenzo de' Medici soon after.[5] In short, *The Prince* seems to have been completed by May or June 1515.

Finally, we know that a number of manuscript copies of *The Prince* were circulating among Machiavelli's friends, and beyond, by 1516–17, and circumstantial evidence suggests that these manuscripts contained something like the entirety of Machiavelli's work as we now have it.[6] Interestingly, a work that borrowed heavily from *The Prince* appeared in 1523 by Agostino Niso, an important philosopher of the time, suggesting that *The Prince* was fairly widely circulated by that time.[7]

As for Machiavelli's intentions in writing *The Prince*, from his letter to Vettori it is clear that he wrote the book for at least two reasons. The first reason, as he notes, was to convert the understanding he has gained from communing with the ancient authors in his nocturnal reading into knowledge. In this regard, therefore, *The Prince* is a book about knowledge of politics, or a work of political theory. The second reason, also obvious from his letter, is that he hoped that the work would help him regain political office under the new Medici rulers by showing that "during the fifteen years I have been studying the art of the state I have neither slept nor fooled around."[8] As we shall shortly see, the relationship between these two purposes of *The Prince*—a work of political theory and a job résumé sent to a prospective employer—will be important for understanding Machiavelli's intention in *The Prince* and its intended audience.

Machiavelli's first purpose in writing *The Prince* of composing a work that contains what he has learned from his experience and reading has, of course, been achieved as testified by the fact that his book has attained the status of one of the most important works of political theory. His second and more immediate purpose nonetheless seems to have failed. Once again, we do not know for certain whether the book was ever actually presented to either Giuliano de' Medici or Lorenzo de' Medici. Nonetheless, an unconfirmed story has long circulated that Machiavelli's "little book" was indeed presented to Lorenzo, but not favorably received. The story is that on the same day that he received *The Prince*, Lorenzo was also presented with a pack of hunting dogs, which he found far more interesting. Machiavelli is said to have sworn that his little book would itself ultimately wreak his revenge against the Medici.[9] Was Machiavelli's intention in *The Prince* to advise princes, including the Medici, or to somehow undermine them? This story, whether or not it is apocryphal, once again points to the difficulty of discerning Machiavelli's intention in *The Prince*.

NOTES

1 Machiavelli to Francesco Vettori, December 10, 1513, in Machiavelli 2004, 264 (translation altered).

2 Ibid.

3 Friedrich Meinecke was among the first to make this argument in his 1923 translation of *The Prince*. See Black 2011 for a review of the literature.

4 See Baron 1991.

5 Connell 2013. Cf. Black 2011, who argues that Machiavelli did not write the Dedicatory Letter to Lorenzo de' Medici until late 1515 or early 1516.

6 See Niccolò Guicciardini to Luigi Guicciardini, July 29, 1517, in Machiavelli 2005a, 143–44.

7 For selections from Niso's work, see Machiavelli 2005a, 153–58.

8 Machiavelli to Francesco Vettori, December 10, 1513, in Machiavelli 2004, 265.

9 See Connell 2013, 513. For an account of the supposed episode, see Connell's edition of *The Prince* (Machiavelli 2005a, 142).

3

THE TITLE AND DEDICATORY LETTER

The title and Dedicatory Letter to Machiavelli's brief work seem entirely straightforward: the title is *The Prince*, or *Il Principe* in Italian, and the work is dedicated to "the Magnificent Lorenzo de' Medici the Younger." As with many aspects of *The Prince*, however, things turn out to be more complicated upon further examination. A consideration of the title and Dedicatory Letter will enable us to better understand the form and style of *The Prince*, thereby introducing the reader to some of the stylistic features of Machiavelli's writing in order to reveal, so to speak, his "tricks of his trade" as an author. This analysis will also lead us to entertain the question of Machiavelli's intended audience or audiences.

THE TITLE

Machiavelli's work is universally known as *The Prince* (*Il Principe*), but this does not appear to be the title he intended to give the work.

Since we do not possess a manuscript of *The Prince* in Machiavelli's own handwriting, and since he did not publish the work in his lifetime, we cannot be sure what title he wanted to give the book. The handful of manuscripts of the work we do possess, which were circulated during Machiavelli's lifetime, do not bear that title. Furthermore, the two direct references to the work in his other major political writing, the *Discourses on Livy*, provide at best ambiguous evidence of the intended title since Machiavelli refers to the work as "our treatise of principalities" (II.1, 128) and "our treatise of the prince" (III.42, 302). In fact, the title *Il Principe* only appeared in the first published edition of the work of 1532. This edition was published a full five years after Machiavelli's death, and since we do not know whether it was based on a manuscript version written by him, the published title cannot provide clear testimony about the intended title. What, then, was his intended title? Only once does Machiavelli unambiguously refer to his book by a title, and that is in his letter of December 10, 1513, to Francesco Vettori, which was mentioned in previous chapters when discussing the composition of *The Prince*. There he refers to the work he is writing as *De Principatibus*, the Latin for *Of Principalities*.

What difference does it make for our understanding of the work if Machiavelli actually intended to title it *De Principatibus*, or *Of Principalities*, instead of the title by which it is now known, *Il Principe*, or *The Prince*? The answer to this question is obviously conjectural, but let us nonetheless consider two differences in the titles that immediately strike the eye: they are in different languages, Latin versus Italian, and they indicate two different subjects, principalities versus princes or even "the" prince.

First, a Latin title for the work would make sense since all the chapter titles, as well as the salutation in the Dedicatory Letter, are in Latin. In contrast, the text throughout (except for a few brief Latin quotations) is in Italian. Machiavelli thereby juxtaposes the language of antiquity and the traditional language of humanistic learning and of the Church, Latin, to the vernacular language of his own time and place, Italian (or, more accurately, the Tuscan dialect, which would later become the basis for standard Italian). Giving his work a Latin title would invite comparison to the sorts of works presented to princes and typically written in Latin, notably works in the mirror-of-princes genre. These works hold up a kind of "mirror" of a virtuous prince to the ruler who receives the book, offering examples of praiseworthy rulers and generally advising the prince to be a just ruler who looks to the good of his people and to avoid the temptations of tyranny. A sense of the genre can be gleaned from Petrarch's contribution to the genre a century and a half before Machiavelli in the form of a letter to a ruler in Padua: "And I want you to look at yourself in this letter as though you were gazing in a mirror."[1] Scholars have therefore long suggested that *The Prince* should be considered as an example of the mirror-of-princes genre, or more generally of the political advice books of the humanist tradition of the fourteenth and fifteen centuries in Italy and elsewhere.[2] The debate among those scholars who situate *The Prince* within this genre or context concerns the extent to which Machiavelli's work differs from those of his predecessors, and whether the continuities or the discontinuities between *The Prince* and its antecedents are more revealing for understanding the work. If Machiavelli did intend to give his little treatise a traditional exterior, by way of a Latin title, and a new or modern interior, by way of the Italian text, he would be confronting us with this very question: to what extent has he put new wine in old bottles? The Latin title of *De Principatibus* would thus further underscore the juxtaposition of tradition and novelty already apparent in several ways in the work.

Second, the title *Of Principalities* (*De Principatibus*) as opposed to *The Prince* (*Il Principe*) might suggest a somewhat different subject matter for Machiavelli's treatise than we often suppose. To be sure, the title itself—*Of Principalities* (*De Principatibus*)—is unremarkable; one can easily imagine a traditional advice book written for a prince with this title, and in fact there were books with similar titles. Machiavelli's new approach comes to light when that title is considered in light of his summary of the work's contents in the letter to Vettori mentioned above: "debating what a principality is, of what kinds they are, how they are acquired, how they are maintained, why they are lost."[3] Rather than beginning with the prince, or the virtues and actions proper to princes, Machiavelli begins with principalities: that is, what princes—and especially new princes—want to acquire, maintain, and avoid losing. In keeping with his novel emphasis on "new" princes, Machiavelli thereby shifts attention to the acquisition of political power. Different kinds of principalities require different methods of acquisition and maintenance, different virtues (and vices); the virtues and actions of a prince must be considered relative to the object of acquiring and maintaining power. Notably, if Machiavelli's particular interest is in new princes, then these princes usually have to acquire political power from someone who already holds it, from already established princes or republics. By placing his emphasis on the new prince or would-be prince, Machiavelli already signals the distance he is creating between his treatise and more traditional works, in which the hereditary prince and his already established power are held up as exemplary.

Whatever Machiavelli's intentions were, his little treatise is now universally known by the title *The Prince*, and that is how I will continue to refer to it throughout this book. Before turning to the Dedicatory Letter, however, we should take the opportunity to clarify the meaning of "prince" (*principe*). By "prince" we usually now refer to royalty, namely either the son of a king or queen, such as the Prince of Wales, or the ruler of an independent principality, such as the Prince of Monaco. However, this is not the primary meaning of the word for Machiavelli and his contemporaries. The word "prince" shares the same etymological root as "principal," meaning either what is first or foremost, as in "my principal reason for writing this guide is to help the reader of *The Prince*," or a person who holds chief authority, such as the principal of a school. Hence a "prince" is not necessarily a monarch or royal personage for Machiavelli and his contemporaries, but instead refers to the "first" or "foremost" person—or persons—in a state in terms of political power or authority. Thus, while in *The Prince* Machiavelli typically uses the term "prince" to refer to an individual holding political power, in keeping with his focus on states in which a single ruler holds sway, in the *Discourses on Livy* he regularly speaks of "princes" in the plural within a given state, in keeping with his main focus there on republics, that is on states in which more than one person wields political authority at the same time. Even more striking, he sometimes refers there to the people as the "prince" of a republican state (e.g., I.58, 117–18). To our ear, the phrase "princes of republics" sounds odd, almost oxymoronic, and referring to the people as "prince" seems nearly nonsensical, but in Machiavelli's usage of the term "prince" doing so makes sense. Indeed, insofar as such uses of the word are meant by him to be deliberately jarring, we might say that his intention is to be brutally frank or realistic: whether we like it or not, all states are in fact ruled by one person or a small group of people who should therefore be considered "princes."

The background of the term "prince" in Roman history is particularly revealing for understanding *The Prince*.[4] The "prince," or *princeps* in Latin, originally referred during the period of the Roman Republic to the member of the Senate who had the privilege to speak first in the assembly and who was considered first among equals, the *Princeps Senatus*. With the fall of the Roman Republic, the *princeps* was the emperor. Importantly, however, the facade of republican rule endured, especially during the early period of the Roman Empire, and the emperor was not formally considered to be a monarchical ruler, but instead the fiction was maintained that he was still only first among equals.[5]

One reason this Roman background is useful for understanding *The Prince* is that the "prince" to whom Machiavelli dedicates his work, Lorenzo de' Medici, was not formally the ruler of Florence, for the Florentines, too, carefully maintained the fiction that it was still a republic. Just as the Medici had dominated the Florentine Republic during most of the 1400s, attaining the role of "prince" without any formal title, so too did they reprise that role when they reassumed power in 1512 with the fall of the Florentine Republic Machiavelli served. Indeed, only in 1530, when the Medici recaptured control of Florence once again after a very brief revival of the republic, was the pretense that Florence was a republic dropped and the Medici formally became hereditary rulers of the city. By addressing Lorenzo de' Medici as a prince, therefore, Machiavelli is being somewhat cheeky as he, so to speak, goes to the "effectual truth" of Florentine politics and beyond the appearances the Medici wished to maintain.[6]

THE DEDICATORY LETTER

The Dedicatory Letter addressed to Lorenzo de' Medici that opens *The Prince* undoubtedly serves one of Machiavelli's purposes in writing the book, namely his goal of regaining political office, but it also reveals a great deal about the style and form of his treatise and its ultimate intended audience.

The heading of the Dedicatory Letter, like all the chapter titles, is in Latin: "Nicolaus Machiavellus Magnifico Laurentio Medici Iuniori salutem," or "Niccolò Machiavelli to the Magnificent Lorenzo de' Medici the Younger: greetings."[7] Once again, by writing the heading of the Dedicatory Letter and the chapter titles in Latin, Machiavelli gives his work a traditional exterior that contrasts with a novel interior, signaled by his decision to write the text in Italian.

The contrast between what is traditional and what is novel is apparent from the very beginning of the text of the Dedicatory Letter. He begins: "It is customary most of the time for those who desire to acquire favor with a prince to come before him with those things among their own that they hold most dear, or in which they see him delight the most." The very first word of the text of *The Prince*, "Sogliano," translated here as "It is customary," calls attention to what is traditional, in this case what those who want to acquire favor or "grace" (*grazia*) with a prince customarily present to him.[8] Note that Machiavelli began the Dedicatory Letter by stating that those who desire to acquire favor with a prince present him either with things *they themselves* care for or with things they see most please *the prince*. He thereby opens up a possible gap between what the giver values and what pleases the recipient. This gap nonetheless seems to close right away because the list of things he says one customarily sees presented to princes seems to be of things that are seen to please the prince: horses, arms, cloth of gold, precious stones, and similar adornments. Either the giver has sacrificed what he considers valuable and instead presents the prince with what he sees pleases him or, alternatively, the giver and the recipient agree on what is customarily held to be valuable or pleasing. As for Machiavelli, he indicates in the very next sentence that he will break from this customary practice by

presenting Lorenzo with something he himself values, not necessarily with what Lorenzo or any other prince who likes horses,
arms, cloth of gold, and such would find pleasing:

> Therefore, since I desire to offer myself to Your Magnificence with
> some evidence of my devotion to you, and since I have not found
> among my valuables anything that I hold more dear or estimate so
> highly as the understanding of the deeds of great men, which I have
> learned through long experience with modern things and constant
> reading about ancient things, these I have with great diligence over a
> long time thought out and examined, and now, reduced into a small
> volume, I send them to Your Magnificence.

Whereas others offer gifts that please the prince, Machiavelli will
offer his prince what he himself cares for and esteems. Machiavelli
asserts his own judgment concerning what is truly estimable: not
horses, arms, gems, and other baubles, but knowledge. Will Lorenzo
esteem what Machiavelli esteems?

Lorenzo will receive "understanding of the deeds of great
men," or rather he will receive a book that contains such knowledge,
if only he will read the book and understand what the author
himself has come to understand. Surely princes have traditionally
been presented not only with horses, gems, and the like, but also
with books. Notably, they have been presented with mirror-of-
princes treatises, as discussed above. Yet Machiavelli goes out of
his way to distinguish his own book from the books customarily
given to princes. "I have not embellished this work, nor stuffed it
with fulsome phrases or with pompous and magnificent words or
with any of the other pandering or outward adornment with which
many are accustomed to describe and embellish their material."
Such ornamental touches may be pleasing, but they are not to
be truly esteemed. Machiavelli would have his work judged by
"the variety of the material and the weightiness of the subject."
Once again, in presenting his own work he breaks from what is
customarily done.

Standing between giver and recipient is the gift itself, and if the
gift is a book then we have the further relationship between
author and reader. Unlike a horse or arms or precious stones, the

knowledge contained in a book can be shared by both author and reader, or at least possessed in common in a way a horse cannot. But in order for such knowledge to be shared, the reader must be both willing to read the book and capable of understanding it. Machiavelli therefore turns in the Dedicatory Letter to the relationship between himself and Lorenzo, author and reader. "And, although I judge this work unworthy of your presence," he writes, "nonetheless I very much trust that on account of your humanity it may be accepted, considering how no greater gift could be given by me to you than to give you the ability in a very short time to understand all that I, in so many years and through so many hardships and perils to myself, have come to know and understand." Of course, Lorenzo could agree with Machiavelli's initial assessment that his short, unornamented book is in fact unworthy of his presence, and therefore not accept or read it. (In fact, if the story of Lorenzo preferring a pack of hunting dogs to *The Prince* is true, then he evidently did not find the book worthy of his presence.) For Machiavelli's great gift to be accepted the recipient or potential reader must first admit to a lack of knowledge or understanding which reading the book promises to remedy. Will Lorenzo admit that he lacks knowledge or understanding?

The relationship between Machiavelli and Lorenzo is further complicated by the fact that Lorenzo is a prince and Machiavelli is not. Why should Lorenzo believe that Machiavelli has anything to teach him about being a prince? "Nor do I want it to be imputed presumption if a man of low and basest state should dare to discourse on and give rules for the conduct of princes," Machiavelli tells Lorenzo, and then justifies his presumptuous act with a metaphor that proves pregnant: "For just as those who sketch landscapes place themselves low in the plain to consider the nature of mountains and of high places, and to consider the nature of low places they place themselves high atop mountains, similarly, to understand well the nature of peoples it is necessary to be a prince, and to understand well the nature of princes it is necessary to be of the people."

At first glance, the analogy seems clear: as a prince, Lorenzo is like the mountain whose "nature" can be known only by someone in the lowly position of being one of the people, such as

Machiavelli. Likewise, the "nature" of peoples is accessible only for those who are princes. Perhaps the first thing to note about this metaphor is that both the prince and the people have only a partial perspective or partial knowledge. In fact, if they can see only the other and not themselves, they both seem to lack the most important sort of knowledge: self-knowledge. If the exhortation inscribed above the Temple of Delphi, "Know Thyself," is the beginning of wisdom, then Machiavelli indicates that most political actors are ignorant, that they are not aware of their ignorance or at best possess only incomplete knowledge. Lorenzo would probably gladly agree that he knows more about the people than the people do, whether or not he in fact does. But would he accept that he lacks self-knowledge as a prince? Further, would he accept that someone of the people, for instance Machiavelli, knows more about princes than princes themselves do? Perhaps Lorenzo would be right in at least this respect, for does Machiavelli's claim that someone of the people necessarily knows the nature of princes better than do princes themselves ring true? To take a contemporary example, doesn't it seem likely that the president of the United States, the British prime minster, and even the premier of China have more insight into one another as leaders, or "princes," than their peoples do?

Perhaps we should challenge Machiavelli's metaphor. Is it true that the "nature" of mountains or valleys is best known from a distance, or at least only from a distance? Or wouldn't one better know the "nature" of something by examining it up close? Machiavelli's artist only "sketches" (*disegnano*) the mountain or valley, a verb that suggests more of an outline than a full picture, as he "considers" them from afar. The verb Machiavelli uses throughout this metaphor, "to consider" (*considerare*) has the basic sense of looking at something from a distance, such as a star (*sidus*, or "star" in Latin, likely being the root of *considerare*), and only comes by extension to mean "to examine" or "to think about carefully." Although I do not want to insist upon this point, the reader will now notice that Machiavelli sometimes writes "consider" alone and sometimes modifies the verb, for example writing "if one considers this well" or "diligently considers," thus indicating that someone might also "merely consider" something or view it superficially.

Later in *The Prince* Machiavelli will write of the prince: "And men as a whole judge more with their eyes than their hands, because everyone is permitted to see, but few are permitted to touch. Everyone sees what you seem to be, few feel what you are" (chap. 18, 95). Does considering the prince from the distant perspective of the people, or the people from the distant perspective of the prince, put one in danger of being taken in by appearances? Once again, upon closer examination, Machiavelli's metaphor underscores the fact that politics is a realm of appearances and partial perspectives.

Machiavelli's metaphor nonetheless also contains a possible solution to overcoming the problem of partial perspectives. If he distributes the knowledge of the nature of princes and peoples between the two groups, in his metaphor the artist has the potential to have knowledge of both mountains and plains, princes and peoples, because he is capable of changing perspective by moving from one place to another, from mountain to the plain and back again. A sufficiently talented artist would thereby come to know the "nature" of both mountains and plains from both near and afar. By implication, a sufficiently intelligent author could likewise have knowledge of both princes and peoples. Later in the work, Machiavelli will urge the prince to think constantly of war, suggesting that a proper means for doing so is hunting. Riding about his lands, the prince should "learn the nature of terrains, and to recognize how mountains rise, how valleys open up, how plains lie, and to understand the nature of rivers and marshes, and in this take very great care" (chap. 14, 85). Machiavelli's prince does not sit atop his mountain, occasionally turning his glance to the less fortunate in the plains below; he is constantly on the move in order to understand the nature of his terrain, both literally and metaphorically. To return to the metaphor in the Dedicatory Letter, although he humbly claims to be one of the people, Machiavelli is analogous to the artist. He will unapologetically discuss the natures of both princes and peoples in his work. The experience of modern things, as well as the reading of ancient things, which he puts forward as proof of his competence to discuss the art of politics, has given Machiavelli the capacity to consider matters from the perspectives of both princes and peoples.

Machiavelli's experience and reading have given him a more synoptic knowledge of politics than is possible from a single perspective.

The Dedicatory Letter concludes with Machiavelli once again considering his relationship to Lorenzo, and in doing so he alludes to his metaphor of mountains and plains. "And if Your Magnificence, from the peak of Your Magnificence's height, sometimes will cast your eyes on these low places, you will understand how undeservedly I endure a great and continuous malignity of fortune." Although he has justified his presumption in writing about princes by stating that one must be a member of the people (in the plains) in order to understand the nature of princes (on the mountain), Machiavelli now reveals that he "undeservedly" inhabits "these low places" because of bad luck. In other words, he signals that he is not essentially or simply one of the "people," and perhaps he is implying that he in truth has the nature of a prince. Machiavelli's apparent inferiority to Lorenzo, having tumbled back into the valley of the people by "a great and continuous malignity of fortune," masks his superiority as a kind of artist of politics. What about Lorenzo? If the author of *The Prince* is undeservedly placed among the people through misfortune, has the addressee of the work attained his lofty perch deservedly or has he become a prince solely through good luck? These questions raise the issue of the intended audience of Machiavelli's *Prince*.

THE AUDIENCE OF *THE PRINCE*

The answer to the question, "Who is the intended audience or reader of *The Prince*?" would seem to be obvious: the person to whom Machiavelli dedicates it, Lorenzo de' Medici. Nonetheless, the text of the Dedicatory Letter itself has already led us to raise doubts about whether Lorenzo will appreciate, read, or understand Machiavelli's work. The slyly ironic manner in which Machiavelli quietly raises these doubts ought to persuade us that he shares them, leading us to wonder whether he has other, even more important audiences in mind for his book. The way in which he concludes the Dedicatory Letter both reinforces our doubts about whether Lorenzo is in fact the principal audience

Machiavelli has in mind for *The Prince* and hints at its true or ultimate intended audience.

Having explained why he should not be held to be presumptuous for daring to "discourse on and give rules for the conduct of princes" given that he himself is not a prince, Machiavelli concludes the Dedicatory Letter by addressing himself to Lorenzo: "May your Magnificence therefore take up this small gift in the spirit with which I send it." What is the "spirit" with which Machiavelli sends his gift? If the doubts raised about Lorenzo thus far are justified, Machiavelli would seem to have sent his book as a kind of challenge. The challenge is indicated with the implied question with which he begins the next sentence: "So that *if* it is diligently considered and read by you ... ." Will Lorenzo read Machiavelli's book, much less diligently consider it? Machiavelli leaves open the possibility that he will not. "So that *if* it is diligently considered and read by you, you will recognize in it my extreme desire that you should arrive at the greatness that fortune and your other qualities promise you." Anyone even casually acquainted with *The Prince* knows that a major theme of the book is the contrast between virtue and fortune. Those who rely on their own virtue rather than on fortune, or luck, are more likely to acquire and maintain power. Fortune may provide the opportunity for a virtuous person to succeed, but ultimately virtue is necessary. Note, then, that Machiavelli only attributes "fortune" to Lorenzo, along with other unspecified "qualities," which may or may not be virtuous qualities, whatever that turns out to mean. Machiavelli is studiously silent about whether Lorenzo is virtuous. Lorenzo has attained princely power through fortune or luck; he was born into the Medici family. Lorenzo's good fortune may turn out to be the opportunity to exhibit his virtue, but he has yet to prove himself. Interestingly, Machiavelli also attributes only fortune to himself— the "great and continuous malignity" he speaks of at the very end of the Dedicatory Letter that contrasts with Lorenzo's good fortune. Nonetheless, Machiavelli indirectly speaks of his virtue when he claims to have knowledge of princes and how they should rule, and also when he says his own bad fortune is undeserved. Whether or not Lorenzo reads Machiavelli's work is a sort of test of his virtue or his capacity to attain virtue. Will Lorenzo diligently consider and read the book? Will he admit that he does not possess the knowledge Machiavelli promises his book contains and therefore read it? Will he have the capacity to understand it if he does read it? Machiavelli issues a challenge to Lorenzo, and to any reader of *The Prince*.

The doubts Machiavelli subtly raises in the Dedicatory Letter about whether a fortunate prince such as Lorenzo possesses the virtue and intelligence to be the proper audience for his work are dramatically seconded by the very different dedication to his other major political work, the *Discourses on Livy*. Machiavelli's book on republics is addressed to two young men of his acquaintance: Zanobi Buondelmonti and Cosimo Rucellai. If he commences the Dedicatory Letter to *The Prince* by speaking of what is customarily presented to princes and only quietly signals that he is breaking from these customs, in the dedication to the *Discourses* he positively proclaims his untraditional approach. He explains: "I have gone outside the common usage of those who write, who are accustomed always to address their works to some prince and, blinded by ambition and avarice, praise him for all virtuous qualities when they should blame him for every part worthy of reproach. Hence, so as not to incur this error, I have chosen not those who are princes but those who for their infinite good parts deserve to be" (Dedicatory letter to the *Discourses*, 3). Machiavelli almost seems to mock his own dedication to *The Prince*. At any rate, he further raises our doubts about Lorenzo de' Medici as the dedicatee of *The Prince*.

Finally, before moving on to the main body of *The Prince*, a brief consideration of two stylistic features of Machiavelli's writing already displayed in the Dedicatory Letter will help us better address the question of his true or ultimate intended audience as well as alert us to some of the "tricks of the trade" he uses as a writer.

First, as just noted, a major theme of *The Prince* as a whole is the contrast between virtue and fortune, and many readers of the work have noticed that Machiavelli frequently presents his consideration of topics in the form of binary terms: virtue vs. fortune, one's own arms vs. others' arms, princes vs. peoples, principalities vs. republics, etc. Sometimes these binary terms seem to be opposites, but often upon closer examination they turn out to be complements to one another, or are in a kind of dialectical relationship. For example, Machiavelli will state that fortune provides the opportunity for virtue to show itself, thus suggesting that fortune is a perhaps a necessary complement to virtue, even if virtue is ultimately what is most necessary. Second, and related, in writing Machiavelli often uses two different verbs or formulations where we might expect one, surely a remarkable feature of a work its author characterizes as short and unornamented. To take one example we have already seen, and to which we shall return shortly, Machiavelli writes of his gift to Lorenzo, "So that if it is diligently considered and read by you ...," using two verbs ("consider" and "read") where we might easily imagine him having used a single one. What does using both verbs add or suggest that either one of them alone does not? When we begin to notice Machiavelli's fondness for binary terms and seemingly redundant paired phrasing, it is striking how many examples of these features we already see in the Dedicatory Letter. What do they tell us about how he writes?

Two pairs of binary terms introduced by Machiavelli in the Dedicatory Letter can help us appreciate the scope and aim of his book: ancients vs. moderns and princes vs. peoples. In characterizing his gift to Lorenzo, Machiavelli claims that it contains "the knowledge of the actions of great men, learned by me from long experience with modern things and continuous reading of ancient ones." (Note that we now have another binary pair: "experience" vs. "reading.") *The Prince* will contain both ancient and modern examples, often juxtaposed with one another. Why? Of course, it could very well be that a reader of Machiavelli's time would expect to see ancient examples for a number of reasons, including as evidence of the author's credentials in the traditional humanist disciplines revived during the Renaissance. But perhaps Machiavelli has a more serious purpose, for example to highlight both differences and continuities between ancient and modern times. Machiavelli makes this purpose more obvious and thematic in his *Discourses on Livy*, where he complains that his contemporaries admire and seek to imitate the ancients in some ways, for example in sculpture, but do not think to imitate them in the most important ways, notably in politics. "This arises, I believe, not so much from the weakness into which the present religion has led the world, or from the evil that an ambitious idleness has done to many Christian provinces and cities, as from not having a true knowledge of histories, through not getting from reading them that sense nor tasting that flavor that they have in themselves" (I Preface, 6–7). We have already discussed the binary pair of princes vs. peoples, and now we see that the binary pairing of ancients and moderns has a similar purpose of giving the reader a more synoptic perspective, and therefore more comprehensive knowledge, than would be possible by focusing on one element of the pair alone. Just as Machiavelli urges readers of ancient history to read those works in such a way as to get their proper "sense" or "flavor," so too ought we, as readers of *The Prince*, read his work in accordance with his advice. By entering into a conversation with the text of *The Prince*, the reader should learn to savor the particular flavor of ancient things, and by comparing ancient and modern examples the reader should gain a clearer perspective on both.

As for Machiavelli's fondness for seemingly redundant phrasing, which he usually does as pairs of verbs or phrases, there are a number of examples in the Dedicatory Letter, but I will focus on two related examples, leaving it to the reader to examine other cases. As for the first example, having informed Lorenzo that he will be presenting him with a book, Machiavelli states that he is confident it will be accepted "considering how no greater gift could be given by me to you than to give you the ability in a very short time to understand all that I, in so many years and through so many hardships and perils to myself, have come to know and understand." Why does Machiavelli include both "come to know" and "understand"? Apparently learning or being familiar with something (the verb being translated "come to know," *conoscere*, meaning either to learn or to be familiar with) is necessary but not sufficient for understanding it. Recall in this light Machiavelli's statement in his letter to Vettori explaining why he has written down what he has come to understand through his conversations with ancient authors: "And because Dante says that to have understood without retaining does not make for knowledge, I have noted what capital I have made from their conversation and have composed a little book *De Principatibus*."[9] Reading the ancient authors is a form of learning, but "conversing" with them and tasting their proper "flavor" is necessary for true understanding. Yet Machiavelli says that even understanding does not fully produce "knowledge." This is perhaps the case for the person who thinks he understands (and we have all undoubtedly had the experience of thinking we understand something until we try to explain it to another person), but definitely so for the person to whom we are trying to communicate that knowledge, for example in a book. Machiavelli invites the reader of *The Prince* to enter into a conversation such as he had with the books he himself reads. The active type of reading necessary for understanding also explains why Machiavelli informs Lorenzo that reading his book will give him "the capacity to be able to understand" what he himself has come to understand, and not the understanding or knowledge itself. Conversing with Machiavelli through his book, or discoursing alongside him as one reads, is a kind of training that develops a capacity to understand on one's own.

This preceding example of seemingly redundant, but revealing, phrasing on Machiavelli's part helps us comprehend the second example I would like to consider, namely the phrasing in his challenge to Lorenzo already discussed above: "So that if it is diligently considered and read by you ... ." How do "diligently considered" and "read" differ? The difference is clear if the suggestion above about the meaning of "to consider" (*considerare*) is correct, namely that in Machiavelli's usage "to consider" usually has the meaning of considering something from afar, and therefore potentially superficially. Imagine Lorenzo taking up Machiavelli's book, looking at its cover, glancing at the Dedicatory Letter, leafing through the book—very much like I have done many times, and I am sure you have as well. This is "considering" the book. Given what we have learned about the difference between "learning" and "understanding" in the other case of seemingly redundant phrasing we have examined, then even simply reading Machiavelli's book would remain at the level of "considering" it. The book demands to be considered and read "diligently" if it is to be understood. Once again, in his Dedicatory Letter Machiavelli issues a challenge to

Lorenzo, or any other reader, as to whether he has the capacity to understand his book.

These considerations of Machiavelli's signature style as an author lead us back to the question of the ultimate audience of *The Prince*, especially given the reasons we have seen for doubting that Lorenzo de' Medici could be the true or ultimate intended audience. Machiavelli himself answers the question, but only for the reader who has persevered through more than half of his book. The answer comes in chapter 15:

> It remains therefore to see what should be the ways and conduct of a prince, whether with his subjects or with his allies. And because I know that many people have written about this, I worry in writing about it too that I shall be held presumptuous, especially since in debating this material I shall depart from the orders of others. But since my intent is to write a thing that is useful for whoever understands it, it seemed to me more appropriate to go after the effectual truth of the thing than the imagination of it.
>
> (Chap. 15, 87)

We shall return to this extremely important passage in its proper place, but for now we can note several aspects that bear on understanding the audience and purpose of *The Prince*. Machiavelli reveals that he has written his book for "whoever understands it." Of course, it is an open question whether Lorenzo, or any other reader, will in fact understand it. In this regard, note the echo in the passage of the Dedicatory Letter: just as he fears he may be held to be "presumptuous" for discussing how princes should rule when he himself is not a prince, so too here he warns that he may be held "presumptuous" for writing of what so many before him have already written, especially since he will depart from what they have written. If the Dedicatory Letter opens with what is "customary," namely what is customarily given to a prince to earn his favor, by chapter 15 Machiavelli is ready to reveal his novelty. Only the reader who has engaged in the back and forth of conversation with the author by engaging with his book will be prepared to understand what Machiavelli has understood.

NOTES

1 Petrarch, in Kohl and Witt 1978, 41.
2 See Gilbert 1938; Skinner 1978. As for Machiavelli, his only apparent reference to the mirror-of-princes genre occurs in the *Discourses on Livy*, where he recommends that princes who depart from ancient laws and customs should take "for their mirror the lives of good princes" (III.5, 217). This recommendation occurs immediately before the chapter devoted to conspiracies (III.6), which is as much a guide to princes in how to avoid conspiracies as it is a guide to conspirators in how to execute a successful conspiracy—not a typical subject for works in the mirror-of-princes genre.
3 Machiavelli to Francesco Vettori, December 10, 1513, in Machiavelli 2004, 264.
4 See Stacey 2007 for a comprehensive discussion of the Roman background to the Renaissance prince.
5 In this light, it is revealing to consider Cicero's concern with what he describes as an "appetite towards preeminence," "preeminence" translating *principatibus*, which he argues leads some individuals to overstep justice and law, pointing to the dangerous example of Julius Caesar. See *On Duties* I.13, I.26, I.63–64.
6 See Benner 2013, 13–14.
7 By specifying Lorenzo de' Medici *the Younger*, Machiavelli both differentiates his addressee Lorenzo de' Medici (1492–1519) from his more famous grandfather of the same name, Lorenzo de' Medici (1449–92), and flatteringly associates him with his illustrious forbearer. Some of the manuscripts do not include "the Younger" (*Iuniori*) in the salutation.
8 For a reading of the Dedicatory Letter very similar to the one offered here and which focuses on Machiavelli's presentation of himself in *The Prince*, see Tarcov 2013a.
9 Machiavelli to Francesco Vettori, December 10, 1513, in Machiavelli 2004, 264.

4

ACQUISITION AND THE EMERGENCE OF THE NEW PRINCE

In chapter 1 of *The Prince*, Machiavelli begins with a schema for classifying different types of states and the modes by which they are acquired. The first type of principality he lists is a hereditary principality, and he therefore dutifully follows his schema by treating hereditary principalities in chapter 2. Nonetheless, Machiavelli's tidy schema quickly breaks down over the next several chapters, or so I will suggest, and at the same time that the various types of principalities become blurred, the modes by which they are acquired come to the fore. As Lefort explains: "Thus, when we approach the work, the landscape changes; the borders, at first so clear, that circumscribed the fragments of the discourse become indistinct. First of all, we must give up the idea that the introductory chapter contains a plan, admit rather that it furnishes a substitute for one, and prepare to seek the meaning at once in the line of what is said and beyond it, in the still underdetermined region it merely delimits."[1]

With acquisition of political power becoming the primary consideration, the hereditary prince, traditionally the primary subject of works on the proper virtues and actions of a prince, is supplanted by Machiavelli's model of the "new" prince. The "new" prince is the announced subject of chapters 6 and 7, and Machiavelli's focus in treating such a prince is the modes by which he acquires power. More specifically, his focus there is the last set of modes for acquiring power that he lists in chapter 1: "either with the arms of others or with one's own, either by fortune or by virtue." In examining chapters 1–5, therefore, we will see how the tidy schema of types of states Machiavelli presents in chapter 1 breaks down, and how his discussion through chapter 5 prepares the emergence of the main theme of *The Prince*: the new prince and the interplay between virtue and fortune.

CHAPTER 1: HOW MANY KINDS OF PRINCIPALITIES THERE ARE, AND BY WHAT MEANS THEY ARE ACQUIRED

The title to chapter 1 is already revealing about Machiavelli's new perspective in *The Prince*: he will discuss not only the various types of principalities, but the modes by which they are acquired. By contrast, the audience of more traditional books presented to princes is customarily a hereditary ruler who claims a long pedigree, a prince who does not have to "acquire" his state. Although the title promises a discussion of types of principalities, the opening sentence of chapter 1 takes a larger view: "All states, all dominions that have had and do have command over men, have been and are either republics or principalities." The reader expecting a discussion of the types of principalities immediately learns that a principality is a form of "state," the other form being a republic. Not only principalities, but republics too will turn out to be the object of acquisition, and in fact some of the most chilling advice Machiavelli offers in *The Prince* concerns how to acquire a republic. We will take up the difficult question of what Machiavelli means by the term "state" (*stato*) momentarily, but an initial definition is offered in the first sentence: "dominions that have held and do hold command over men." States or dominions exercise "command" over men, either as subjects in the case of a principality or fellow citizens in a republic. "Command" (*imperio*) might be translated "political power." "Command" is not the simple exercise of force, but the recognized power to rule, and in this sense Machiavelli anticipates something akin to Weber's definition of the state as an entity having a monopoly on the legitimate use of force. Machiavelli's definition of the state seems "empirical" as opposed to "theoretical," or to borrow language from later in *The Prince*, he goes to "the effectual truth of the thing." All states "that have had and do have" command over men "have been and are" either republics or principalities. What matters is "having" command, and what republics and principalities "are," and have always been, depends on who exercises this command.

After this opening proposition about "all states" being either republics or principalities, Machiavelli turns to his promised enumeration of the types of principalities and the modes by which they are acquired. "Principalities are either hereditary, in which the lineage of their lord has been prince for a long time, or they are new. The new ones are either completely new, as was Milan for Francesco Sforza, or they are like limbs added to the hereditary state of the prince who acquires them, as is the Kingdom of Naples for the king of Spain."

Whereas Machiavelli gives one example each for the two types of "new" principalities he lists, he gives no example here of a hereditary principality. A hereditary principality is defined here as a principality in which "the lineage of their lord has been prince for a long time," that is where the current "lord" (*signore*) comes from a family that has been "prince" (*principe*)—that is, has held the status of prince—"for a long time." How long is "a long time"? Hereditary princes probably do not like to be reminded that at some point their principality was "new," was acquired by someone, so perhaps Machiavelli declines to give an example of a hereditary principality because doing so would raise this delicate question. This consideration already blurs the tidy distinction Machiavelli draws between hereditary and new principalities. This blurring is also evident in his example of Francesco Sforza as ruling a "completely new" principality. Sforza was in fact the son-in-law of the previous Duke of Milan, who died without any heirs, and the Milanese, after a brief period of unsuccessfully attempting to reestablish a republic, granted the duchy to Sforza. Since the duchy passed to Sforza's son after his death, what was in some sense a "new" principality was transformed into a hereditary one. Perhaps all principalities, even all states, are in fact a mixture of "old" and "new." If so, then the example of the king of Spain adding the Kingdom of Naples to his hereditary state like adding a new "limb" to the "body" of his dominion would in fact be the typical case for all principalities or states. In chapter 3 Machiavelli will term this type of principality or state "mixed." Once again, we see how the binary categories Machiavelli often uses, here "hereditary" vs. "new," are not as clear and distinct as they initially seem.

The emphasis on acquisition becomes thematic when Machiavelli turns from the types of principalities to the modes by which they are acquired. "Dominions that are thus acquired are either accustomed to living under a prince or used to being free, and they are acquired either with the arms of others or with one's own, either by fortune or by virtue." Just as he presents the types of states as a series of binary categories—republics vs. principalities, hereditary vs. new principalities—so too does he list the modes of acquiring dominions in a series of pairs: accustomed to living under a prince vs. used to living free, acquired with the arms of others vs. acquired with one's own arms, acquired by fortune vs. acquired by virtue. We will have to watch carefully to see how these seemingly exclusive categories fare as the work progresses.

Let us now return to what Machiavelli means by a "state" (*stato*). What Machiavelli means by "state" is not what we mean today, so we must first try to understand his conception of a "state."

Today we are accustomed to using the word "state," or its relative the "nation-state," to denote an impersonal entity: "the state." "The state" so conceived is somehow distinct from its people, or its government, or even its form of government. That is, the people or population of the state might change (e.g., through birth, death, and immigration), its government might change (e.g., from a Republican to a Democratic administration), and even its form of government might change (e.g., from a democracy to an autocracy) without "the state" itself considered to have changed. The state so conceived is somehow the locus of legitimate power, or sovereignty, within its borders or dominion and it stands as an equal alongside other such "sovereign states" in the international realm, for example in the United Nations. This conception of "the state" fully emerged more than a century after Machiavelli wrote *The Prince*. Within the realm of politics, the fully modern idea of the state is usually dated from the Peace of Westphalia of 1648, the series of treaties that ended the Thirty Years War, the long political and religious conflict generated by the Protestant Reformation, by establishing the principle of state sovereignty with which we are still familiar today. Within the realm of political theory, the first theorist of the modern state and sovereignty is often said to be Thomas Hobbes, whose major work *Leviathan* was published in 1651. At any rate, other political theorists such as Jean Bodin who might be said to have developed the concept of the sovereign state wrote in the same period, well after Machiavelli. In short, the political and theoretical events that led to the full emergence of the concept of the sovereign state as we now know it today occurred more than a century after Machiavelli's lifetime.

What, then, does Machiavelli mean when he uses the term "state" (*stato*)? This issue turns out to be complex and controversial.[2] Broadly speaking, though, if the modern conception of the state is impersonal, then the conception of the "state" found in Machiavelli is essentially personal. To return to the first sentence of chapter 1, Machiavelli characterizes "states" as "dominions that have had and do have command over men." To simplify somewhat for starters, then, the state in this sense is the person or persons actually exercising political authority, or the "regime" in the sense of the reigning power in a given place (a "dominion") at a given time. For example, we might speak of the "state" or the "regime" of Henry VIII of England (a younger contemporary of Machiavelli's), meaning not just that Henry VIII happened to be king of England at the time, but that his exercise of command or his rule in a sense defined or constituted the state or regime then reigning in England. This usage will be familiar to readers of Shakespeare, who for example refers to the king of France as "France," as though the king *is* France or France is the king's personal property. More informally, we might refer to the period during which a sports team, or a company, or some other entity was under the dominant leadership of someone as a "regime," for example the "Vince Lombardi

Regime" for the Green Bay Packers or the "Bill Gates Regime" at Microsoft. More colloquially, we might say that Serena and Venus Williams "ruled" the tennis world in the early twenty-first century. Conceived in this way, states can be "acquired," that is the position of command or political authority can be acquired, for Machiavelli and his contemporaries in a way that is difficult for us to grasp with our modern impersonal conception of the state.

Machiavelli nonetheless does not simply identify a state with the person or persons exercising command, but rather for him a state is constituted by who has the *status* of exercising command. In other words, he distinguishes between the given person exercising political authority at a given time from the position or status of ruling. For example, in chapter 1 he states that in hereditary principalities "the blood of their lord has been their prince for a long time." The current ruler, the "lord" (*signore*), is distinct from the "prince" (*principe*). This distinction reveals something essential about Machiavelli's use of the term "prince." In addition to referring to a specific individual who exercises the power of his principality, or the current "lord," the term "prince" refers to the *status* of the person within the regime: the "lord" holds the status of "prince," his "status" as prince is recognized. We can understand something of what he means by recalling that the words "state" and "status" are related, as is the word "estate." In its original or more traditional meaning, "state" denoted *someone's* state, in the sense of his possession or "estate." Similarly, the nobility had estates and titles that they came to possess through inheritance, grant, or otherwise, and this gave them a certain "status" or made them members of different "estates," for example the nobility, the clergy, and the people (the "third estate") in the old regime in France before the Revolution. Machiavelli evokes this traditional meaning when he writes in the Dedicatory Letter: "Nor do I want it to be imputed presumption if a man of low and basest state [*stato*] should dare to discourse on and give rules for the conduct of princes" (Dedicatory Letter, 40). Machiavelli's "status" is being a member of the people, as opposed to having the "status" of being a prince. In short, Machiavelli's conception of the state is not simply personal, in the sense of being bound up with what person or persons are wielding power at a given time, and to that

extent his conception of the state is impersonal and might be said
to prepare the modern understanding of the state. Nonetheless,
and most importantly, his conception of the state remains personal
in the sense that he insists that *someone* is always exercising
command and that the actual exercise of this command defines
the state.

Since the fact of who has the status of exercising command
differs from one state to another, there are different forms of state.
In *The Prince* Machiavelli confines himself to two: republics and
principalities. In so doing, he silently rejects more traditional
understandings of political regimes. Most famously and influen-
tially, Aristotle categorized regimes along two dimensions: correct
vs. deviant (based on whether the rulers aimed at the common
good versus their own good), and the number of rulers (one, few,
many). This typology produced six forms of regime: kingship,
aristocracy, and polity (a correctly tempered or "mixed" regime)
being the correct forms, and tyranny, oligarchy, and democracy
(the rule of the many for their own benefit, or what we might call
"mob rule") being the deviant forms. Other ancient and medieval
authors offered similar categorizations. We know that Machiavelli
was familiar with these traditional categories. For example, in the
Discourses on Livy he writes: "some who have written on republics
say that in them is one of three states [*stati*]—called by them
principality, aristocrats, and popular—and that those who order a
city should turn to one of these according as it appears to them
more to the purpose. Some others, wiser according to the opinion
of many, have the opinion that there are six types of government, of
which three are the worst; that three others are good in themselves
but so easily corrupted that they too come to be pernicious"
(I.2, 11). In the *Discourses on Livy* Machiavelli will largely reject
the traditional categorization of regimes and, as in *The Prince*,
speak of principalities and republics, but at least he commences
his discussion of the forms of states by acknowledging the traditional view. In *The Prince*, by contrast, he silently sweeps away
the traditional understanding of regimes. Once we recognize what
is missing from his discussion, the boldness of the first sentence of
chapter 1 is apparent: "*All* states, *all* dominions that *have had and
do have* command over men, *have been and are* either republics or

principalities." Once again, Machiavelli seems to go directly to "the effectual truth of the thing," indicating that whatever names one wants to give to the state or regime, the truth of the matter is that someone is exercising command over men. If one individual has command, it is a principality; if a number of individuals share command, it is a republic.

Perhaps most notably, even shockingly, Machiavelli dispenses in *The Prince* with any distinction between a prince and a tyrant. This distinction is not only crucial to Aristotle's categorization of regimes, as well as those of other political theorists, but to perhaps every single writer in the mirror-of-princes genre to which *The Prince* at least superficially seems to belong. When teaching a prince about the virtues he should have and how he should behave, these writers insisted that the prince not give into the temptation to become a tyrant. Yet the word "tyrant" is nowhere to be found in *The Prince*. This omission is all the more striking because Machiavelli freely uses the term in his other works, including the *Discourses on Livy*. Indeed, he even refers there to the very same individuals in that work as "tyrants" whom he calls "princes" in *The Prince*. For example, in chapter 6 of *The Prince* he brings forward Hiero of Syracuse as an example of a new prince, as someone who rose from being a private citizen to become a prince, whereas in the *Discourses* he refers to Hiero as an example of a tyrant who brutally ruled his people for his own benefit (II.2, 130). Whether Machiavelli's prince is a tyrant, and whether or not the people benefit from his rule, is one of the central questions of *The Prince*.

CHAPTER 2: ON HEREDITARY PRINCIPALITIES

In chapter 1 Machiavelli began by stating that there are two types of states, republics and principalities, and he opens chapter 2 by putting aside republics: "I shall leave out reasoning on republics because on another occasion I have discussed them at length." He appears to refer to the *Discourses on Livy*, a work he probably began at about the same time as he was completing *The Prince*. The relationship between his discussion of republics in the *Discourses on Livy* and his advice to princes in *The Prince* has long been a subject of debate, and a topic to which we shall return in Chapter 11. For the present it suffices to say that he does not entirely put aside republics in *The Prince*. Among other things he recommends to princes that they should follow the harsh modes used by the Roman Republic in acquiring republics and he discusses how a new prince might rise to power in a republic. For now, however, he turns to a discussion of the governance and maintenance the first type of principality he enumerated in chapter 1: hereditary principalities.

Hereditary principalities turn out to be hardly worth discussing, or so it seems. "I say therefore that in states that are hereditary and accustomed to the lineage of their prince there are many fewer difficulties in maintaining them than in new ones, for it suffices only not to break with the orders of one's ancestors and then to govern according to circumstances. So that if such a prince is of ordinary industry he will always maintain himself in his state, unless an extraordinary and excessive force deprives him of it." The hereditary prince, it seems, merely has to show up for work. But how reliable are the "orders," or political institutions, of one's ancestors in the face of changing circumstances? Further, one of the main arguments of the *Discourses on Livy* is that all states need to be regularly reordered because their "orders" tend by their nature to lose their original effectiveness (III.1). Likewise, even if it is true that a prince of "ordinary industry" can maintain his state with relative ease, how unusual or how far away is the "extraordinary and excessive force" that will deprive him of his state, and how well equipped will this "ordinary" prince be for such "extraordinary" events?

The example Machiavelli gives to reassure his "ordinary" prince is hardly reassuring. "We have in Italy, among our examples, the duke of Ferrara, who survived the attacks of the Venetians in 1484 and those of Pope Julius in 1510 for no other reason than that he had grown old in that dominion." Machiavelli actually refers here to two dukes of Ferrara as though they were one, in keeping with the notion that in a hereditary principality the "prince" remains the same even if the "lord," or present ruler, changes. The first duke is Ercole I d'Este, who was defeated by the Venetians in 1482 but then restored to his principality by a coalition of

Italian states, but only after he ceded part of his dominion. The second duke is his son Alfonso I, who lost his state to Pope Julius in 1510, but then regained it the following year due to his military prowess. Although it is true that these dukes of Ferrara maintained their states in the face of extraordinary force, thus supporting Machiavelli's thesis of the ease with which hereditary principalities are maintained, surely he could have chosen a more apt example of how easy it is to maintain a hereditary principality, and even more certainly he could have provided numerous examples of them being lost. First of all, the "extraordinary" forces faced by the dukes were not so extraordinary, for in a little over twenty-five years they faced two perilous forces that nearly led to the loss their state. Second, they did not regain their state merely because their bloodline was ancient, for the first duke regained it through the arms of others, and only after the humiliation of losing part of his dominion, and the second duke was hardly a prince of "ordinary industry." As is often the case in *The Prince*, Machiavelli's examples turn out to be more complicated than they first appear.

With his less than reassuring example in place, Machiavelli concludes his chapter on hereditary principalities by explaining why such states are supposedly more easily maintained than new ones. "For the prince by birth has fewer reasons and less need to offend, from which it proceeds that he is more loved; and, if extraordinary vices do not make him hated, it is reasonable that his own subjects naturally should wish him well." The phrase translated here as "the prince by birth" is *principe naturale*, or "natural prince." This term was common in an era when hereditary rule was often deemed the most "natural" form of state, and "natural princes" were presumed to be as natural to a dominion as its mountains and plains. It is thus "reasonable" that the "natural prince" of ordinary virtue and industry should be "naturally" loved and wished well by his subjects, Machiavelli writes. The hereditary prince has "*fewer* reasons and *less* need to offend" compared with the new prince. While this may be true, this prince at least sometimes has reason or need to offend. Machiavelli therefore concludes his chapter on hereditary principalities by reminding the prince that his state was once new and required such offense: "And in the antiquity and continuity of his dominion the memories of revolutions [*innovazioni*] and the reasons for them are extinguished." The hereditary principality seems ancient because the memory of its former novelty, the "revolutions" or "innovations" by which it was founded, has been extinguished. We might even say that it is less the affection of the subjects for their hereditary prince than the fact that they are accustomed to being oppressed that explains their quietude. But do the "reasons" for such innovations ever truly disappear? How different in the end is a hereditary principality from a new one when it comes to the modes necessary for maintaining it? Machiavelli addresses these issues in the following chapter.

CHAPTER 3: ON MIXED PRINCIPALITIES

"But the difficulties are in the new principality." With this abrupt statement Machiavelli begins chapter 3, and he does so with a qualifying "But" that links this chapter to the previous one on hereditary principalities and suggests that the discussion in the preceding chapter requires qualification or is somehow incomplete. He shifts his focus from hereditary principalities, where at least superficially there did not appear to be many difficulties in maintaining power, to new principalities, where the difficulties are greater or perhaps more obvious. Turning from hereditary to "new" principalities, Machiavelli begins with a discussion of principalities that are somewhere in between old and new, or what he terms "mixed" principalities. "And first," he continues, "if it is not wholly new, but like a limb (so that all together it may be called almost 'mixed'), its troubles arise at once from a natural difficulty that exists in all new principalities, which is that men willingly exchange their lord if they believe they will be better off, and this belief makes them take up arms against him." Machiavelli here alters his perspective, moving from the view from the "mountain" of the hereditary prince of chapter 2 to the "plains" of the would-be new prince who intends to assault the mountain and topple the present lord.

Let us begin with the term "mixed" principality. If the title of the chapter announces that it will be on "mixed" principalities, Machiavelli immediately qualifies this terminology in the text by calling it "almost" (*quasi*) mixed, or we might say "quasi-mixed." One reason he may hedge in calling this principality simply "mixed" is to avoid the terminology of the "mixed regime" favored by Aristotle and other classical and contemporary theorists, a regime that mixes monarchical, aristocratic, and popular elements.[3] By calling attention to the fact that he is avoiding this traditional terminology, however, he simultaneously thereby calls it to mind. In addition to being "mixed" in the sense of a prince adding new territory to his dominion like a limb to his body, the "mixed principality" he is discussing turns out to be "mixed" in the sense that it is composed of different elements. Explaining why the people are deceived in their hopes that they will be better off under a new prince, he writes: "This follows from another natural and ordinary necessity that stipulates that one always has to offend those of whom one becomes a new prince, both with men-at-arms and with the infinite other injuries that a new acquisition brings with it. The result is that you have as enemies all those you have offended in occupying that principality, and you cannot maintain as friends those who have put you there, because you cannot satisfy them in that way that they had earlier supposed … ." The newly acquired dominion is a mixture of friends and enemies. In fact, every principality will turn out to contain both friends and enemies to the regime, a consideration Machiavelli politely declined to raise in chapter 2 on hereditary principalities, where he spoke only of the loving subjects of the "natural" prince. The "mixed" character of principalities will continue to occupy him throughout *The Prince*, and among the considerations he will raise is the relationship between the prince, the aristocracy or elite (or "the great," as he will call them), and the people. These are the various groups or elements central to more traditional treatments of the "mixed" regime, but Machiavelli treats these elements from the novel perspective he adopts of the acquisitive new prince.

If the hereditary prince, or the "natural" prince as he called him in chapter 2, should "naturally" have the affections of his people, Machiavelli now reveals that nature is not so kind to princes. Discussing the difficulties of new principalities in general, including "mixed" ones, he states: "its troubles arise in the first place from a natural difficulty that exists in all new principalities, which is that men willingly change their lord if they believe they will be better off, and this belief makes them take up arms against him." Of course, if men willingly change their lord, then this "natural difficulty" would also affect hereditary princes. Our suspicion that hereditary princes faced considerably more difficulties in maintaining their state than Machiavelli let on has been confirmed. Machiavelli will say that the people are mistaken in their belief that they will profit by this change, and the reason for this arises from yet another "natural and ordinary necessity," namely that a new prince "always has to offend" some of the people, thereby creating enemies, and also cannot completely satisfy his friends in their hopes, thereby disappointing his friends. These "necessities" Machiavelli reveals all relate to human passions—love, fear, hope, etc.—and their variability. He claims here that the new prince, whom he now addresses as "you," cannot "use strong medicines" against his disappointed supporters "since you are obligated to them." Later in this chapter, when discussing sending colonies to the new part of the "mixed" principality, Machiavelli will no longer tell the prince to worry about such obligation, and will instead pointedly note: "men should either be coddled or eliminated."

In our discussion of chapter 1 we saw that Machiavelli's generalizations and the examples he uses to illustrate them are more complicated than they first appear, and the very first example he provides in chapter 3 is a good example of such complexity. As an example of a new prince being initially welcomed when he overthrows the former prince, and of the people then repenting of the change, Machiavelli offers up King Louis XII of France's capture of Milan from its prince, Ludovico Sforza. Louis first captured Milan in September 1499 and then Sforza recaptured the city five months later in February 1500 when the Milanese realized that they were deceived in their hopes with regard to the French king. This would appear to be an apt example of Machiavelli's point. However, he immediately complicates it. "It is indeed true that when lands that have rebelled once are regained for a second time they are lost with greater difficulty, for their lord, having taken the occasion from their rebellion, is less hesitant to secure himself." (Again, no more talk of obligation restraining the prince in his actions.) In order to illustrate his statement, Machiavelli continues with the story of Louis XII and Ludovico Sforza. He explains that if Louis lost Milan easily to Sforza the first time in February 1500, regaining it "for the second time" in April of the same year, he only lost it with difficulty "the second time" (in 1512) and only because he had "all the world against him" (a league of states led by Pope Julius II), a seemingly extraordinary and almost miraculous event. Machiavelli is therefore constrained to admit at the conclusion of his example: "Nonetheless both the first and the second time it was taken from him." What are we to make of this example?

It seems doubtful that the example of Louis' twice losing Milan proves the truth that it is difficult to lose a state a second time, but the other example quietly contained within this exemplary story positively refutes it, for if Louis gained and lost Milan two times, then Sforza must have also twice lost his state to Louis. Indeed, after regaining Milan the second time in February 1500, Sforza died in captivity in France some years later, a defeat that only becomes more bitter when we consider that Sforza was a hereditary prince, in fact the son of the exemplary new prince of chapter 2, Francesco Sforza, further undermining Machiavelli's argument that maintaining a hereditary principality is easy. Focusing our attention on the king of France, Machiavelli causes us to lose sight of Ludovico Sforza, who twice lost Milan and rather easily so. The truism that it is difficult to lose a state a second time turns out to be cold comfort. If Machiavelli undermines the truism through his example, he simultaneously underscores the main point with which he began the chapter concerning the instability of princely rule due to the acquisitive desires from both within and without the state.

With the example of Louis XII of France Machiavelli also introduces the historical context that overshadows *The Prince* and his political writings in general: the invasion of Italy by foreign powers, initially by Charles VIII of France in 1494, then again by Louis XII in 1499, and subsequently by a number of foreign powers over the next several decades. These invasions of Italy made clear to Machiavelli and many of his contemporaries the vulnerability of a divided Italy, and also the role of the Church in this division, a point he will first raise later in this chapter. Much of the remainder of chapter 3 is consumed with Machiavelli's analysis of the reasons why Louis lost his Italian acquisitions, including Milan, and his recommendations on how that loss could have been prevented. He thereby teaches his reader how to successfully acquire Italy—a seemingly odd thing for a self-professed Italian patriot to do. Nonetheless, the project of acquiring Italy could also simultaneously be a plan for uniting a disunited Italy. A united Italy would be able to defend itself against foreign invasion by the newly united states, the budding nation-states of Europe, to which it had been prey.

Successfully conquering Italy from without or successfully uniting it from within would both require acquiring political power, and in this light we should note Machiavelli's striking remark in this chapter on the natural and ordinary desire to acquire. In the middle of his analysis of Louis XII's failed invasion of Italy, and specifically when discussing Louis' disastrous decision to satisfy the Church's and the king of Spain's own desire to acquire in Italy by allowing them to become powerful, Machiavelli suddenly offers a general thought: "It is a thing truly very natural and ordinary to desire to acquire. When men do it who are capable, they will always be praised or not criticized. But when they are not capable and want to do it anyway, here is the error and the blame."[4] Machiavelli's application of this general remark to the specific case of Louis XII has the effect of justifying his invasion of Italy as an instance of the "very natural and ordinary" desire to acquire. It simultaneously has the effect of blaming him—not for his desire to acquire, but for his failure to do so. What Machiavelli here accepts as "truly" the case (the first time he uses the word "true" or "truly" in *The Prince*) flies in the face of the traditional classical and Christian attitudes toward desire to acquire. In the traditional view, even if the desire to acquire is somehow "very natural and ordinary," it ought to be restrained, in the view of such classical authors as Plato, Aristotle, Cicero, and others, or viewed as evidence of our sinful nature, in the Christian context. For example, both Aristotle and the Church Fathers, among others, had condemned practices such as the lending of money at interest, or usury, as vicious or sinful. With something like a shrug of the shoulder Machiavelli dismisses these condemnations of our natural desire to acquire. Once again, his focus in *The Prince* is on how to acquire and maintain political power, and the "effectual truth" is that humans are naturally acquisitive.

Let us turn now to Machiavelli's extended analysis of the French king's failure to keep his Italian acquisitions, which Machiavelli writes he will do in order to instruct "whoever is in his circumstances" how to succeed. Machiavelli immediately starts raising issues concerning the acquisition of new or mixed principalities he has not yet mentioned. The first factor is whether or not the new part being added to an existing state is of the same province and the same language. By "province" Machiavelli usually means a broadly geographically homogenous area, so that Italy or perhaps just the north of Italy would qualify as a province. He claims that if they are of the same province and language then the new part is more easily acquired, but he also immediately raises further issues when he states that this is especially the case "when they are not used to living in freedom, and to possess them securely it is enough to have eliminated the line of the prince who was ruling them." His seeming indifference to freedom and his offhanded advice to eliminate the line of the ruling prince—that is, to kill or otherwise eliminate his family—is all the more chilling for its being so casually offered. Further discussing how such acquisitions can be maintained, he says that the acquiring prince should have two concerns: "one is that the bloodline of their former prince be eliminated; the other is to alter neither their laws nor their taxes." Once again, his murderous advice is chilling. But what about his advice not to alter the laws or taxes of the newly acquired part of the principality? Despite his remarks in chapter 2 concerning the love peoples show toward their hereditary prince, it seems that the people care more about their own safety and property. As for Machiavelli, he cautions against invading the property of these new subjects not because of his concern for property rights or the like, but as a counsel of prudence.

His example here of a "mixed" principality whose parts are of the same province and language is interesting given that he is analyzing the king of France's failure to acquire Italy, an acquisition that is not of the same province or language: France itself. Although we today think of France as a unified nation-state, in

Machiavelli's own time what we now know as France had only recently been created by the addition of the various formerly independent or nearly independent states which Machiavelli lists here as having "been with France for so much time": Burgundy, Brittany, Gascony, and Normandy. Indeed, it was the acquisition of Brittany in 1491, just twenty some years before Machiavelli wrote *The Prince*, that created more or less the geographic entity we now see as France. Brittany was acquired through marriage (though with great reluctance on the part of the Bretons), but other provinces were not acquired so easily, for example Gascony, which was alternately in French and English hands until the final defeat of the English in 1453. Apart from suggesting that cobbling together a "mixed" principality of the same province and language is only relatively easier to do than acquiring new domain where the province and language are different, Machiavelli's example of France itself as a "mixed" principality further blurs the difference between a hereditary and new or mixed principality, since France might be considered as any of these depending on what point of view one takes.

Having dealt with new acquisitions of the same province and language, Machiavelli turns to the more difficult case of acquiring "a province that is foreign in its language, customs and orders." Before he spoke of language and customs, Machiavelli now quietly adds another element: "orders." What does he mean by "orders" (*ordini*)? This term does appear in *The Prince*, but it is much more prominent in the *Discourses on Livy* where it refers to what we might term "institutions" broadly speaking, especially political institutions, but also other formal and informal institutions, including religion. Machiavelli's advice for a prince in this situation is itself fairly straightforward, it seems: the prince should either go live in the newly acquired dominion so that he can deal with issues on the spot as they arise and inspire the people with both love and fear or, even better Machiavelli says, he should send colonies, that is groups of his own subjects to live among the newly acquired people.

His choice of examples of these two methods is perhaps what is more interesting. For the remedy of going to live there he points to "the Turk" going to reside in Greece, that is the Ottoman

Sultan making Constantinople the capital of his empire after successfully capturing the city in 1453 from the Byzantines, the successors to the Roman Empire in the east. For the remedy of sending colonies, he gives the example of the Romans, that is the Roman Republic, in their own conquest of Greece. Machiavelli even underscores his choice of this example of a general Roman policy by explicitly specifying his choice: "And I want the province of Greece to suffice as my single example." In both cases, then, Greece is the example of the province being acquired, first by the Ottoman Turks in modern times and second by the Roman Republic in ancient times. In fact, his example of Rome here is the first instance in *The Prince* in which Machiavelli draws on his "constant reading about ancient things" of which he spoke in the Dedicatory Letter when explaining his credentials for writing about political affairs. Apparently we can learn something from an ancient example that we cannot learn from a modern one.

One other thing these two examples have in common is that both of the conquering states are non-Christian, as opposed to the main example of chapter 3 of the king of France attempting to seize Italy. Perhaps religion is among the "orders" Machiavelli has in mind in explaining the difficulties of acquiring a mixed state with different "language, customs and orders." As we shall see momentarily, the presence of the Papal Court in Italy turns out to be a central factor in Machiavelli's analysis of the failure of the French to acquire Italy, and also of the difficulties in unifying Italy along the model of France, among other states. For the moment, though, his choice of examples may also explain why he states that sending colonies is a better remedy than going to live there in such cases. Namely, as he explains in his *Florentine Histories*, it was the removal of the capital of the Roman Empire from Rome to Constantinople, specifically by the Emperor Constantine (the first Christian emperor) in 324 CE, that began the process of the decay of the Roman Empire in the west and its eventual fall to the invading barbarians a century and a half later.[5] So, at minimum, if a prince goes to live in his newly acquired province he has to leave his former state, and the gains in attending on the spot to difficulties that arise in the new state have to be balanced against the losses of not being able to attend to any problems in the old dominion.

Machiavelli's example of the Romans in this context is interesting in yet another way. Namely, having explained in chapter 2 that he will not reason about republics since he has done so at length elsewhere, Machiavelli nonetheless offers a republic, Rome, as an example that should be followed by princes: "For the Romans did in these circumstances what all wise princes should do." What did the Romans do? Machiavelli emphasizes that the Romans were not only aware of "present disorders," but more importantly anticipated future disorders and dealt with them right away. Machiavelli likens these disorders to an illness, consumption (that is, tuberculosis), which he says is difficult to diagnose at the beginning because its symptoms are difficult to recognize but easy to cure if diagnosed, but easy to diagnose and difficult to cure when it becomes manifest. The rare "prudent man" who foresees dangerous disorders from a distance, as the Romans did, can remedy them before they arise. Machiavelli contrasts the "virtue and prudence" of the Romans to "the wise men of our times" who, he says, are constantly voicing the adage "to enjoy the benefit of time."[6] Whereas the ancients, represented by the Romans, put their trust in present virtue and prudence to forestall future evils, the moderns, "the wise men of our times," abandon virtue and prudence and instead place their faith in future good. Perhaps what lies behind Machiavelli's contrast of the practice of the ancients and the moderns here is religion, for Christianity famously puts its faith in the future goods promised by a beneficent deity and savior. Machiavelli is much more explicit about this contrast, and its political consequences, in the *Discourses on Livy*. Notably, after remarking on the fact that in ancient times there were many more free peoples in Italy than in his own times, he discusses the reasons for this difference and identifies religion as the key factor. "For our religion, having shown the truth and the true way, makes us esteem less the honor of the world, whereas the Gentiles, esteeming it very much and having placed the highest good in it, were more ferocious in their actions" (II.2, 131). Thus, a difference between the ancients and moderns due to the "orders" of religion helps explain their difference in approach to acquiring new states, and their success or failure in doing so.

Having digressed from his planned analysis of the failure of the French to acquire Italy by pointing to the successful methods of the Turk and the Romans, Machiavelli finally turns to that analysis by admitting he has digressed: "But let us return to France." We might well suspect that his supposed digression is actually more important than the main analysis. Be that as it may, he returns to the French invasion of Italy. Although he mentions Charles VIII's invasion of 1494, he says that he will focus on Louis XII's invasion of 1499. His diagnosis of the French failure takes the form of promulgating a series of rules, presumably learned from his digression on successful acquisitions, that the French king failed to follow. A list of the rules will be useful:

1   To go live in the newly acquired state;
2   To send colonies;
3   To make oneself head and defender of the less powerful states in the province;
4   To weaken the powerful states in the province;
5   To prevent another powerful foreigner from entering.

In brief, defying (1) Louis XII did not go to live in Italy, nor did he send colonies there, contravening (2). As for (3) the rule of making himself the defender of the less powerful states there, he failed to do so by violating (4) the rule of weakening the powerful states in Italy when he aided Pope Alexander VI in increasing the already powerful Papal States by helping ruin the less powerful states in the area in the northeast of Italy known as the Romagna and later weakening the Venetians, who were traditionally a countervailing force to the Papal States. The increased power of the Church is particularly important in Machiavelli's account: by aiding the Pope, he explains, Louis did not realize that he was making the Church strong "by adding to its spiritual power (which gives it so much authority) so much temporal power." Machiavelli will return to an explanation of the growing temporal power of the Church in chapter 11, "On Ecclesiastical Principalities." Finally, given that he could not conquer the Kingdom of Naples and Sicily on his own, the French king agreed to split the dominion with Ferdinand of Spain, thereby breaking (5) the rule against allowing a powerful foreigner to enter.

Rather than following Machiavelli through all of his analysis, it would be more useful to examine his promulgation of these rules more generally. His propensity to offer one rule after another gives *The Prince* the appearance of a guidebook for princes, an appearance that has inspired countless "Machiavellian" guidebooks to politics, business, and even child-rearing. *The Prince* is filled with rules either deduced by Machiavelli from historical examples, as in the case of the discussion of the Turk or Romans in chapter 3, or asserted by him and then buttressed by such examples. Oftentimes, he presents these rules in an emphatic fashion, asserting that such and such a rule "never" fails. It is understandable, therefore, why numerous readers and scholars have taken *The Prince* to be something like a handbook for princes.[7] If only princes would follow the rules of statesmanship Machiavelli provides, it seems, they could not fail to acquire and maintain power. How accurate or satisfying a characterization this is of *The Prince* would require a detailed analysis of the various rules he promulgates, but a closer look at his analysis of Louis XII's failure to acquire Italy because he did not follow the rules Machiavelli provides actually undermines the appearance that the work is a series of simple and surefire rules for acquiring and maintaining power.

When he begins his analysis of Louis XII's failure, the first thing he does is excuse the king for violating rule (4), that is strengthening rather than weakening a strong state, in this case strengthening Venice, which Machiavelli excuses because the king's alliance with the Venetians was the only way he could enter Italy. Machiavelli even praises this violation: "And it would have resulted in a decision well taken for him if in his other actions he had not made any errors." Louis' next mistake was a further violation of rule (4) by helping the Church to become more powerful, so it seems that sometimes it is excusable to violate this rule and sometimes not. His next mistake was to divvy up the Kingdom of Naples and Sicily with the King of Spain, thus violating rule (5) by allowing a powerful foreigner to enter. Having gone through these mistakes, Machiavelli summarizes Louis' actions by enumerating his "five errors," but having done so he then surprisingly remarks: "These errors, so long as he was alive, could not have harmed him still, if he had not committed the sixth, which was to take their state away from the Venetians." Yet this decision, far from being an error, would seem to be an instance of following rule (4) of weakening a powerful state. Machiavelli explains that it was nonetheless a mistake because Louis had previously broken rule (4) by strengthening and not weakening the Church and rule (5) by allowing the king of Spain to enter Italy. In short, Machiavelli's rules cannot be followed simplemindedly; rather, their application—by following or even breaking them—requires prudence.

When discussing Machiavelli's statement in the Dedicatory Letter that careful reading of his work will give Lorenzo, or at least any reader who understands his work, the "capacity" to understand what Machiavelli has come to understand through his experience of modern things and his reading of ancient things, I suggested that this "capacity" is earned by entering into a dialogue with him. Merely following rules without critically analyzing them is not a dialogue. It is therefore fitting that chapter 3 also includes two sorts of dialogues at the end of the chapter. In the first case, having concluded his analysis of the French failure to acquire Italy, Machiavelli enters into a kind of dialogue with an imagined skeptical reader: "And if anyone should say King Louis surrendered the Romagna to [Pope] Alexander and the Kingdom of Naples to Spain in order to avoid a war, I reply with the reasons stated above, that one should never allow a disorder to happen in order to avoid a war, because it is not avoided but it is deferred to your disadvantage," a lesson he himself drew by looking back at the practices of the Romans. Having addressed one imaginary reader, Machiavelli turns to another: "And if anyone else should invoke the promise that the king had given to the pope, to make that invasion for him in exchange for the annulment of his marriage and the cardinal's hat for Rouen," that is, Louis' powerful minister, "I reply with what will be said by me below concerning the promises of princes and how they ought to be observed." Machiavelli thus refers the reader forward to chapter 18, where he famously counsels the prince to keep his promises only when it is advantageous to do so, and shockingly adduces as his example of a serial oath-breaker none other than Pope Alexander. In these two imagined dialogues with readers who object to his analysis, Machiavelli first asks the reader to look backward to what he had already written, and moreover to look along with him backward in time to the Romans and their foresight, and in the second case he asks the reader to look forward to what he will write later, which is appropriate since keeping promises involves faith that they will be kept in the future. Recall that Machiavelli earlier contrasted the foresight of the Romans in dealing with evils before they arose to the "wise men of our time" who put their faith in future anticipated good, and the suggestion there that this contrast had something to do with the difference between the ancients and the moderns concerning religious faith. By sending his reader forward to his own discussion of keeping faith in promises, Machiavelli further embraces the Roman practice of enjoying the benefit of "their own virtue and prudence," which he has learned from his "constant reading about ancient things."

The second dialogue Machiavelli reports concludes chapter 3, and this dialogue involves none other than Machiavelli himself, providing testimony to the "long experience of modern things" he puts forward in the Dedicatory Letter as the other source of his knowledge about political affairs. Concluding that Louis XII's failure was no "miracle" but instead a "very ordinary and rational" thing, that is something capable of being understood and, with prudence, better managed, Machiavelli reports a conversation he had with the French king's minister, the Cardinal of Rouen. He specifies that this conversation took place at the very time that Pope Alexander was increasing his dominion in the Romagna through his son, Cesare Borgia, with Louis XII's assistance, or what Machiavelli has identified as the French king's critical mistake. "For when the Cardinal of Rouen told me that the Italians did not understand war, I replied to him that the French did not understand the state, since, if they understood it, they would not allow the Church to come into such greatness." Machiavelli does not gainsay Rouen's criticism of the Italians, for he agrees that they no longer understand war and, in fact, he will point in chapter 12 to this lack of understanding of arms as a principal cause of Italy's ruin. What about his criticism of the French for not understanding "the state"? First, and as already noted, by allowing the Church to become great the French king made a critical mistake that fatally undermined his attempt to acquire Italy. From the French failure Machiavelli deduces "a general rule that never or rarely fails," namely, "that whoever causes someone else to become powerful is ruined." Second, and more subtly, Machiavelli points to a crucial factor that explains why Italy remains divided: the temporal power of the Church. He will return to this subject more explicitly in chapter 11.

CHAPTER 4: WHY DARIUS' KINGDOM, WHICH ALEXANDER HAD OCCUPIED, DID NOT REBEL FROM ALEXANDER'S SUCCESSORS AFTER HIS DEATH

Having followed Machiavelli through his lengthy analysis of the French failure to acquire Italy in chapter 3, the second longest chapter in *The Prince*, we now find ourselves in a relatively brief chapter (with a rather lengthy title) that concerns a successful conquest. As the title announces, this successful acquisition is Alexander the Great's conquest of the Persian Empire of King Darius III, and the subject of the chapter is less Alexander's conquest than the failure of the conquered to rebel against his successors. Both acquiring the state and maintaining it seem miraculous: "When the difficulties that exist in holding a newly acquired state are considered, anyone might marvel" at Alexander's becoming "lord of Asia" in a few short years, and then further marvel at the fact that the conquered subjects did not rebel, even though such rebellion would seem "reasonable" to have expected. Although we might at first wonder at Alexander's rapid success, what Machiavelli draws our attention to as most wondrous of all was his successors' maintenance of the acquired territories without facing any rebellion.

The way in which Machiavelli begins this chapter links it to the previous chapter in at least two ways. First, in speaking of the "difficulties that exist in holding a newly acquired state," he seems to refer to his analysis in chapter 3 of the difficulties faced by the king of France in his failed invasion of Italy. Louis' failure will turn out to be much less surprising than Machiavelli let on in chapter 3 when we consider the difficulties inherent in the enterprise. Second, having stated at the end of chapter 3 that the French failure was no "miracle," but instead "very ordinary and rational," Machiavelli begins chapter 4 by stating that Alexander the Great's successful conquest, and especially his successors' ability to maintain it, would make "anyone"—that is anyone who considered the difficulties involved—"marvel." Machiavelli thus initiates another dialogue, this time with a reader who marvels at Alexander's and his successors' success after having learned about the difficulties of conquest in chapter 3. The author therefore replies—"I reply ..."—by introducing new considerations about the acquisition of states and the maintenance of that acquisition. Machiavelli's dialogue with his astonished interlocutor will take the form of a distinction he draws between two different kinds of state and the opportunities and difficulties faced in conquering each type. The achievement of Alexander and his successors will turn out to be no more marvelous than France's failure. We may therefore also wonder whether he is simultaneously continuing his analysis in chapter 3 of how to conquer Italy, a question that should lead us to ask which type of state Italy most resembles.

To his interlocutor who "marvels" at the astonishing success of Alexander the Great and his successors, Machiavelli says: "I reply that the principalities of which there is a memory are found to be governed in two different ways: either by a prince, with everyone else as his servants" who administer the prince's state "by his grace and leave," or "by a prince and by barons, who hold that rank not by the grace of their lord but by the antiquity of their bloodlines." Note that Machiavelli oddly specifies that he is speaking of principalities "of which there is a memory." As we shall see, a people's memory of its former freedom and particularly the loss of that memory will turn out to be critical for explaining how conquests are successfully maintained. At any rate, Machiavelli further explains that in the second type of principality the barons have states and subjects of their own, subjects who "have a natural affection toward them." We have already seen how fickle the people are in their "natural" affection for their princes, even hereditary princes. What will turn out to be more important in this case is the fact that the barons have authority and privileges that are acknowledged both by their peoples and (reluctantly) by their prince. As for the first type of principality, there is no one but the prince himself whose dominion is recognized and "toward the prince alone do they bear particular love." Once again, it will turn out that it is not the "particular love" shown by the people toward their lone prince that matters in Machiavelli's analysis, but rather the fact that once this prince is eliminated, along with his bloodline, there are no rivals for power over the subject people.

In order to illustrate his argument concerning these two types of government Machiavelli brings up two examples "in our times," that is modern examples. The Turk, in other words the Ottoman Sultan, is his example of a principality with a single lord, whereas the king of France is an example of a king surrounded by "an ancient multitude of lords" each of whom has his own subjects. (Tellingly, Machiavelli might have used the contrast between the Turk and France to employ the familiar terminology of classifying regimes as "despotic" versus "monarchical," but as with the term "tyrant" he silently refuses the opportunity.[8]) We have already encountered the Turk and the king of France in chapter 3, with the Turk there being Machiavelli's example of how a prince should go live in his newly acquired territory. His other example in chapter 3 was the Roman Republic, which took the alternative remedy of sending colonies in newly acquired states, and we shall soon again encounter the example of the Romans in chapter 4. Interestingly, if the example in chapter 3 of a successfully conquered province was the same for both the modern Turk and the ancient Romans, namely Greece, in chapter 4 Machiavelli will consider the conquest or potential conquest of more or less the same province in both ancient and modern times: namely, the historical conquest of Persia by Alexander the Great and the hypothetical conquest of the Turk's state. The conquerors of chapter 3 become the conquered in chapter 4. In turn, instead of considering the difficulties in conquering Italy, as he did in chapter 3, in the present chapter he entertains the difficulties one would face in conquering France. Perhaps we are meant to wonder whether the difficulties in conquering—or unifying—Italy are more similar to the case of France or of the Turk.

According to Machiavelli, kingdoms like those of the Turk are difficult to acquire but very easy to hold, whereas kingdoms like France are in some respects easier to seize but difficult to maintain. He explains to a would-be conquering prince that the kingdom of the Turk is difficult to enter because there are no disaffected princes or anyone else who is able to call "you" into the state, the reason being that there is a single prince there ("the Turk" himself) and everyone else around him "are all slaves." If the kingdom of the Turk is difficult to enter, once one successfully overcomes its prince then the state is easy to hold because there is no one who has credit with the people, and the only remaining threat comes from "the bloodline of the prince" (and we have already seen Machiavelli's recommendation concerning what to do about that). Turning to the opposite kind of state, a state such as France, Machiavelli explains that it is easy to enter because there are barons to welcome "you" into the state, "for always one finds some malcontents and some who want to revolt." Yet this state is difficult to hold because now you have friends (those who helped you) and enemies (those who opposed you), neither of which can be fully contented or entirely eliminated. Furthermore, the very reason why you were able to enter so easily, namely the discontent and propensity to revolt of these barons, now creates "new troubles" that make it difficult to maintain your acquisition. Note Machiavelli's change in emphasis here from when he first described states like France just two paragraphs prior. There the "lords" or barons in the state were described as "recognized by their subjects and loved by them," but now he speaks only of the discontent and ambition of these barons as the key factor in explaining why such states are relatively easier to acquire but difficult to maintain. The main reason why the states of the Turk and France differ, it seems, is whether or not they contain independent and rival princes or a single prince.

With his analysis of these contrasting types of states in place, Machiavelli turns back to the subject announced in the chapter title. The nature of Darius' government, he explains, was similar to the kingdom of the Turk. Once Alexander the Great defeated Darius, it was easy for him and his successors to hold it for the reasons he has explained. However, Machiavelli now emphasizes what he had only mentioned at the outset, namely that even if Alexander's successors did not face rebellions from their conquered peoples, they in fact did not hold the conquered state as a united kingdom but instead quarreled amongst themselves and divided it. "And his successors, if they had been united, could have enjoyed it for themselves at their leisure." In fact, Alexander's quickly acquired and briefly held empire was divided up into five main states. Machiavelli therefore considers less a historical example than a hypothetical one, namely what Alexander's successors "could have" done if they had been united, in keeping with his consideration of the difficulties "you" would encounter in your hypothetical conquest of the Turk or of France. Why the emphasis now on the failure of Alexander's successors to keep his conquests united?

Machiavelli may indirectly answer this question in the immediate sequel. Having explained the supposed ease in maintaining Persia and Alexander's other conquests after his death by stating that Darius' state is similar to the kingdom of the Turk, he contrasts this example with what would have been the case if Persia had instead been like the kingdom of France, stating that it would have been impossible to have possessed it so easily. Having said this, he applies his reasoning to a new example: "From this fact arose the frequent rebellions against the Romans by Spain, by France, and by Greece. On account of the many principalities that existed in those states the Romans were always uncertain of their possession so long as the memory of these endured. But when the memory of these principalities was eliminated through the power and duration of their empire, the Romans became their secure possessors."[9]

Several things should be noted about the Roman example. First, it seems that the Roman Empire—that is, the dominion of the late Roman Republic and then the Roman Empire beyond Italy—was more like the modern kingdom of France, a state that contains independent "lords" or barons, or now "principalities," making it easy to make new conquests but difficult to maintain them. Second, the example of the Romans' difficulties in Greece is particularly interesting, because "Greece"—that is, various separate principalities or kingdoms in the general area of what is now Greece, Turkey, and the vicinity—includes some of the very states established and held by Alexander the Great's successors. The same would be true of Rome's other eastern conquests, for example Egypt, which was ruled by the Ptolemaic rulers beginning with Ptolemy I after Alexander's death and ending with Cleopatra in 30 BCE, when Egypt was formally incorporated into Rome. In other words, even if Alexander's successors retained his conquests, though as separate kingdoms, they ultimately lost them to a new conqueror, Rome. Perhaps we should consider Rome as the most important successor of Alexander as "lord of Asia." Third, also notable is the reason for Rome's success: it eliminated "the memory of these principalities," meaning it eliminated their memory of being independent, and in that sense "free," states. Machiavelli expands on this fact when he continues: "And since the bloodlines of their former lords were eliminated, the provinces recognized only the Romans." Earlier I noted Machiavelli's curious phrasing in saying that he will consider "principalities of which there is memory," and now we see that the Roman Republic, his model for any prince who would like to acquire, succeeded through a ruthless elimination of the bloodlines of princes and, more importantly, the memory of freedom or independence in the states it acquired.[10]

If Machiavelli begins chapter 4 by entering into a dialogue with anyone who would "marvel" at Alexander the Great's and his successors' ability to maintain their acquisitions, he ends the chapter by dispelling this wonder. "Thus, when all of these things are considered, no one will marvel at Alexander's ease in keeping his state in Asia, and at the difficulties that others, such as Pyrrhus and many others, have had in keeping what they acquired. This is a thing that arises not from the great or small virtue of the victor, but from the difference in their situations." In the end it seems that the qualities of the conquered matter at least as much, if not more, than the virtue of the conqueror. Namely, the slavish subjects of the Persian Empire in ancient times and of the parallel Turkish sultanate in modern times make it easy to hold once conquered, whereas the numerous independent states of Gaul in ancient times and of the parallel of France in modern times make the state difficult to maintain, unless, that is, the memory of freedom is extinguished in imitation of the Roman example.

Curiously, now we have no more talk about Alexander's successors, and instead we are told that Alexander himself kept "his state in Asia," echoing Machiavelli's characterization of Alexander at the outset of the chapter as "lord of Asia." In what sense could this be true given that Alexander died very shortly after acquiring this state? Does Alexander's empire or dominion somehow last after his death, through his memory? We might be reminded in this of Julius Caesar, whose memory endured in the Roman Empire when his own successors called themselves "Caesar," or, as Machiavelli later writes in *The Prince*, they ruled "under the title of Caesar" (chap. 19, 101).[11] Likewise, why does Machiavelli unexpectedly mention Pyrrhus? Pyrrhus of Epirus (319/318–272 BCE) was among the last and almost successful foes of Rome, a Greek prince who attacked Italy and was initially successful but ultimately overextended himself (hence a "Pyrrhic victory"). Mentioning Pyrrhus' failure to keep what he had acquired, namely his possessions in Italy, serves to remind us again of Rome's own success in unifying Italy under its authority and then of expanding its empire. If ancient Rome conquered the world, it extinguished those states that were once free and even the very practice or memory of liberty in their conquests and ultimately in Rome itself. As Machiavelli writes in the *Discourses on Livy*, "the Roman Empire, with its arms and its greatness, eliminated all republics and all civil ways of life. And although that empire was dissolved, the cities still have not been able to put themselves back together or reorder themselves for civil life except in very few places of that empire" (II.2, 132). Once again, perhaps Rome is the most interesting example of the successors of Alexander the Great in conquering Asia here in chapter 4, just as it was the example of the most successful conquering state in chapter 3.

CHAPTER 5: BY WHAT MEANS CITIES OR PRINCIPALITIES ARE TO BE ADMINISTERED THAT, BEFORE THEY WERE OCCUPIED, LIVED BY THEIR OWN LAWS

When outlining the different types of states and modes by which they are acquired in chapter 1, Machiavelli mentioned as his first consideration whether these states "are accustomed to living under a prince or used to being free," and so far he has not directly discussed the acquisition of free states. The title of chapter 5 does not mention freedom, but it does announce that he will discuss how to administer "cities" and principalities that "lived by their own laws" before being occupied, and so states that are "free" in the sense of being independent. He does, however, add the word "liberty" in the first sentence of the chapter, although it is as yet unclear what he means by it: "As has been said, when those states that are acquired are accustomed to live with their own laws and in liberty, there are three ways of trying to hold them." He enumerates these ways: "The first is to destroy them. The second is to go there in person to live. The third is to allow them to live with their own laws," but to exact tribute from them and to establish an oligarchical regime there that depends on you since "it is easier to hold a city used to living in freedom by means of its own citizens." Where has Machiavelli discussed these three modes? He did discuss the second mode in chapter 3 when he gave the example of the Turk going to live in his newly acquired territories, but he has not explicitly spoken of the other two modes. Nonetheless, our examination of his example in chapter 4 of how the Romans succeeded in their conquests by eliminating the memory of the principalities they acquired should prepare us for his bluntly offered first mode: "to destroy them."

As examples of the use of these modes Machiavelli offers the Spartans and the Romans. The Spartans are his example of the third mode of setting up friendly oligarchic governments in subject states, as happened for example to Athens after its defeat by the Spartans in the Peloponnesian War. The result was not good: the Spartans "lost them again." The Romans initially used the same mode as the Spartans, trying to hold Greece by allowing the conquered states to live by their own laws, and they too failed. Instead, they turned to Machiavelli's chilling first mode of destroying these states, a mode he notes they successfully employed with Capua, Carthage, and Numantia. "For in truth there is no secure way to possess them other than their destruction." He does not discuss the second mode of going to live in these states used to living freely. In chapter 3 he noted the successful use of this mode of the Turk making Constantinople his capital, but perhaps the reason why Machiavelli does not discuss this mode in the present context is because of what he now writes about free states: "And whoever becomes master of a city accustomed to living in freedom and does not destroy it may expect to be destroyed by it, because in rebellion it always takes refuge in the name of liberty and its ancient constitution, which neither through the passage of time nor through benefits are ever forgotten." We saw in chapter 4 that the Romans were able to eliminate the memory of freedom in at least some of the states they conquered. Now we know more about how they did so: they effectively destroyed these states. The example of Capua is instructive, and was meant by the Romans to be instructive. When the Capuans defected to Hannibal in his war against Rome, the Romans besieged the city and took it in 211 BCE, and then executed its leaders, sold most of the men, women, and children into slavery, and then exiled all of the remaining inhabitants. A similar fate met the other examples Machiavelli lists here, Numantia and Carthage.

As an example of a state that was not destroyed and therefore kept its memory of freedom alive, Machiavelli offers the only modern example in the chapter. This is Pisa, which was under Florentine dominion from 1405 to 1494 and then resisted Florence's lengthy campaign to retake it, a campaign directed in large part by Machiavelli himself in his role as administrative head of Florence's militia. The implication of his analysis is clear: the Florentines should have followed the ancient Roman mode and destroyed Pisa.[12] Later in the work, in chapter 17, Machiavelli will criticize the Florentine's rule over another subject city, Pistoia, and blame them for misguided compassion and for failing to employ cruelty "well used" (chap. 17, 90–91). The moderns, or at least the modern Florentines, have qualms about cruelty. The ancient Romans had no such compunction.[13]

This chapter concludes with an explicit comparison between acquiring states not accustomed to living freely and those that are so accustomed. As for states used to living under a prince, once the prince's bloodline is eliminated, the people "do not know how to live in freedom" but are instead used to obeying, do not know how to create a new prince amongst themselves, and offer little resistance. As for "republics," and Machiavelli now uses this term to describe cities that live in freedom, "there is greater life, greater hatred, more desire for revenge. Nor does the memory of their ancient liberty ever allow them to rest, nor can it, so that the most secure way is to eliminate them or live there." At the very end of the chapter, then, Machiavelli finally mentions the second mode he enumerated above for holding a state used to living freely, namely going to live there. Given what he has said so far, it is difficult to see how such a mode would succeed under such a restless and freedom-loving people. If this advice is meant for Lorenzo de' Medici, a prince who has acquired a republic and has come to live there, the implications of Machiavelli's analysis are alarming to contemplate for his beloved city.

NOTES

1 Lefort 2012 [2005], 102.
2 See Mansfield 1983; Vatter 2013, 42; Vivante 2013, appendix.
3 See Tarcov 2000, 30. The analysis of chapter 3 is indebted in many respects to Tarcov's detailed interpretation of the chapter.
4 In the *Discourses on Livy* he explains: "nature has created men so that they are able to desire everything and are unable to attain everything. So, since the desire is always greater than the power of acquiring, the result is discontent with what one possesses and a lack of satisfaction with it. From this arises the variability of their fortune; for since some men desire to have more, and some fear to lose what has been acquired, they come to enmities and to war, from which arises the ruin of one province and the exaltation of another" (I.37, 78).
5 See Machiavelli, *Florentine Histories* I.1. See Tarcov 2000, 36.
6 As Hörnqvist (2004, 98ff.) shows, by the "wise men of our times" Machiavelli refers to the elites who controlled Florentine politics during his time in office who adhered to a policy of temporizing in dealing with Florence's subject cities which Machiavelli himself unsuccessfully opposed.
7 E.g., Butterfield 1962.
8 See Lefort 2012 [2005], 120.
9 Machiavelli discusses the love of freedom among the peoples Rome conquered at length in the *Discourses on Livy* (II.2).
10 See Sullivan 2013 for this point and for a detailed analysis of chapter 4 of *The Prince* to which the interpretation here is indebted on many points.
11 See Sullivan 2013, 522–23, 532–33.
12 For Machiavelli's critique of Florence's methods of holding Pisa, see *Florentine Histories* VII.30.
13 See *Discourses on Livy* (III.27, 274–75) where Machiavelli discusses the Florentine policy toward Pistoia and attributes the city's unwillingness to use harsher policies to the difference in modern "education" which makes it seem impossible to imitate the ancients in this regard, thereby referring the reader to his discussion in II.2 of the crucial difference between ancient and modern "education" due to the difference in religion.

5

THE NEW PRINCE

We have seen the new prince and, relatedly, the theme of the acquisition of political power emerge in the first five chapters of *The Prince*, and now the new prince finally comes to the fore in chapters 6 and 7. These two chapters form a pair, like pendant portraits, that is, a pair of portraits meant to be hung together. This is intentional pairing as is already evident from their titles, with chapter 6 titled "On New Principalities That Are Acquired by One's Own Arms and by Virtue" and chapter 7 "On New Principalities That Are Acquired with the Arms and Fortune of Others." The titles of these chapters signal two other important themes of the work that also come into focus here: first, whether someone acquires and maintains power through virtue or fortune and, second, whether someone does so through his own arms or depends on the arms of others. Machiavelli mentioned these two pairs of considerations in acquiring a new principality in chapter 1 when he enumerated the various modes of acquisition used to acquire a principality, but they will turn out to be the key considerations for both acquiring and maintaining power. Machiavelli asks his reader to compare these two chapters in order to understand the roles of virtue and fortune, and how having one's own arms differs from having to depend on the arms of others in acquiring and maintaining a principality.

Chapters 6 and 7 also raise the issue of which princes are exemplary and should be imitated. In chapter 6 Machiavelli urges his reader—"you"—to imitate the greatest examples, listing Moses, Cyrus, Romulus, and Theseus as the "most excellent" new princes. Yet he is not particularly forthcoming about precisely what actions undertaken by these exemplary princes should be imitated. Chapter 7 confronts the reader with a further puzzle, for his main example in this chapter of a prince who acquires his state by the fortune and arms of others is Cesare Borgia, about whom he declares "I would not know what better precepts to give to a new prince than the example of his actions." Unlike chapter 6 on Moses and his fellow exemplary princes, Machiavelli gives a detailed account of Cesare Borgia's actions, and yet in the end Cesare Borgia failed to acquire and maintain his state. What kind of example is Cesare Borgia, then? In approaching Machiavelli's discussion of new princes in these two chapters, then, we need to ask ourselves what is—and what is not—worthy of imitation for the would-be prince reading his book.

CHAPTER 6: ON NEW PRINCIPALITIES THAT ARE ACQUIRED BY ONE'S OWN ARMS AND BY VIRTUE

"Let no one marvel whether I shall introduce the greatest examples in the speech I shall make concerning principalities that are wholly new, both in their prince and in their state." The reader with whom Machiavelli enters into dialogue has been told on several occasions not to "wonder" or "marvel" at the events he recounts, but perhaps we should indeed marvel at the "greatest examples" contained in chapter 6, for the deeds of his exemplary princes— Moses, Cyrus, Romulus, and Theseus—do indeed seem to be marvelous. Machiavelli announces in the first sentence of the chapter that he will make a "speech" (*parlare*), and in fact the chapter does sound like a sermon, a fitting tone for a discussion of armed and unarmed "prophets," as we shall see. With Machiavelli in the pulpit, the reader sits in the congregation listening in awe at the marvelous events he says he will recount. Finally, he explains that he will speak of "wholly new" principalities, "both in their prince and their state." In other words, this is a chapter about *founding* a new state, or the greatest possible example of acquiring and maintaining power.

Machiavelli explains that he will introduce "the greatest examples" as exemplary princes whom he urges a would-be prince to imitate. "For, since men always walk in paths beaten by others, and they proceed by means of imitation in their actions, and since one cannot completely hold to the paths of others, nor arrive at the virtue of those whom you imitate, a prudent man should always enter by paths beaten by great men and imitate those who have been most excellent, so that if his virtue does not arrive there, at least it gives off some scent of it." On the one hand, Machiavelli counsels his reader—"you"—to be a "prudent man" who imitates the trails blazed by the greatest men. On the other hand, however, he suggests that the person who imitates these examples is not likely fully to succeed in doing so. He therefore suggests that this person should act like "prudent" archers who, knowing that the strength or "virtue" of their bow is insufficient, aim much higher than their intended target in order to reach it. Perhaps Machiavelli emphasizes that we can imitate these great men only to an imperfect degree because the examples he is about to introduce of entirely new princes in entirely new states are legendary or mythical figures. For how are we to imitate the actions of princes who are the stuff of legend, even semi-divine or inspired by God himself? Indeed, oddly enough, Machiavelli is quite vague about what actions of entirely new princes we should imitate. Why give us these examples, then, and why stress that we can only imperfectly imitate them? Despite Machiavelli's reputation for being a clear-eyed realist with his gaze fixed on the "effectual truth" rather than the "imagination of it," as he will say in chapter 15, he asks his reader—or rather listener, for he has said he is making a speech—to imagine a world beyond what is ordinarily seen.[1] In this light, it is interesting to note that none of the exemplary princes he will mention imitated others.

The subject of this chapter, which Machiavelli describes as "wholly new principalities" with an entirely "new prince" or, alternatively, "becoming a prince from being a private man," gives him the opportunity to introduce one of the main themes of *The Prince*: virtue and fortune. We will have to wait to see what Machiavelli means by "virtue" (*virtù*), which is a complicated issue, but by "fortune" (*fortuna*) he means essentially "luck," whether good or bad luck, for the goddess Fortuna is notoriously fickle. We have already seen Machiavelli remark in the Dedicatory Letter on Lorenzo de' Medici's good fortune and on his own "great and continuous malignity of fortune," but now the theme of virtue and fortune comes to the fore. Both virtue and fortune mitigate the difficulties in founding a new principality, he states, but "he who has relied less on fortune has kept more of what he has acquired." The relationship between virtue and fortune introduced here will be the main subject of chapters 6 and 7, the two chapters on the entirely "new" prince.

Having thematically introduced the question of virtue and fortune, Machiavelli finally produces the "greatest examples." "But to come to those who by their own virtue and not by fortune became princes, I say that the most excellent are Moses, Cyrus, Romulus, Theseus and similar persons." By adding "similar persons" to his list Machiavelli invites us to use our imagination to produce other examples. Who might he have in mind? Strangely, Machiavelli begins his discussion of the examples we are urged to imitate by telling us that we should not reason about the first one: Moses. "Although one ought not to reason about Moses, since he was a mere executor of the things that were ordered of him by God, yet he should be admired, if only for that grace that made him worthy of speaking with God." How are we supposed to imitate Moses if we are not allowed to reason about what he did? Are we supposed to hope that we too have sufficient "grace" to attract God's attention? Machiavelli puts aside Moses and turns to his other examples: "But let us consider Cyrus, and the others who have acquired and founded kingdoms. You will find them all admirable, and if their particular actions and orders are considered they will appear no different from those of Moses, who had so great a teacher." So he will reason about Moses after all! Does he demote Moses to the level of Cyrus and the other new princes, implying that his "actions and orders"—supposedly actions commanded by God and laws and other "orders" given to Moses by his great "teacher"—were no more miraculous or beyond rational understanding than theirs? Or, alternatively, does he raise Cyrus, Romulus, and Theseus to the level of Moses? Perhaps he does both.

Machiavelli has told us that these exemplary princes "by their own virtue and not by fortune became princes," and, having introduced them, he comments: "And if their actions and life are examined, it is not seen that they got anything from fortune other than opportunity, which gave them the material so as to be able to introduce into it whatever form they chose. And without that opportunity, the virtue of their spirit would have been wasted; and without that virtue, the opportunity would have come in vain." Let us begin by reasoning about Moses, following Machiavelli by breaking his injunction against doing so. Just above he characterized Moses as "a mere executor" of the things ordered by God, though admirable for the "grace" that made him worthy of speaking with God. Now he drops any mention of God and speaks only of "fortune" giving Moses and his fellow, entirely new princes an "opportunity." Moreover, rather than talking about the "grace" that made Moses worthy of conversing with the divinity, now he speaks of his "virtue of spirit" or plain "virtue." It seems it was Moses' own virtue, not God's grace, which made him worthy of any divine attention he may have received. What Moses and his fellow new princes got from God or fortune was opportunity, and they seized it.

Machiavelli describes this opportunity as giving Moses and the others "material" so as to be able to introduce into it "whatever form they chose." He thereby uses the traditional philosophic language of "form" and "matter" developed by Aristotle and running through medieval thought. When applied to an object such as a wooden chair, for example, the "matter" (or "material cause" in the traditional terminology) would be the wood and the "form" (or "formal cause") would be the form or shape of the wood that makes it capable of serving as a chair. Considering the material and form as "causes" brings us to the two other "causes" in the Aristotelian view, namely the end or purpose for which the chair is made, which is known as the "final cause," and the cause that fashioned this material into that form for such-and-such a purpose, known as the "efficient cause," in this case the wood-worker who made the chair. When applied to politics, the concept of "form" (or the "formal cause") of the political association referred to the particular "regime" that made the city the kind of city it was, for example a monarchy, aristocracy, or democracy. The "material" of the city, that is the citizens and other inhabitants, were given a certain arrangement or constitution according to the "form" of the regime. In this way, a given city might be made up of precisely the same "material" but given a new "form" by a change of regime, as from an oligarchy into a democracy. In turn, in this traditional conception the "form" of the regime is related most importantly to the "end" (or "final cause") in the sense of the purpose or aim of the political association, for example the "end" of an oligarchy being wealth and the "end" of an aristocracy pro-perly so-called being virtue. We have already noted in discussing chapter 1 that Machiavelli silently dismisses any talk of regimes as traditionally understood, and reduces all states to two types: republics and principalities. When he employs the traditional language of "form" and "material" when discussing the actions of Moses and other entirely new princes, then, Machiavelli uses the concepts in a new way that conceives of the "material" of a state, that is human beings, as lacking any determinate "form" and of the act of giving them a "form" as an essentially creative act. This creative act resembles more the creation of form out of nothing-ness attributed to the Judeo-Christian deity than giving "form" to "material" in order to achieve an "end" dictated by nature, as in the traditional Aristotelian framework.[2] Indeed, nowhere does Machiavelli speak of the "end" of the state in anything like the traditional way, and when he does speak in *The Prince* of ends or goals (especially in chapter 15), he identifies the end of the prince as acquiring and maintaining power. We will have to keep asking whether he conceives of any other end or purpose of politics.

With the general claim that Moses and his fellow entirely new princes owed nothing to fortune other than the opportunity to exercise their virtue by giving "whatever form they chose" to the material they found, Machiavelli now describes the actions of his four exemplary princes. "It was therefore necessary for Moses to find the people of Israel in Egypt, enslaved and oppressed by the

Egyptians, so that in order to escape servitude they were disposed to follow him," he begins, and then goes on to comment on Romulus being rejected by his own city and therefore able to become king of Rome and "the founder of that fatherland," on how Cyrus found the Persians discontented under Median rule, and on Theseus being able to demonstrate his virtue because the Athenians were "dispersed."

Let us begin again with Moses. Nowhere in Machiavelli's description here do we find any mention of a divine plan or divine assistance, but only of Moses being able to exercise his virtue because of the condition of the "material" he found, namely Israelites who were "disposed to follow him" because of the oppression they were suffering. The same explanation is given about Cyrus finding the Persians discontented and Theseus giving form to formless or "dispersed" Athenians. In short, their actions do not seem different from those of Moses, as Machiavelli himself forewarned us. Interestingly, the case of Romulus is somewhat different, for Machiavelli here mentions only how Romulus turned his bad fortune (being exposed at birth and rejected from his own fatherland of Alba Longa) into good fortune (becoming king of Rome and father of a new fatherland). Perhaps Machiavelli means to draw our attention to Romulus by treating him differently. What he obviously does not mention about the story of Romulus is that he murdered his own brother, Remus, to become sole king of Rome. If Machiavelli conspicuously fails to mention this deed in *The Prince*, in the *Discourses on Livy* he goes out of his way to justify Romulus' fratricide. Replying to someone who might object that such a terrible crime would provide a bad example for founders, Machiavelli excuses Romulus by using him as an example of a general rule: "that it never or rarely happens that any republic or kingdom is ordered well from the beginning or reformed altogether outside its old orders unless it is ordered by one individual" (I.9, 29). Romulus' crime is justified by the need to be "alone" in founding, and Machiavelli also states that the "means" he used were also justified by the "end" he had in mind, though he is not entirely clear about what that "end" might have been.[3]

If the example of Romulus is unsettling, Machiavelli's other exemplars of new princes turn out to be no less chilling. As for

Moses, Machiavelli is once again more forthright in the *Discourses on Livy*. Speaking of how those who order or reorder a state encounter resistance or "envy" regarding the orders they want to introduce, he writes: "And whoever reads the Bible judiciously will see that since he wished his laws and his orders to go forward, Moses was forced to kill infinite men who, moved by nothing other than their envy, were opposed to his plans" (III.30, 280). (Also, Machiavelli pairs his example of Moses there with that of Savonarola in this context, just as he is about to do in *The Prince*.) Putting aside the small matter of the death of all the firstborn sons of Egypt, Machiavelli seems to refer here to an episode recounted in Exodus (32:27–29) when Moses, having ascended the mountain to receive the tablets inscribed with the Ten Commandments, descends to find the Israelites worshipping the golden calf. Aside from breaking the tablets (the part of the story we tend to remember), he orders the slaughter of 3,000 Israelites (the part of the story we tend to forget). If Moses had "so great a teacher," we now learn what sort of lessons he received. Closer inspection of Cyrus' actions in leading the Persians against the Medes reveals him to be a practitioner of fraud, including effectively seizing power from his uncle Cyaxares, king of the Medes, in order to rise to power. Yet again Machiavelli is more forthcoming in the *Discourses on Livy*. Drawing on Xenophon's *Education of Cyrus* (*Cyropaedia*), to which he will refer in chapter 14 of *The Prince*, he explains: "Xenophon in his life of Cyrus shows this necessity to deceive, considering ... that he makes him seize his kingdom through deception and not through force ... . Besides this, he makes him deceive Cyaxares, king of the Medes, his maternal uncle, in several modes; without which fraud he shows that Cyrus could not have attained that greatness he came to" (II.13, 155). As for Theseus, Machiavelli may be alluding to a story told in Plutarch. After having successfully navigated the labyrinth in Crete and killed the Minotaur, Theseus sailed back to Athens with his ship bearing black sails instead of the white sails he had said he would hoist if he was successful, an oversight (?!) that led his father to leap to his death from the cliffs overlooking the sea when he spotted the returning ships, leaving Theseus as king of Athens. In this light, Theseus could be considered to have committed patricide.

Perhaps we should not be surprised that Machiavelli is so vague about the actions taken by his exemplary new princes whom he urges a prince to imitate.

"Those who, like these men, become princes in virtuous ways," Machiavelli tells us, "acquire their principalities with difficulty, but hold them with ease." The main reason for this difficulty is that these new princes must introduce "new orders and methods" in order to "establish their state and their security." By "orders" (*ordini*) Machiavelli refers to institutions broadly conceived, including not only formal political institutions but also religious and other institutions. In turn, by "methods" or "modes" (*modi*) he refers to the ways in which political power is wielded, whether by what he sometimes terms "ordinary" means, that is through these institutions, or by "extraordinary" or extralegal means. In the present context, these "new orders and methods" are the institutions a new prince establishes and the actions he takes to give "form" to the "material" he opportunely finds in establishing a state. "One should consider how there is nothing more difficult to realize, nor more doubtful of success in, nor more dangerous to manage than to make oneself a leader [*capo*] who introduces new orders," Machiavelli proclaims. He explains that the reason for this difficulty is that the entirely new prince who introduces these "new orders" encounters "enemies" in those who are doing well under the "old orders" and "defenders" of these new orders who turn out to be "lukewarm" in their support because they fear the new prince's enemies and also are not yet firm in their belief concerning these new orders.

With this explanation we encounter a puzzle. Machiavelli announced at the beginning of chapter 6 that he was going to discuss principalities that are "wholly new, both in their prince and in their state," and he has described these entirely new princes as being able to introduce "whatever form they chose" into what seemed to be formless material. Now it seems that these founders who introduce "new orders" as founders of a state actually encounter "old orders" and an existing "form" of the state that among other things divides the "material" of the state into supporters of the "old orders" and lukewarm defenders of the "new orders." In what way, then, are we engaged in a discussion of principalities that are "wholly new, both in their prince and in their state"? At least two possibilities come to mind. First, perhaps these "new orders" constitute a "wholly new" prince and state insofar as the prince who institutes them effectively wipes away the "old orders," giving an entirely new "form" to existing "material." Such an action would be what we would term a "revolution," or what Machiavelli terms an "innovation." In this case, then, all founding or ordering is a radical refounding or reordering, and in fact this is how he treats introducing new orders in the *Discourses on Livy* (see I.9, III.1). Second, and related, perhaps the actions of an entirely new prince are paradigmatic for what is required of *any* prince in acquiring and maintaining power. If so, this would explain why he urges the reader of chapter 6 to imitate the "greatest examples" he will discuss.

Having commented on the difficulties the introducer of "new orders" encounters concerning "enemies" and "lukewarm" defenders of those orders, Machiavelli shifts his focus slightly. "It is necessary, therefore, if one wants to discuss this part well, to examine whether these innovators stand by themselves, or if they depend on others." He thus introduces the other part of his subject announced in the title to the chapter: one's own arms. He explains that these innovators either have to "beg" (or "pray"—*pregare*) for support or they can use "force." Standing by oneself therefore turns out to mean having "force" or "arms" to make oneself obeyed. "From this it arose that all the armed prophets were victorious and the unarmed ones were ruined." Why does Machiavelli unexpectedly introduce "prophets" into his discussion? Of course, Moses was a prophet, and this was the reason Machiavelli initially said one should not reason about his actions. Perhaps Machiavelli has elevated Cyrus, Romulus, and Theseus to the status of "prophets." When discussing the problem that arises from the "lukewarmness" of the defenders of the "new orders," Machiavelli explained this tepidness as owing in part to the "incredulity" of men, "who do not truly believe in new things unless they see that they arise from solid experience." He now follows up this thought with regard to armed and unarmed prophets, explaining that while it is easy to persuade "peoples" of something new due to their "nature," it is difficult to keep them persuaded. (Recall from the beginning of chapter 3 that the hope of the people that they will profit by changing princes is one of the "natural difficulties" that make it possible to acquire a new principality.) "For this reason it is suitable for them to be ordered in such a way that when they no longer believe, one can make them believe by force," Machiavelli recommends, giving Moses, Cyrus, Romulus, and Theseus as examples of successful "prophets" because they were so armed. The case of Moses is particularly instructive. In the story from Exodus related above Moses failed to keep the Israelites firm in their belief while he ascended the mountain to receive the Ten Commandments, but his brutal use of force when he discovered the Israelites worshipping the golden calf made them believe again. In sum, in Machiavelli's analysis it was Moses' own virtue and own arms that led to his success, not any divine instruction or assistance.

Machiavelli contrasts the success of his "armed prophets," especially Moses, to an "unarmed prophet," namely Brother Girolamo Savonarola. Savonarola was the Dominican friar whose preaching helped bring down the Medici from power in 1494 and reestablish the Florentine Republic with Savonarola himself as a leading figure behind the regime. When Pope Alexander VI grew tired of Savonarola's incessant preaching about the corruption of the Church and the Florentines began to weary of Savonarola's condemnation of their own sinful ways, the once powerful friar fell from power in 1498 and was executed and burned at the stake in the public square by the Florentines. Machiavelli comments: "He was ruined in his new orders when the multitude began not to believe him and he had no way to hold firm those who had believed, nor to make the unbelieving believe." So Savonarola too faced unbelieving enemies and "lukewarm" believers in introducing his "new orders."[4] Machiavelli claimed that all "unarmed prophets" are ruined and he has given us one example of such failure. But is it true that *all* "unarmed prophets" have failed to keep the people believing in the new orders they bring? By his very silence Machiavelli seems to beg us to think of an example of an extremely successful unarmed prophet. Perhaps he would tell us that we should not reason about this prophet, but as with Moses perhaps he would thereby be inviting us to do just that.

Chapter 6 concludes with a surprisingly mundane example given the marvelous ones Machiavelli has discussed and invited us to imagine. "To such lofty examples I want to add an example that is lesser, but that still has some similarity with those, and I want it to suffice for all the other similar examples, and this is Hiero the Syracusan." He explains that Hiero rose from being a private citizen to become prince of Syracuse, getting nothing from fortune other than the opportunity, just as he had said of Moses and his other exemplary new princes. He goes on to relate that the Syracusans elected him as their captain, "hence he was worthy of being made their prince." Finally, he states that Hiero showed "such great virtue" at all points in his career that, quoting an ancient historian, "'he lacked nothing appropriate to kingship save a kingdom,'"[5] and relates that he put his state on an entirely new foundation. What Machiavelli does not reveal here is that Hiero *seized* the principate of Syracuse and ruled as a tyrant. I have already noted that nowhere in *The Prince* do we find the word "tyrant." Machiavelli does not hesitate to use the term in his *Discourses on Livy*, however, and in fact does so with reference to Hiero. In order to illustrate how a "virtuous tyrant" acts, he refers his reader to another work by Xenophon, *Of Tyranny*, the full title of which is *Hiero: or, Of Tyranny* (II.2, 130).[6] Does Machiavelli introduce Hiero as an admittedly "lesser" example to display the distance between a tyrant, even if he is "virtuous" in some sense, and the "lofty examples" of Moses, Cyrus, Romulus, and Theseus? Or does he do so in order to draw our attention to their similarity?

CHAPTER 7: ON NEW PRINCIPALITIES THAT ARE ACQUIRED WITH THE ARMS AND FORTUNE OF OTHERS

As noted above, chapters 6 and 7 constitute a pair, with chapter 6 on new principalities acquired by one's own virtue and arms and chapter 7 on new principalities acquired "with the arms and fortune of others," as the title tells us. Note already that the question in chapter 7 is therefore not merely relying on the arms of others and fortune but, worse, on the fortune of others. To rely on the fortune of others is to be doubly reliant on fortune. The "greatest examples" of new princes in chapter 6 relied on fortune solely for the opportunity to exercise their virtue, but now it seems Machiavelli will discuss new princes who continue to rely on fortune, and even the fortune of others, beyond the initial opportunity. Such princes, he tells us, acquire their states with little trouble but can only maintain themselves with a great deal of labor, the opposite of the case of the new princes of chapter 6, who acquire their states with great effort but then maintain them with relative ease. As noted in the introduction to this chapter, the status of Machiavelli's main example in chapter 7 of a new prince who acquires through the fortune and arms of others, Cesare Borgia, is problematic. Although Machiavelli comes to Cesare's defense by claiming that his ultimate failure was not his fault but instead "arose from an extraordinary and extreme malignity of fortune," we might suspect that Cesare's downfall was instead due to his continuing to rely on the fortune and arms of others. Or are we to applaud Cesare's apparent attempts to free himself of reliance on others, even if he ultimately failed? In short, what sort of exemplar is Cesare Borgia?

Before turning to modern examples of princes who rely on the fortune and arms of others, and especially to his discussion of Cesare Borgia, Machiavelli first presents us with a few brief ancient examples of a state being obtained by money or by someone else's "grace." He cites the petty tyrants the Persian king Darius set up in Greece (Darius I the Great, who ruled in the fifth century BCE, and not the Darius III we encountered in chapter 4 who was defeated by Alexander the Great) and those Roman emperors who owed their becoming emperor to the army, which quickly made and just as quickly unmade these emperors, a subject to which Machiavelli will return in chapter 19. "These persons rely simply on the will and fortune of whoever has granted it to them, and those are two things that are very volatile and unstable, and they neither know how nor are able to maintain that rank." That said, Machiavelli does allow that if fortune throws a state in a prince's lap, he might succeed if he is "a man of great genius and virtue" and acts quickly—"right away," he writes—to lay foundations to maintain the state. In other words, such a virtuous prince would thereby succeed in becoming like one of those princes discussed in chapter 6 who owe nothing more to fortune than the opportunity and strike with their virtue while the iron is hot. Machiavelli thus invites us to ask what the modern princes he will discuss in chapter 7 failed to do in order to be reckoned among those great examples.

In chapter 6 all of Machiavelli's models of new princes who acquired a principality by their own virtue and arms were ancient examples, but now he presents us with two modern examples, and in fact he goes out of his way to underscore this by stating that he will adduce examples "that took place during days that are within our memory." Is there something about modern times that makes princes less likely to rely on their own virtue and own arms, or more likely to rely on the arms and fortune of others? At any rate, these contemporary examples of new princes who have acquired their state by the arms and fortune of others should be of particular interest to the dedicatee of *The Prince*, Lorenzo de' Medici, who is himself in this situation. Perhaps Machiavelli offers Lorenzo these two recent examples to see which he will choose to imitate.

The way in which Machiavelli introduces these two examples forces us to compare them. "Concerning the first and the second of the modes stated for becoming a prince, by virtue or by fortune," he writes, "I want to adduce two examples that took place during days that are within our memory, and these are Francesco Sforza and Cesare Borgia." He describes Sforza as rising from private individual to become duke of Milan by "proper means and with great virtue of his own." As noted when we first encountered Sforza in chapter 1 as an example of an entirely new prince, Machiavelli exaggerates somewhat in characterizing him as an entirely "new" prince, given that Sforza was the son-in-law of the previous duke. Now he also overstates the "proper means" through which Sforza attained his principality, for the brief and tumultuous republican government that was established after the death of Sforza's father-in-law capitulated to Sforza under threat of arms and granted him the duchy. What seems to be essential about the example of Sforza, then, is the "great virtue of his own," and we can add having his own arms as well since Sforza rose to prominence as a successful mercenary captain, in fact using his "own arms" to threaten Milan. Why didn't Machiavelli mention Sforza in chapter 6? If Sforza is an example of a prince who attained his state by virtue, Cesare Borgia is Machiavelli's example of a prince who rose to power through fortune. "On the other hand, Cesare Borgia, who was called Duke Valentino by the people, acquired his state through his father's fortune, and on the same account he lost it, even though he took every care, and did all those things that ought to have been done by a prudent and virtuous man to put down roots in those states that the arms and fortune of others had granted him."

Several things should be noted by the way in which Machiavelli introduces Cesare. First, he is said to have acquired his state not only through fortune, but through the fortune (and arms) of someone else: his father, Pope Alexander VI. The example of Cesare therefore matches the subject announced in the title of chapter 7. Second, Machiavelli goes out of his way to point to Cesare's relationship with "the people" by mentioning that he was popularly called "Duke Valentino" (a reference to his being duc de Valentinois), and so it seems we are being asked to pay particular attention to the relationship between Cesare and the people. Third, and most importantly, despite having stated that Cesare gained and lost his state through the fortune and arms of others, Machiavelli nonetheless presents him as having done "all those things that ought to have been done by a prudent and virtuous man to put down roots in those states that the arms and fortune of others had granted him." Note that Machiavelli does not himself actually say that Cesare was prudent or virtuous, but instead circuitously characterizes him as having done those things which a prudent and virtuous man should do, namely to "put down roots" in states given to him by the arms and fortune of others. Machiavelli retains this emphasis on putting down roots when he goes on to explain why he will focus on Cesare: "For, as was said above, he who does not lay his foundations in advance may, with great virtue, lay them afterward, although they be laid with pain for the builder and peril for the building." Such actions would convert a prince who comes to power through the arms and virtue of another into an example of a prince who acquired a state through his own virtue, as we saw above. "Thus if one will consider all the steps of the duke," Machiavelli continues, "one will see that he lay great foundations for his future power. These I do not judge superfluous to discuss, for I would not know what better precepts to give to a new prince than the example of his actions. And if he did not profit by his orders, it was not his fault, because this arose from an extraordinary and extreme malignity of fortune."

Again, what sort of example is Cesare meant to be? Is he an example that should be followed, or an example of what should be avoided? If he was indeed as prudent and virtuous as Machiavelli suggests, or almost suggests, then why did he fail? We are told that "an extraordinary and extreme malignity of fortune" was the cause of his failure (thereby also reminding us of what Machiavelli says in the Dedicatory Letter about his own "great and continuous malignity of fortune"). But was Cesare indeed not at fault for allowing this to occur? We will have to follow Machiavelli in his extended analysis of Cesare's actions to identify the causes of his ultimate failure.

Given that the case of Cesare Borgia is Machiavelli's most extensive treatment in *The Prince* of any example he gives, and given the ambiguity surrounding the lesson we are supposed to learn from this example, it would be useful to briefly provide some historical background before turning to this analysis. As noted, Cesare Borgia was the son of Pope Alexander VI, and we should note that it was not uncommon for Renaissance popes to have children, though since the practice was not condoned these offspring were often claimed to be the "nephews" and "nieces" of a pope. Pope Alexander was named Rodrigo Borgia (or Borja) and came from Spain. After his uncle was created Pope Calixtus III in 1455, Rodrigo Borgia entered a career in the papal service and later became a cardinal, and was himself elected pope in 1492 as Alexander VI. Like his uncle and many other popes before and after him, Alexander VI used his power to aggrandize his family, in his case his children, notably Cesare and Lucrezia, the latter of whom he married off to several princes in order to create alliances. Cesare Borgia (b. 1475/76) was originally destined for a career in the Church, becoming a bishop at the age of fifteen and a cardinal at eighteen. After the death in 1497 of Cesare's elder brother Giovanni (allegedly Cesare's own doing), who was Captain General of the papal forces, Alexander VI turned to Cesare to realize his dynastic goals. Cesare resigned his cardinalate in 1498 and on the very same day was made duc de Valentinois by Louis XII of France as part of a deal where the pope annulled Louis' marriage in exchange for the duchy for his son. Cesare then began a military career, with the French invasion of Louis XII of 1499 providing the opportunity to begin to carve out a state in the Romagna and the Marche, roughly the eastern region of the Italian peninsula lying south of Venice and east of Florence, an area that had traditionally been under the domination of the Papal States. In 1500, Cesare was able, thanks to his father, to hire mercenary forces and to expand his campaign of conquest. In addition, he threatened Florence and was paid handsomely not to attack the city. During this period Machiavelli himself witnessed many of the events he recounts in *The Prince* since during this period he was sent by his Florentine superiors on a series of diplomatic missions to Cesare's camp as well as to the Papal Court in Rome. Pope Alexander VI died in August 1503 and Cesare was also seriously ill at the time, allegedly because he and his father mistakenly drank poisoned wine intended for a cardinal. Cesare was nonetheless able to control the conclave of cardinals, arranging for the election of the elderly Pius III, who reaffirmed Cesare's role as head of the papal forces. However, when Pius died after just twenty-six days, Cesare witnessed the election of his longtime enemy Giuliano della Rovere as Pope Julius II. Julius had promised Cesare that he could continue his conquests in the Romagna, but then the new pope promptly turned on him. Cesare was betrayed by an ally, imprisoned, and his conquered territories were taken by the pope. Cesare managed to escape and served for the next few years as a military captain for the king of Navarre before being killed in an ambush on March 11, 1507. As we shall see, Machiavelli alternately condenses and expands the time frame of these historical events in his own narrative.

Tellingly, Machiavelli begins his analysis of Cesare's career as a new prince not with Cesare, but with Pope Alexander. "Alexander VI, when he wanted to make a great name of the duke, his son, had many difficulties, both present and future." The Pope, not Cesare, seems to be the prime mover in this story, a point Machiavelli will fully confirm later in the work. The difficulties faced by Alexander concerned the present balance of political forces in Italy and his inability to trust the military arms of other princes or states, which had reason to fear the power of the papacy. "Thus it was necessary that those orders should be disturbed, and the states of those men put in disorder, so that he could securely assume the lordship of part of them." The occasion for sowing disorder amidst this order came with the events that led to the French invasion of 1499, an event that Alexander facilitated by annulling the French king's marriage. Once the French had successfully taken Milan, the Pope borrowed troops in order to invade the Romagna. Only at this point does Cesare enter the picture. "When, therefore, the duke had acquired the Romagna and defeated the Colonnesi, and he wanted to maintain it and proceed farther ahead, two things impeded him." Namely, he realized that his mercenary forces were not faithful to him and also that he could not trust the king of France, who held Cesare back from further attacks after his initial successes. So far, then, we have Pope Alexander maneuvering to make a name for Cesare by disrupting the existing political order in Italy, and Cesare acting as a successful military captain using the arms of others and coming to realize that those arms were not dependable.

"Whence it was that the duke decided no longer to depend on the arms and fortune of others," Machiavelli suddenly writes, adding the "fortune" of others to the "arms" of others he has just discussed. To what degree did Cesare succeed in making himself no longer so dependent? Machiavelli relates that Cesare took advantage of the partisan rivalries in Rome, especially between the Orsini and Colonna clans, in order to divide and conquer, making their adherents his own. This was part of his strategy of no longer relying on the arms of others since these powerful Roman families and their allies were the source of much of the funds and many of the military forces upon which Cesare had relied to this point. After the Orsini realized too late that the fall of their rivals was augmenting "the greatness of the duke and of the Church," they rebelled, and Cesare was able to maintain his conquests in the Romagna only with French help. Wanting to rid himself of dependence on the French as well, Cesare turned to deceit. After reassuring the Orsini and plying one of their leaders with "money, clothing and horses" (gifts reminiscent of those

Machiavelli stated in the Dedicatory Letter are customarily given to princes), he lured them into a trap at Senigallia and had them all murdered. (Machiavelli himself was present on this memorable occasion.) So far, then, Cesare had at least begun to lay plans to no longer depend on the arms of others.[7] What about the fortune of others?

Machiavelli now pauses in his narrative to consider Cesare's accomplishments to this point. He states in his own name that Cesare "had thrown down very good foundations for his power, since he had all of the Romagna and the duchy of Urbino," and then adds, writing now from Cesare's viewpoint, "and it appeared to him that he had especially acquired the friendship of the Romagna and won its peoples wholly to himself because they had begun to savor their own well-being." To what extent Machiavelli agrees with how things "appeared" to Cesare is unclear, although we know that he argues that appearances are often treacherous. For the present it should be noted that these peoples had only "begun" to experience well-being, suggesting that Cesare's "very good foundations" were only just in place.

Continuing with his analysis, Machiavelli emphasizes what he is about to write by calling the reader's attention to its importance: "And because the following point is worthy of notice and should be imitated by others, I do not want to leave it out." He explains: "After the duke had taken the Romagna, since he found it commanded by impotent lords who preferred to despoil their subjects rather than correct them, and who had given them motive for disunion not unity, so that that province was completely full of robberies, feuds and every other kind of insolence, he judged it necessary, since he wanted to render it peaceful and obedient to the royal power, to give them good government." Before turning to the chilling example Machiavelli provides of how he did so, let us note that he attributes to Cesare the motive of wanting to render his conquered province "peaceful and obedient," not to give it "good government" for its own sake. "Good government" seems to be a means toward the end of acquiring and maintaining Cesare's own power, and the previous lawlessness of the states in the Romagna provided him with the opportunity to do so. Nonetheless, it would seem that Cesare's actions, even if self-serving, had a positive effect for these peoples. One way of reading *The Prince* based in part on this passage is that Machiavelli's intention is to harness the ambition of princes to act in ways that benefit peoples. In this case we would have to contrast the rapacious actions of the lords who previously ruled in the Romagna to Cesare's apparently more effective methods, methods that simultaneously benefited himself and the people. Even if Cesare and these petty princes were all driven by the same desire to acquire and maintain power, Cesare's mode of doing so would seem to be more successful, at least potentially, and therefore to be imitated. We will continue to test this reading of *The Prince* as we proceed.

In order to illustrate how Cesare brought "good government" to the Romagna, Machiavelli relates a chilling story. Cesare appointed a certain Messer Remirro de Orco, "a cruel and expeditious man," who in short order made the province peaceful and united, "and had a very great reputation." He goes on to state that Cesare now "judged that such excessive authority was not necessary because he worried that it would become hateful." Was Cesare perhaps instead worried that Remirro's growing reputation was a threat to his power? Perhaps, but Machiavelli continues by relating how Cesare set up a civil tribunal in the province to hear cases.[8] But once again he raises our suspicions about Cesare's motives when he continues: "And because Valentino knew that the past rigors had generated some hatred toward him, to purge the spirits of those peoples and to win them wholly to himself, he wanted to show that if any cruelty had taken place, it was caused not by himself, but by the harsh nature of his minister." Of course, Remirro's actions were taken on Cesare's orders, and so any hatred directed at Cesare for these cruel deeds would rightly be attributed to him and not solely to his minister. So he makes Remirro a scapegoat. Machiavelli writes that Cesare seized an opportunity that arose and had Remirro placed in two pieces—namely his head and his now headless body—in the town square in Cesena, a city in the Romagna, with a piece of wood and a bloody knife at his side. "The ferocity of that spectacle left those peoples at once satisfied and stupefied," Machiavelli comments. And he would know: he was present at that event as well. The hatred of the people, now directed at Remirro, was "satisfied" by this bloody spectacle, but they are also left "stupefied"—speechlessly afraid—and thus motivated to obey Cesare. Such were Cesare's methods in bringing "good government." As though having hardly written anything remarkable, Machiavelli returns to his narrative: "But let us return to where we left off."

Returning to his account, Machiavelli states that, having taken these actions, Cesare ended by "finding himself very powerful and in part secure against present dangers." (Machiavelli's formulation, that Cesare "finding himself"—*trovandosi*—in this situation seems to suggest that this is Cesare's own estimation of his position, and not necessarily Machiavelli's.) Therefore, he turned to the problem of the French king holding him back from making further acquisitions and tried to form other alliances so that he would no longer be dependent on the French. "His intention was to secure himself against the French, which he would have succeeded quickly in doing if Alexander had lived. And such was his conduct as regards present things." How does Machiavelli know Cesare would have succeeded in doing this? Did Cesare focus on "present things" to the detriment of looking toward the future, and especially the death of his father, who recently turned seventy? Machiavelli continues: "But as regards future things, he had to worry, first, that a new successor to the Church might not be his friend, and might try to take away what Alexander had given him." In other words, Cesare still remained dependent on his father and the Church. Machiavelli enumerates four ways in which Cesare thought to defend himself against an unfriendly new pope: first, to eliminate the bloodlines of those lords he had despoiled to prevent them from becoming the means of revenge against him; second, to win over the noblemen of Rome to hold a new pope in check; third, to gain as much influence in the College of Cardinals as possible; fourth, and most importantly, to acquire as much of a dominion of his own so as to be able to resist an unfriendly pontiff. Machiavelli claims that Cesare had accomplished the first three goals at the death of Pope Alexander, but not the fourth.

Machiavelli's discussion of Cesare's progress on the fourth goal, of acquiring enough power to stand on his own, is curious for its hypothetical language.[9] "As for the new acquisition, he had planned to become lord of Tuscany ... ." Such were Cesare's "plans," but how realistic were they? "And as soon as he did not have to fear France ..." (although Machiavelli parenthetically remarks that in fact he no longer did have to fear France, whether or not Cesare was aware of this) "... he would have jumped to Pisa." Note the conditional phrasing: *if x* had happened, Cesare *would have* done *y*. Machiavelli continues with this conditional language: "After this, Lucca and Siena would have surrendered immediately ... and the Florentines would have had no remedy." In other words, Machiavelli lays out a hypothetical plan for Cesare to become "lord of Tuscany" which Cesare in fact never carried out. Indeed, it is not clear whether this plan was Cesare's or Machiavelli's own. "If this had succeeded for him (it would have happened in the same year that Alexander died)," Machiavelli concludes his plan, "he would have acquired so many forces and such a reputation that he would have been able to stand alone, and he would not have depended any longer on the fortune and forces of others, but on his own power and virtue." In other words, without saying so directly, Machiavelli indicates that Cesare in fact still depended on the fortune of others, namely his father's fortune. What about his "virtue"? The sentence just quoted is in fact the first time Machiavelli ever refers to Cesare's "virtue." Yet even this reference is conditional: if things had happened thus, he "would have" depended on his own power and virtue.[10] We will further entertain the possibility that the plan laid out is less Cesare's than Machiavelli's when wrapping up the analysis of this chapter.

Recall that at the outset of chapter 7 Machiavelli considers the possibility that a prince who gains a state through the arms and fortune of others might possibly succeed if he is "a man of great genius and virtue" and acts quickly—"right away"—to lay foundations to maintain the state. One interpretation of his analysis of Cesare's failure to accomplish his fourth goal of making sufficient acquisitions to hold on to his power was that he acted too late, perhaps because he was not fully aware of how dependent he was on his father's fortune. This possibility is underscored by how Machiavelli continues his analysis: "But Alexander died five years after he had started to draw his sword."[11] Who is "he" in this sentence? Alexander or Cesare? We have already seen from the way that Machiavelli begins his analysis of Cesare's career that Alexander was in fact the prime mover. Alexander's death left Cesare with only his state in the Romagna consolidated, and that not for long. Machiavelli comments: "Yet there were such a great ferocity and so much virtue in the duke, and so well did he understand how men are won or lost, and so strong were the foundations that he had made in so little time, that, if he had not had those armies on top of him, or if he had been healthy, he would have stood through every difficulty." Such is Machiavelli's counterfactual evaluation; but, of course, the fact is that Cesare did not do these things.

If Machiavelli's assessment so far of Cesare's would-be actions raises doubts as to whether Cesare had indeed acted to make himself no longer dependent on the fortune of others, the way in which he concludes his narrative sows further doubts.[12] "And one could see that his foundations were good, since for more than a month the Romagna waited for him," he begins. That a month does not seem like a very long time is bad enough, but in fact Cesare's subjects in the Romagna, the only area where his state was relatively consolidated, were already in rebellion at this time. As for his being able to at least prevent anyone he did not want to become pope from doing so, if this was true then Cesare's action in this regard was his fatal undoing, as we shall see momentarily. "But if on the death of Alexander he had been healthy, everything would have been easy for him," Machiavelli claims, but as we saw in the brief historical background about his life presented above, Cesare was in fact able to control the initial conclave of cardinals that elected his ally Pius III despite being ill. In his account, Machiavelli fails to mention this first conclave and instead discusses only the second conclave a month later after Pius' death that elected Julius II, as we shall see. Before summing up with an evaluation of Cesare's actions, Machiavelli reports a conversation with him: "And he told me, in the days when Julius II was created pope, that he had thought through what might happen if his father died, and for everything he had found a remedy, except that he never thought that at his father's death he too would be close to death."[13] Does Machiavelli agree with Cesare that he had found a remedy for what would happen with his father's death?

Or is he reporting wishful thinking on Cesare's part? Whatever his planned remedies, Cesare nonetheless continued to be dependent on the fortune of his father and the Church.

The conversation Machiavelli reports having had with Cesare should remind us of another conversation he has related, namely at the end of chapter 3 when he reports responding to Cardinal Rouen's remark that the Italians did not understand war by saying that the French did not understand the state, "since, if they understood it, they would not allow the Church to come into such greatness" (chap. 3, 50). What is common to these two reported conversations is the growing temporal power of the Church, a power augmented by Pope Alexander and Cesare, whatever their own intentions.

Having narrated the story of Cesare's career, Machiavelli concludes chapter 7 with an assessment. "Thus, having summarized all of the actions of the duke, I would not know how to reproach him. On the contrary, I would like to put him forward, as I have done, as one to be imitated by all those who have risen to rule through fortune and the arms of others. For, since he had a great spirit, and his intention was high, he could not conduct himself otherwise." And yet, as Machiavelli himself has underscored, Cesare failed.[14] He attempts to exculpate this new prince: "And only the brevity of the life of Alexander and his own sickness opposed his designs." Yet Alexander was over seventy when he died, hardly a brief life for the time. And to what extent was Cesare's own sickness an excuse rather than an explanation? Machiavelli explains that he can find "no fresher examples" of the sort of qualities and actions of Cesare, such as succeeding through force and fraud, but Cesare nonetheless remains an ambiguous example for a new prince given his failure. Machiavelli finally accuses Cesare: "Only in the creation of Julius as pontiff, since he made a poor choice, may the duke be criticized."[15] Machiavelli alludes at the very end to the fact that Julius had been a long-time enemy of Cesare and his father when he writes: "And whoever believes, in dealing with great personalities, that new benefits make old injuries forgotten deceives himself. Thus the duke erred in this choice, and it was the cause of his final ruin." In other words, Cesare deceived himself, and in doing so he allowed Julius to deceive him. As Tarcov explains: "Cesare Borgia is here revealed to have been a believer, one who believes in the possibility of forgiveness for the injuries he has committed ... . He turns out to have been Christian in this decisive respect. His belief weighed more heavily than his arms in determining his ultimate ruin."[16]

Once again, however, Cesare also seems to have deceived himself that he could stand alone and not depend on the fortune of others.[17] After the death of Pope Alexander, he was still dependent on the pope for his arms and finances, a weakness that Julius immediately exploited by taking away both. In a more subtle way, Machiavelli may also signal Cesare's dependence on the Church, and more broadly the weakness of Italy caused by the growing temporal power of the Church. After blaming Cesare for his so-called "choice" of Julius as pontiff, Machiavelli lists a number of cardinals whom Cesare had "offended" and who would therefore be disastrous choices, among them "St. Peter in Chains." Machiavelli refers here to the future Pope Julius II, Giuliano della Rovere, who was cardinal of the church of San Pietro in Vincoli, or St. Peter in Chains (which is now famous for Michelangelo's statue of Moses, part of the tomb of Julius II). Could he also be referring to the papacy itself, for the martyred St. Peter was the first pope, the rock upon whom Jesus said he would build his church?

Let us return in conclusion to the vexing question of why Machiavelli chose Cesare Borgia as his example of a new prince who attains his state through the arms and fortune of others, and what lesson we are to learn from his account. While analyzing Machiavelli's narrative of Cesare's actions, I noted two possible themes or issues that might be important for learning from Cesare's example without necessarily having to answer the question as to how a prince who ultimately failed in his enterprise could serve as an exemplar. First, Machiavelli himself directs attention during the course of his account to a particularly important point, a point "worthy of notice" that "should be imitated by others," namely how Cesare brought "good government" to the Romagna and gave its peoples peace, security, and unity where they had previously been subject to impotent lords who despoiled their subjects. Throughout *The Prince* Machiavelli will urge the prince to build his power on the people, and his description of

Cesare's actions, again notwithstanding his ultimate failure, is his first extended example of how that strategy might succeed. Second, I noted that oftentimes during his account of Cesare's actions, and especially his supposed plans for no longer depending upon the fortune and arms of others, the plans seem to be less Cesare's than Machiavelli's own (hypothetical) plan for how Cesare might have successfully acquired and maintained his power, again despite Cesare's own failure to do so. In this light, an influential interpretation of *The Prince* has been that Cesare Borgia's plan to carve out an independent state in the regions of the Romagna and the Marche is a model for what Machiavelli hopes a new prince who reads his book might accomplish. In support of this interpretation, scholars often point to the concluding chapter of *The Prince* where Machiavelli calls on a new prince, and specifically the Medici prince to whom he addresses his book, to unify Italy or at least a portion of Italy, noting that Lorenzo de' Medici is in a parallel position with regard to the current pope, his uncle Pope Leo X, as Cesare was with regard to his father Pope Alexander VI. Whether or not Cesare himself succeeded, a new prince who finds himself in power through the fortune and arms of others, such as Lorenzo de' Medici, might learn from Cesare's successes and failures and thereby accomplish what Cesare failed to do.[18]

Without further attempting to resolve the question over what sort of example Cesare Borgia might be, I will note that the debate over Machiavelli's intention in *The Prince*, and in his political thought as a whole, is mirrored in how different readers have answered it. Scholars have long debated the issue, with some seeing Cesare as Machiavelli's "model" prince and as an example for the dedicatee of *The Prince*, Lorenzo de' Medici, to follow and others detecting an ironic or even satirical streak in Machiavelli's presentation of the actions of the duke. These varying assessments are also seen in philosophers who came after Machiavelli. Two examples will suffice. Writing about 250 years after Machiavelli wrote *The Prince*, Montesquieu and Rousseau came to opposite conclusions about the meaning of the example of Cesare Borgia and therewith of Machiavelli's intention. As for the Baron Montesquieu, whose *Spirit of the Laws* (1748) so influenced the conception of the separation of powers in the US Constitution of 1787, he writes that "Machiavelli was full of his idol, Duke Valentino."[19] Writing about a decade later, Jean-Jacques Rousseau came to a different conclusion in his *Social Contract* (1762): "Machiavelli was an honest man and a good citizen. But being attached to the house of the Medici, he was forced during the oppression of his father-land to disguise his love of freedom. The choice of his execrable hero alone is enough to manifest his secret intention ... ."[20] The role of Cesare Borgia in *The Prince* continues to perplex.

NOTES

1 See Viroli 2007.

2 For a strong version of the argument that Machiavelli's new prince gives form to the state in a way traditionally associated with the Judeo-Christian divinity, see Newell 2013.

3 See Warner and Scott 2011 for a discussion of Machiavelli's treatment of Romulus.

4 In using the terms "lukewarm" and "lukewarmness," Machiavelli refers to Savonarola's own language in his sermons in reference to his enemies. Inter-estingly, he reverses Savonarola's usage by attributing "lukewarmness" not to his enemies, but to his friends. See Scott 2014. See also Revelations 3:15–16 (RSV Bible): "'I know your works: you are neither cold nor hot. Would that you were cold or hot! So, because you are lukewarm, and neither cold nor hot, I will spew you out of my mouth.'"

5 Justin, *History* XXIII.4 for the phrase. See also Polybius, *Histories* VII.8.

6 In the Dedicatory Letter to the *Discourses on Livy* Machiavelli also references the ancient historians concerning Hiero: "Writers praise Hiero the Syracusan when he was a private individual ... for Hiero lacked nothing other than the principality to be a prince" (4).

7 As Najemy (2013, esp. 545) notes, however, Cesare in fact depended on mercenary and other arms to the very end.

8 The tribunal was announced in October 1502, but only began functioning in mid-1503, shortly before Cesare's ultimate fall.

9 See Najemy 2013.

10 Benner 2013, 105.

11 In his translation Connell takes "he" in this sentence to refer to Cesare or "Valentino," but the Italian is ambiguous.

12 In his analysis of this chapter, Najemy (2013, 550–52) cites Machiavelli's own reports back to Florence from this very same time, noting Cesare's weak position.

13 Najemy (2013, 554) quotes from a diplomatic report Machiavelli sent back to Florence concerning his conversations with Cesare: "'he let himself go on at length with words full of poison and anger ... . I did not lack for things to

reply ... but decided instead to calm him down and got away from him as deftly as I could, although it seemed to take a thousand years.'"

14 As Benner (2013, 110) comments concerning Cesare Borgia as an exemplar: "Machiavelli does not say that *every* prince should imitate Borgia, but only a particular, deficient class of princes: namely, those who have 'risen to empire' by 'fortune and the arms of others.'"

15 To what degree Cesare "chose" Julius is doubtful because by the time of the election his control of the conclave had diminished to a mere four of twenty-eight cardinals (Najemy 2013, 549–50).

16 Tarcov 2013b, 580.

17 For a suggestion as to how Cesare might have ended his dependence on his father and the Church, see Scott and Sullivan 1994.

18 See Baron 1991.

19 Montesquieu, *Spirit of the Laws* XXIX.19 (Montesquieu 1989 [1748], 618).

20 Rousseau, *On the Social Contract* III.6 (Rousseau 2012, 218).

6

CRIMINALS, CITIZENS, POPES, AND OTHER TYPES OF PRINCES

When he outlined the various types of principalities and the modes by which they are acquired in chapter 1, Machiavelli stated that they are acquired "either with the arms of others or with one's own, either by fortune or by virtue." Even if the distinctions between hereditary and new principalities, entirely new and mixed principalities, break down over the course of the first five chapters and beyond, as I have suggested, Machiavelli's initial outline nonetheless does prepare us for chapters 6 and 7 where the new prince comes fully to the fore and where the question of one's own arms versus the arms of others and virtue versus fortune become thematic. Chapters 8 through 11 therefore come as something of a surprise since the types of principalities and modes of acquisitions Machiavelli discusses in these chapters were not included among the threads out of which he said in chapter 1 he would weave his book. Chapter 8 deals with principalities attained through crime, chapter 9 with what he terms a "civil principality," chapter 10 with how to measure the strength of all principalities, and, finally, chapter 11 with "ecclesiastical principalities." How do these new types of principalities and modes of acquisition relate to what Machiavelli has discussed up to this point?

CHAPTER 8: ON THOSE WHO HAVE ATTAINED PRINCIPALITIES THROUGH WICKED DEEDS

Machiavelli begins chapter 8 with the word "But," thereby suggesting that there was something missing in the previous chapter or chapters that he now wants to address as something of a qualification of what he has written or as an additional consideration. We saw him do this before, in chapter 3, which he began by writing, "But the difficulties are in the new principality...," thus indicating that his treatment in chapter 2 of hereditary principalities was insufficient, and we saw how he then revealed that maintaining a hereditary principality is not as simple as he first let on. So he begins chapter 8: "But because a private man may become a prince in two further modes that cannot be attributed wholly to fortune or to virtue, I do not wish to leave them out, although one may be reasoned about more extensively when republics are treated. These ways are when either by some wicked and nefarious way one ascends to the principality, or when a private citizen with the favor of his fellow citizens become prince of his fatherland." Machiavelli clearly suggests that his discussion in chapters 6 and 7 of private men acquiring an entirely new principality through virtue or fortune was incomplete. The first mode of attaining a principality through criminality will be the subject of chapter 8, and it seems that the second mode of becoming prince of one's fatherland with the help of one's fellow citizens will be the subject of chapter 9. Machiavelli's remark that "one" of these modes (which one?) will be reasoned about more extensively "where republics are treated" is an unclear reference: does he mean chapter 9 on "civil principalities," or the *Discourses on Livy*, or somewhere else? In fact, both chapters 8 and 9 of *The Prince* contain examples of republics where an individual rises to become prince, whether through crime or citizen support. Does Machiavelli intentionally blur principalities and republics and these modes of acquisition in order to suggest that the same dynamics of acquiring and maintaining power exist in all states? Are the wicked and nefarious modes of acquisition discussed in chapter 8 actually any different from what we saw in chapter 6 (for example, Romulus and his fratricide) or chapter 7 (for example, Cesare Borgia)?[1]

The first mode of attaining a principality through wicked and nefarious means will be the subject of the present chapter, and Machiavelli tells us that he will speak of it "without entering otherwise into the merits of this point." In other words, he will not judge these modes as good or evil, even though he has characterized them as "wicked and nefarious," but simply presents them for "whoever needs to imitate them." He also tells us that he will demonstrate them through two examples, one ancient and one modern. We saw in chapter 6 on new principalities acquired through one's own arms and virtue that he gave only ancient examples, and we saw in chapter 7 on new principalities acquired through the arms and fortune of others that, apart from a brief mention of ancient instances, his examples were modern. If he means to thereby suggest that the moderns are more likely to rely on the arms and fortune of others in comparison to the ancients, for some reason, then his explicit use in chapter 8 of both ancient and modern examples suggests that criminal means of acquiring power apply in all times. We will have to see whether there are any differences between his ancient and modern examples here.

Agathocles the Sicilian is Machiavelli's ancient example. Machiavelli provides the salient details of Agathocles' life and career, from his humble birth as the son of a potter to his rise to become prince of Syracuse and then king of all Sicily, and so we need only add two considerations not wholly obvious in his account. First, although Machiavelli calls Agathocles a "prince," he was commonly called a "tyrant." So, as with the example at the end of chapter 6 of Hiero of Syracuse, among others, Machiavelli pointedly declines to use the word "tyrant" in *The Prince*. Indeed, the fact that both Agathocles and Hiero were tyrants of the same city begs us to compare them and to wonder why Hiero is ranked by Machiavelli among virtuous princes and Agathocles among criminal ones. Second, Agathocles ruled for a considerable time, first becoming ruler of Syracuse in 317 BCE and staying in power until his death in 289 BCE, so for twenty-seven or twenty-eight years. The length of his rule will be one notable difference between Agathocles and Machiavelli's modern example in this chapter.

Concerning Agathocles Machiavelli emphasizes from the outset that he "always led a wicked life through each step of his career," but even so he writes: "Nonetheless, he accompanied his wicked deeds with such great virtue of spirit and of body" in such a way that he successfully rose to the peak of power even though he began from a very low place. We shall see that "nonetheless" and similar words are Machiavelli's signature way of writing in his discussion of Agathocles, as it is throughout *The Prince*. For example, here, after making what seems to be a definitive statement that Agathocles was continually "wicked," he goes on "nonetheless" to take back or qualify what he has said, saying that Agathocles had "great virtue of spirit and of body." Elsewhere in chapter 6, for example, he states that one should not reason about Moses, and nonetheless goes on to reason about Moses.

Machiavelli recounts how Agathocles rose through his military and political skill to become "governor" of Syracuse, but then decided to become prince, "and to hold with violence and without obligation to others what had been granted to him by consent." In other words, Agathocles is an example of the kind of prince Machiavelli will discuss in chapter 9 who rises to power in a "civil principality" through the support of his fellow citizens. Apparently, this was not enough for Agathocles, and he decided to become a prince no longer dependent on others for his power. After murdering all of the senators and the richest citizens, thereby overthrowing the existing regime, he "occupied and held the principate of that city without any internal opposition." Yet Agathocles clearly *established* the principate, meaning that he is in fact an example of a "new prince" in Machiavelli's terminology. Moreover, Machiavelli leaves out of his account the fact that the opportunity that enabled Agathocles to establish his principate was that he gained the support of the people by promising to overthrow the oligarchy in order to establish a democracy, but instead founded a principality. In what way is Agathocles different from the princes who acquired a wholly new principality whom Machiavelli has discussed so far? In fact, in the *Discourses on Livy* (II.13, 155) he writes of Agathocles alongside Cyrus as examples of those who rise from base to great fortune through fraud more than force.

Having recounted Agathocles' rise to power, Machiavelli now offers his assessment. "Thus whoever considers the actions and life of this man will not see things, or will see only a few of them, that he may attribute to fortune ... ." If we cannot attribute Agathocles' success to fortune, can we attribute it to virtue? Apparently not: "And yet one cannot call it virtue to kill one's fellow citizens, to betray one's friends, to be without faith, without compassion, without religion. These modes may be used to acquire rule but not glory." Nonetheless, Machiavelli continues: "For if one considers Agathocles' virtue in entering into and escaping dangers, and the greatness of his spirit in enduring and overcoming adverse things, one does not see why he should be judged inferior to any most excellent captain." So Agathocles is indeed virtuous. Not quite: "nonetheless, his bestial cruelty and inhumanity, with infinite wicked deeds, do not allow that he should be celebrated among the most excellent men. One cannot, therefore, attribute to fortune or to virtue what was accomplished without either one." So Agathocles is not virtuous after all?

What are we to make of Machiavelli's seemingly alternating assessment of Agathocles' virtue? One possibility is that he is not using the term "virtue" (*virtù*) in a moral sense, but in a value-neutral way to denote a kind of "excellence" in the way that we might admire a particularly clever criminal and call him an "excellent criminal," so in that sense a "virtuous criminal." With this in mind, then, some translators of Machiavelli render *virtù* differently in different contexts. In the passage in question, for example, they write of Agathocles' "ingenuity" instead of his "virtue" in "entering into and escaping dangers," but retain the translation "virtue" elsewhere, as with "And yet one cannot call it virtue to kill one's fellow citizens ... ." To be sure, *virtù* has a wide range of meanings, and the word can refer to "virtue" in the moral sense (courage, moderation, etc.). Or it can refer to the "excellence" of something without necessarily giving it a moral evaluation, as with a "virtuous" horse or even our "virtuous" criminal. Or, finally, it can connote "manliness" and the so-called "manly" virtues such as courage, given that the root of *virtù* is *vir*, "man" in Latin (hence our "virile") in the strong sense of a so-called "real man," as opposed to being called "effeminate," pejorative gendered language Machiavelli himself sometimes uses. Machiavelli takes advantage of the full range of the meaning of *virtù*, and in fact he seems to do so intentionally in his alternating assessment of Agathocles.

If we consistently render *virtù* in the passage in question as "virtue," as Connell does in the translation we are following in this guide, then what we see is that Machiavelli is confronting us with a problem: how is "virtue" in the traditional moral sense related to "virtue" in what might be called a "political" sense, that is what qualities and actions are required to acquire and maintain power? Machiavelli in fact signaled that he would do just this at the outset of the chapter. First, he explicitly evoked the moral connotation of "virtue" by stating that the mode of acquisition he will discuss is "some wicked and nefarious way" that "cannot be attributed wholly to fortune or to virtue." Yet, second, he also stated that he would do so "without entering otherwise into the merits of this point," in other words without passing moral judgment. By the traditional standards of virtue and vice, Agathocles' deeds cannot be deemed "virtuous": "And yet one cannot call it virtue to kill one's fellow citizens ... ." The word "call" here— "one cannot *call* it virtue"—is critical: Agathocles' deeds cannot be "called" virtuous according to what people traditionally *say* about virtue and vice. We will see Machiavelli using this same language later in *The Prince* when he turns in chapter 15 to a thematic discussion of the virtues of the prince. For the present, however, once we recognize that what one may "call" virtue is not the same as the qualities needed to acquire and maintain power, Machiavelli's alternating assessment of Agathocles begins to make sense. After telling us that his actions could not be attributed to fortune, Machiavelli tempts us to wonder whether they are due to virtue. But then he tells us that Agathocles' actions cannot be "called" virtuous. "These modes may be used to acquire rule but not glory." "Glory" is a form of reputation: because Agathocles cannot be called virtuous according to traditional standards, he cannot acquire "glory." Likewise, his "bestial cruelty" and "infinite" wicked deeds "*do not allow* that he should be *celebrated* among the most excellent men." In short, his blatantly vicious behavior and apparent disregard for reputation or appearances "do not allow" Agathocles to be called "virtuous" despite his success. Yet the qualities he had that enabled him to acquire rule, what Machiavelli characterizes as "such great virtue of spirit and of body," can be considered virtuous in a different sense. By juxtaposing the traditional moral meaning of "virtue" with a different, "political" meaning in this passage, Machiavelli confronts the reader with a puzzle or even a dilemma concerning the role of virtue and vice in politics, as we shall see later in the work.

Having finished his account of his ancient example, Machiavelli turns as promised to his modern one. He underscores the fact that his example is contemporary by the way he introduces it: "In our times, while Alexander VI was reigning, Liverotto the Fermano ... ." Why specify that the events he is about to recount occurred during the papacy of Alexander VI? Machiavelli goes on to tell how the orphaned Liverotto rose up through the military because he was "clever and gallant in both his person and his spirit." Like Agathocles, Liverotto decided that he did not want to owe his rank to anyone else: "But since it seemed to him a servile thing to follow others," he decided with the aid of some citizens of Fermo to plot to become prince of the city. After entering the city with his troops, Liverotto invited his uncle, the present lord, and the leading men of Fermo to a banquet. Engaging his guests in conversation and "speaking of the greatness of Pope Alexander, and of Cesare, his son, and of their undertakings" (once again, an emphasis on Pope Alexander), Liverotto suddenly suggested retiring to a more secret place to continue their discussion, leading them into a room where he had hidden his soldiers, who then killed his uncle and the others. Afterward he intimidated the magistrates of the city, forcing them to establish a government of which he "made himself prince." Machiavelli concludes the story of Liverotto by twice mentioning that he ruled a mere one year before becoming the victim of Cesare Borgia at Senigallia, referring the reader to his account in chapter 7 of Cesare's murder of Liverotto and his other mercenary captains.

What are we to make of the example of Liverotto and how does it compare to that of Agathocles? Perhaps most obviously, as an example of attaining a principality by crime the modern example of Liverotto pales in comparison to the ancient example of Agathocles. Machiavelli seems to signal this in several ways. First, unlike Agathocles, he does not describe Liverotto as "virtuous," but only as "clever and gallant in both his person and his spirit." Second, he underscores Liverotto's short reign of one year. Indeed, Liverotto was twenty-seven years old when he died, and Agathocles *ruled* for twenty-seven or twenty-eight years. Agathocles was described by Machiavelli as being "without faith" and "without religion." What about Liverotto? We are not told of his faithfulness or religiosity directly, but Liverotto's key mistake was trusting—having faith in—Cesare Borgia. Why does Machiavelli frame his account of Liverotto with Pope Alexander at the beginning and Cesare Borgia at the end, and remind us in the middle of them? First and more obviously, Liverotto's fate as a rising military captain whom Cesare employed and his ultimate fate at Cesare's hands are central to the story, and especially its denouement. Second, perhaps Machiavelli is suggesting that misplaced faith is more characteristic in modern than in ancient times. We saw a similar pattern in chapter 3, with Machiavelli's comparison of the ancient Romans as his example of foreseeing evil from afar and therefore preventing it from arising to "the wise men of our times," who place their faith in future good. In other words, Machiavelli may be pointing to something about modern times that is owing to Christianity. If so, that would explain in part how he continues his analysis, to which we now return.

With his ancient and modern examples in place, Machiavelli returns to his general discussion of attaining a principality through wicked deeds. "Anyone might wonder how it happened that Agathocles, and anyone like him, after infinite betrayals and cruelties, could live for so long securely in his fatherland, and defend himself against external enemies." We have been told before that someone might "wonder" or "marvel" at something that would appear to contradict or be missing from Machiavelli's analysis, and as before our author will demonstrate that we ought not wonder. Moreover, when he returns to Agathocles, Liverotto is nowhere to be seen except by silent comparison to Agathocles, who lived "a long time securely in his fatherland" despite his criminal and cruel behavior. At any rate, Machiavelli now dispels the reader's wonder: "I believe that this comes from cruelties that are badly used or well used. Cruelties may be called 'well used,' if it is permissible to speak well of evil, when they are all done at once, out of the necessity of securing oneself, and when afterward they do not persist, but are converted into as much utility for the subjects as possible. Cruelties 'badly used' are those, even if at the beginning they are few, which instead grow over time rather than eliminating themselves."

Several things should be noted about this striking passage. First, in even daring to call some acts of cruelty "well used," Machiavelli challenges traditional notions of cruelty, rooted both in classical philosophy and especially in Christianity. He calls attention to this challenge in two ways. First, he commences his statement by stating what he believes, "I believe ....," thus indicating that others apparently believe something different about cruelty. Second, he underscores others' contrary belief by apologizing: "if it is permissible to speak well of evil."[2] As for Machiavelli, he will indeed speak well of evil. Second, aside from the temporal aspect of using cruelty well by doing it all at once and getting it out of the way, cruelty "well used" benefits both the prince, who thus secures himself in power, and ultimately the people, since these cruel acts can be "converted" into the "utility" of the subjects if properly done. We saw a similar example of this in chapter 7 concerning how Cesare Borgia's actions in the Romagna benefited, or at least might have benefited, his subjects by giving them security and law and order where they had previously lived without security and lawlessly. In fact, when Machiavelli returns in chapter 17 to the question of cruelty and mercy "well used" and "badly used," Cesare Borgia will be his example of cruelty "well used." For the present, though, he attributes Agathocles' astonishing success to the fact that he used cruelty well, and thereby had some remedy "with God and with men," a curious use of the Italian idiom given that it is used with reference to the irreligious Agathocles. Since Agathocles is his ancient example in this chapter, Machiavelli may be hinting that modern princes are more likely to employ cruelty "badly used" because of their mistaken faith that a few instances of cruelty in the beginning will allow them to avoid greater cruelty later.

Machiavelli concludes chapter 8 by offering advice to someone who plans to "seize a state" and occupy it, although he no longer speaks of the modes, criminal or otherwise, by which it is acquired. Drawing on the example of Agathocles, he counsels this prince to commit all the necessary "offenses" all at once so that he does not have to keep committing them, and to thereby win the subjects over to himself "by benefiting them." Whoever does not do so will have to keep his sword in hand and cannot rely on his subjects. Machiavelli promises that "adverse times" will arise, and a good prince should therefore act like the Romans of chapter 3 by preparing for adversity, in the present analysis by having won over his subjects and making them more reliable through cruelty "well used." The theme of the relationship of a prince and his people continues in the next chapter.

CHAPTER 9: ON THE CIVIL PRINCIPALITY

We have another chapter beginning with "But ...," indicating once again that something remains from the preceding chapter to be discussed. In this case, Machiavelli explicitly ties this chapter to the previous one by announcing that he will take up the other mode of acquisition he mentioned there, namely when a private citizen attains the principality through the assistance of his fellow citizens. In addition, he emphasizes the supposed difference between the two modes by now adding that this second mode is done "not through wickedness or other intolerable violence," as opposed to the cases he discussed in the previous chapter. The type of principality this mode of acquisition creates may be called a "civil principality," Machiavelli tells us, seemingly indicating that this terminology is his own. How a "civil principality" might be related to a republic is not clear, but a prince in this type of principality founds his power more explicitly on the people than the other types of principalities Machiavelli has discussed. Alternatively, he is more explicit here about the degree to which any prince must found on the people. In either case, some interpreters of *The Prince* have found chapter 9 particularly important for ascertaining Machiavelli's intention in his little treatise, arguing that this chapter reveals most clearly that his intention is to urge princes to rule in a more republican manner, by founding on the people, ruling for their benefit, or preparing a transition to a more fully republican form of government, or, somewhat differently perhaps, in a more populist manner, favoring the people rather than "the great."[3] We should keep these interpretations in mind as we proceed.

A "civil principality" is attained through "neither complete virtue nor complete fortune," but rather through what Machiavelli terms "a fortunate astuteness," a phrase that combines elements of fortune and virtue. How "astuteness" or "cleverness" (*astuzia*) is different from the kind of clever wickedness displayed by Agathocles, if it is in fact different, is as yet unclear. In any case, Machiavelli now moves to the main theme of chapter 8, the two "factions" out of which all cities are composed: the people and "the great." He explains: "For in every city these two different humors are found, whence it arises that the people desire to be neither commanded nor oppressed by the great, and the great desire both to command and to oppress the people. From these two different appetites there arises in the city one of three effects: principality, or liberty, or license."

That Machiavelli would wait until now to discuss what seems to be a very important subject relevant to any type of principality is exceedingly strange. By characterizing these two elements in every city as "humors," he uses the medical language of his time, which attempted to explain health and to diagnose illness in terms of the balance of four glandular fluids or "humors" in the human body. Earlier in *The Prince*, in chapter 3, Machiavelli compared political prudence to medical diagnosis, specifically trying to recognize future evils when the symptoms are not clear at present, and in the *Discourses on Livy* he likewise employs a medical analogy when he describes the state as a "mixed body" requiring regular treatment (III.1). Yet Machiavelli here quickly drops the language of "humors" and instead speaks of the "appetites" of the people and the great for wanting not to be commanded or oppressed and wanting to command and to oppress, respectively. As for "the great" (*grandi*), Machiavelli's definition of them in terms of their "appetite" for command and oppression suggests that he is not referring specifically to either aristocrats or oligarchs, and therefore is not relying on a traditional classification of regimes, but rather on political hierarchies that generate different characteristic appetites relating to command and oppression. Finally, he tells us that these appetites have three possible effects: principality, or liberty, or license.[4] Since he introduces his discussion by saying that these two "humors" or "appetites" are found in "every city," he seems to be offering a general classification of regimes that is not restricted to the "civil principality" which is the subject of this chapter. How is this tripartite classification related to the bipartite classification of states into principalities and republics with which he began in chapter 1? Is "liberty" here the same as a "republic"? Machiavelli does not say. What he does do is proceed to discuss the first possible outcome, a principality arising from the conflict between the great and the people, and devotes the remainder of chapter 9 to this subject. He does not discuss the other two possible outcomes, liberty or license, in this chapter. Are we to anticipate that he will do so in the following chapters?

A private individual can attain a civil principality either with the favor of the people or of the great, Machiavelli tells us. As for the great, when they see they cannot resist the people by themselves they fashion one of their own into a prince so that they can satisfy their appetite for command and oppression "under his shadow." As for the people, when they see they cannot resist the great they fashion someone and make him prince in order to defend themselves from the great. Machiavelli explains that those who attain the principality with the help of the great have difficulty maintaining themselves because many of the great consider themselves his equal. We might add that if the great erect someone as prince so as to sate their appetite for command and oppression, their appetite conflicts with that of the prince. By contrast, those who become prince with the favor of the people have an easier time because the people can be more easily satisfied, for, Machiavelli explains, "the end of the people is more honest than that of the great, since the latter want to oppress and the former want not to be oppressed." What exactly Machiavelli means when he states the end of the people is more "honest" or "decent" (*honesto*) is unclear, although we should note that he claims only that their end is "more" honest, not that it is simply honest. The key factor would however seem rather to be that their aim of not being oppressed does not conflict with that of the prince whereas the end of the great does. But the prince presumably shares the same aim as the great, to command and perhaps also to oppress. How should a prince rule so as not to make the people hostile? Machiavelli emphasizes that the prince always has to live with the same people, and thus cannot afford to make them hostile without losing his state. He also claims that the hostility of the great is more dangerous than that of the people because the great have "more astuteness." This is the first time Machiavelli has used the term "astute" since the beginning of the chapter, where he says that princes acquire a "civil principality" through "a fortunate astuteness." The prince seems to share both the desire to command and the quality of astuteness with the great. How is the prince to conduct himself with regard to the great?

In order to clarify his point, Machiavelli says that the great act either in such a way that they are bound to "your fortune" or they do not. Those who are so bound to you can be "honored and loved" as long as they are not too rapacious, that is, as long as they do not excessively indulge their appetite for command and oppression. Those who are not bound to you are of two sorts: either they lack spiritedness, and can be used by the prince for his own purposes, or they are clever and ambitious, and therefore pose a threat. One potential problem with Machiavelli's analysis is that the great, hoping to gratify their appetites under the "shadow" of the prince, do not necessarily reveal which type they are, and therefore whether they pose a threat to the prince, until it is too late. What remedy might exist? Machiavelli drops his discussion of the great and turns to the people. Whether one becomes prince through the favor of the great or of the people, he argues, it is essential to win over the people. The people are more easily won over because "they ask only not to be oppressed" (Machiavelli drops "not to be commanded"). He continues: "The prince may win them to himself in many ways, although, because they vary according to the circumstances, a certain rule cannot be given for them, and for this reason they will be left out."

Is Machiavelli being coy? If winning the favor of the people is so important, shouldn't he discourse on the matter at length and provide some rules? Instead, he gives us an example. Nabis, "prince of the Spartans," he tells us, was able to defend "his fatherland and his state" against hostile Greek enemies and the Romans because the people were his friend. What Machiavelli does not tell us is how Nabis made the people his "friend." He did so by exiling the wealthy from Sparta and dividing up their estates among the people. In the *Discourses on Livy* Machiavelli mentions Nabis as an example of "those tyrants who have the collectivity as a friend and the great as an enemy," and are therefore more secure because of it, and he freely calls him "tyrant of Sparta." Just before mentioning Nabis in the *Discourses on Livy*, Machiavelli explains that "the great part of tyrannies" arise "from too great a desire of the people to be free and from too great a desire of the nobles to command ... . When a people brings itself to make this error of giving reputation to one individual because he beats down those it holds in hatred, and if that individual is wise, it will always happen that he will become tyrant of the city" (I.40, 88–89). Once again, as with Hiero and Agathocles, Machiavelli avoids using the term "tyrant" in *The Prince* when he unhesitatingly does so elsewhere. In fact, Nabis was a notoriously violent tyrant according to Machiavelli's sources, and he was also the last king of an independent Sparta, ultimately losing both "his fatherland and his state," to use the language Machiavelli uses here in *The Prince*, when he was assassinated in a conspiracy and Sparta was defeated.[5] Nabis is an unsettling example of a prince who founds his power on the people, both in terms of the violent means by which he did so and in terms of the outcome. Is Machiavelli warning the people against such princes?

Having offered Nabis the Spartan as an example of a prince who had made the people his "friend," Machiavelli defends himself against a potential objection, although not an objection to his choice of example. "And let there be no one who strikes back at this opinion of mine with that trite proverb that 'He who builds on the people builds on mud.'" Machiavelli admits that the proverb is true if a private citizen "allows himself to think" that the people will "free him" if he is attacked by his enemies or by the authorities or magistrates. Rather than speaking of a prince in a civil principality here, Machiavelli has shifted his attention to a private citizen trying to gain the people's support in a partisan conflict, so perhaps he is discussing the difficulties such a private person has in rising to become prince. His examples attest to the difficulty of doing so: the two Gracchi brothers were tribunes of the people in Rome who promoted agrarian reform and were opposed by the patricians, or what Machiavelli terms "the great," and were assassinated; and Messer Giorgio Scali was a leader of the populist Ciompi regime in Florence from 1378 to 1382, which drew its support from the lesser trade guilds and was opposed by the wealthier trade guilds, and was executed when the populist regime fell. Apparently both ancient and modern populist leaders have falsely believed that the people would simply come to their aid, seemingly proving the "trite proverb" Machiavelli is arguing against true. Yet he continues: "But if he is a prince who builds on the people, who is able to command, and if he is a man of heart, who does not take fright in adversities, and does not fail in his other preparations, and who with his spirit and with his orders keeps the populace inspired, he will never find himself deceived by the people, and he will judge that he has built good foundations." Apart from having the right personal qualities, what sort of "preparations" and "orders" does it require and in what way ought the populace be "inspired" in order to lay these "good foundations"? Machiavelli does not say. His language concerning "good foundations" should make us think of chapters 6 and 7 on new princes and the actions they took to form their peoples and win them over, and perhaps most particularly of Cesare Borgia's spectacular execution of Remirro de Orco, which left the people "at once satisfied and stupefied."

In conclusion Machiavelli turns his focus from the private citizen trying to rise through the support of the people to the moment when the civil order is overturned. "These principalities are usually imperiled when they are about to ascend from a civil to an absolute order." These princes either command by themselves, which is what Machiavelli seems to mean by an "absolute order," or through other magistrates, which is what he seems to mean by a "civil order." If the prince depends on magistrates, he is dependent to some degree on their support and on the good will of the citizens and subjects. Such a prince would seem to be in the same position as the populist leaders Machiavelli brought forward as examples that prove true the "trite proverb" that to found on the people is to found on mud, falsely putting their faith in the people. What is a prince to do? "For a prince of this kind cannot found himself on what he sees in peaceful times, when the citizens have need of his state," and are therefore loyal and promise their lives and treasure, but who then are nowhere to be found in "adverse times." Machiavelli now offers his advice: "For this reason a wise prince must think of a way by which his citizens, always and in every kind of circumstance, have need of his state and of himself, and then they will always be faithful to him." If the mistake made by most princes is to have faith in the promises of their subjects, then the "wise prince" would seem to found himself on more reliable motives. Perhaps the "preparations" and "foundations," and the manner of "inspiring" the people, he mentioned previously as "good foundations" for a prince involve the prince using institutional ("orders") and extra-institutional means ("inspiration") to tie his subjects to him through mutual interest and dependence.

CHAPTER 10: IN WHAT WAYS THE STRENGTHS OF ALL PRINCIPALITIES SHOULD BE MEASURED

This brief chapter is puzzling in many ways, for starters with regard to its seemingly awkward location in *The Prince*. What are the "strengths" (or "forces") which the chapter title announces must be measured? If they are military strength, as much of the content of the chapter seems to suggest, then why isn't chapter 10 placed together with chapters 12–14, which contain Machiavelli's thematic discussion of military arms? Such a location would also make sense since the chapter title mentions measuring the "strengths" of "all" principalities, and Machiavelli only completes his analysis of the various types of principalities in chapter 11, "On Ecclesiastical Principalities." In this way, then, chapter 10 would seem to belong after chapter 11, and the odd placement of chapter 10 therefore has the effect of dislocating chapter 11 and making it stand out as exceptional. If these "strengths" refer to more than military arms, then perhaps chapter 10 is a logical continuation of the previous two chapters with their emphasis on founding on the people, since the friendship of the people might be considered to be the most important "strength" a prince could have. This conjecture would gain support from the fact that Machiavelli begins the chapter by stating: "It is appropriate in examining the qualities of these principalities to consider another thing ...," thereby seeming to add something to the previous discussion of founding on the people. "These principalities" might refer to the types of principalities discussed in chapters 8 and 9, which are acquired neither through virtue (or what can be "called" virtue) nor fortune. Or perhaps "these principalities" encompasses all of the principalities he has discussed so far in the work. If so, then how do we assess the "strengths" of the type of principality he has not so far discussed, the "ecclesiastical principalities" of chapter 11? The odd placement of chapter 10 once again has the effect of underscoring the exceptional character of chapter 11. Indeed, Machiavelli even appears to draw attention to the issue of the location of chapter 10 with an unusual number of references within the chapter that point backward and forward to other parts of the work. For example, in the very first paragraph he writes: "As to the first case, it has been discussed, and in what is coming we shall say about it what is needed," and "as stated above and as will be said below." All of this is a puzzle to be pondered.

The new consideration Machiavelli states he will discuss in chapter 10 is "whether a prince has a state sufficient that he may stand by himself if he needs to, or if instead he always needs to be defended by others." He clarifies what he means by "a state sufficient" (or perhaps, more clearly, "sufficient enough state" or a "sufficiently strong enough state"—*tanto stato*), by stating that he judges that those who can "stand by themselves" are those who have sufficient men or money to be able to put together an adequate army to withstand whoever might attack them. Similarly, he judges that those who do not have "a state sufficient" as those who cannot field such an army and must therefore flee within their walls and try to withstand a siege. "As to the first case, it has been discussed, and in what is coming we shall say about it what is needed." By the "first case" of having enough men or money to field such an army, Machiavelli seems to refer to his discussion in chapter 6 of princes who acquire a principality through their "own arms." As for "what is coming," he appears to refer to chapters 12–14, once again putting chapters 10 and 11 into a kind of limbo. Having thus pointed back and then ahead, he turns to the case at hand of a prince without enough men or money to field an adequate army and who is therefore forced to withdraw behind the walls of his city. He has no advice for such a prince except the obvious: "nothing else can be said, save to advise such princes to fortify and supply their own town, and to pay no attention to the countryside." If such a prince has "managed himself concerning the other affairs of his subjects" according to what Machiavelli has "stated above and as will be said below," he is likely to avoid or withstand a siege. Once again, then, he points back (it seems to chapters 6–9) and ahead (it seems to chapters 15–19). In this case, his references backward and forward mimic the actions of a prince in the position he is discussing, who earlier had the foresight to fortify and supply his town and who now awaits an impending siege and hopes he can withstand it. Should such a prince have instead seen to it that he had "a state sufficient" to field an army?

Without preparation Machiavelli suddenly introduces the cities of Germany, which he characterizes as "very free," and explains that they have little countryside to defend, obey the emperor when they so choose, and do not fear the emperor or any other power. The German cities to which he refers are the largely autonomous cities of Switzerland and southern Germany (e.g., Basel, Augsburg, Strasbourg, Cologne, Nuremberg, etc.) that owed nominal allegiance to the Holy Roman Emperor. What links these German cities to the preceding discussion of a prince who has to withdraw behind his walls is that they are also fortified towns that have armed and fortified themselves so well that no one dares attack them. Machiavelli emphasizes not only their military preparedness, but also their economic preparations in storing up enough materials for the "plebs" to engage in the crafts that are the mainstay of their economies for a whole year. Finally, he adds: "They still hold military training in repute, and, in this regard, they have many institutions for maintaining it." In other words, Machiavelli is discussing something like free commercial states, or even republics, with an armed citizenry.

These German cities are Machiavelli's only historical example in chapter 10, and notably they are modern examples and, moreover, non-Italian examples. The implicit contrast with Italy will be made more explicit by Machiavelli with his discussion in chapter 11 of how Italy came to rely on the arms of others due in large measure to the presence of the Church.

We will see what he has to say in chapter 11 shortly, but for now something he writes in the *Discourses on Livy* (in a passage we will further examine when discussing the next chapter) may help us understand why he refers to these German cities here. Having stated that Italy owes both its corrupt mores and political divisions to the Church, Machiavelli offers a hypothetical test case to prove the truth of his proposition: "Whoever wished to see the truth more readily by certain experience would need to be of such power as to send the Roman court, with all the authority it has in Italy, to inhabit the towns of the Swiss. They are today the only peoples who live according to the ancients as regards both religion and military orders; and one would see that in little time the bad customs of that court would make more disorder in that province than any other accident that could arise there at any time" (I.12, 38–9; see also II.19). What Machiavelli writes in the *Discourses on Livy* suggests that we must compare what he says in chapter 10 of *The Prince* about the armed and free German cities to what he says in chapter 11 about Italy and the role of the Church there. As for the Germans, they "render unto Caesar" when they choose to do so, and they do not owe anything to the Church.

With his pregnant digression concluded, Machiavelli returns to the prince held up behind the walls of his city. If such a prince has a strong city and is not hated by his people, he cannot be attacked or, if he were to be attacked, the attacker "would depart in shame, since the things of the world are so changeable that it is almost impossible that someone should stand idle with his armies for a year to besiege him." Why so optimistic? Don't the same vicissitudes of the world apply to the besieged prince, idle along with his people behind the walls? Perhaps these thoughts have entered the mind of the imagined interlocutor Machiavelli brings forward to object to what he has just said. "And if anyone should reply, 'If the people have their farmlands outside, and they see them burn, they will have no patience, and the long siege and self-interest will make them forget their prince,'" Machiavelli would answer that "a powerful and spirited prince will always overcome all of those difficulties" by managing the hopes and fears of his "subjects" and their obligation to him. A "prudent" prince, he concludes, should not find it difficult to gain and keep up the "spirits of his citizens," at least "so long as he does not lack what is required for living or for their defense." Machiavelli switches here from speaking of the prince's "subjects" to his "citizens." Is he suggesting that there are different ways to "found on the people," as he phrased it in the previous chapter, by treating them as subjects or as citizens? How optimistic should we be that "a powerful and spirited prince" will succeed in preventing the people—whether considered as subjects or as citizens—from "forgetting" him, and how often can we expect these princes to be "powerful and spirited"? Perhaps this prince should have attended to making sure he had "a state sufficient" for resisting the enemy on the battlefield, for example by arming his citizens, rather than having to resort to hoping that he might resist the siege.

CHAPTER 11: ON ECCLESIASTICAL PRINCIPALITIES

"At present it remains only for us to reason about ecclesiastical principalities." The way in which Machiavelli begins chapter 11 has led some interpreters to suggest that this was the concluding chapter to what he originally intended as his small treatise on principalities. While it is true that his discussion of ecclesiastical principalities is the last chapter devoted to the types of principalities and the modes by which they are acquired, Machiavelli none-theless does not in any way prepare the reader for this discussion in the supposed plan he laid out in chapter 1, where there was no mention of ecclesiastical principalities whatsoever. In short, chapter 11 comes as a surprise. It should also be surprising that he discusses ecclesiastical principalities in the plural: not *the* ecclesiastical principality, but ecclesiastical *principalities*. We should remind ourselves that Machiavelli wrote *The Prince* before the Protestant Reformation, so at that time in Western Europe there was supposedly only one church: The Church. By speaking of ecclesiastical principalities in the plural Machiavelli enlarges his perspective beyond his present place and time.

We have been told repeatedly by Machiavelli not to marvel or wonder at the matters about which he reasons, but ecclesiastical principalities seem to be truly marvelous. All of the difficulties consist in acquiring these principalities, and that can be done either through virtue or fortune, but once acquired they are maintained without either virtue or fortune being necessary. He explains:

> For they are sustained by orders that have become ancient in religion, which have been so powerful, and of such a quality, that they keep their princes in their states no matter how they proceed and live. Those men alone have states and do not defend them. They have subjects and do not govern them. And their states, although they are not defended, are not taken from them. And the subjects, although they are not governed, do not care, nor do they think of freeing themselves from their princes, nor are they able to. Thus only these principalities are secure and happy.

Machiavelli's tone here is difficult to discern. Is he being ironic? For example, his remark that these princes maintain their states "no matter how they proceed and live" could be taken to be a reference to the corruption of priests and prelates, and therefore as the expression of stock-in-trade anticlerical sentiments common in his time and before. On the other hand, is he expressing genuine astonishment? How could it be that "only these principalities are secure and happy"? Do ecclesiastical principalities have "orders" that could somehow be employed by other types of principalities? He will not say: "But since they are ruled by superior causes that no human mind is able to grasp, I shall leave out speaking about them, for since they are exalted and maintained by God, it would be the office of a presumptuous and rash man to discuss them." We have seen Machiavelli worry that he will be held to be presumptuous, in the Dedicatory Letter when he admitted that it might seem presumptuous for him to reason about princes, which of course he goes on to do. We have also seen him say that he will not reason about something and then proceed to do so, notably when he said that one should not reason about Moses since he was the executor of the things ordered by God, but then promptly go on to reason about Moses. What about in the present case? He will in fact go on to gratify the curiosity of someone who wants to understand how the Church came to have such great temporal power, but he will not dare to reason about its spiritual power.

Before turning to his explanation of how the Church acquired its temporal state, let us pause over the puzzle of ecclesiastical principalities in the plural. If we take Machiavelli to be not simply or solely ironic in his description of these principalities as not needing to defend their states or govern their subjects, then what he says is false, or at least a great exaggeration, for the Church did in fact have to defend its territories and govern its subjects. But perhaps this is just the clue we have been looking for. Could it be the case that he is not speaking about the Church when discussing ecclesiastical principalities?[6] The spiritual power of any religion, that is the power it exercises over people's thoughts and actions through their beliefs, may be Machiavelli's subject here. What might be just as interesting to Machiavelli as the temporal power of the Church, or even more interesting, is the spiritual power it exercised before it acquired such temporal power. Indeed, if we broaden our horizons beyond the late fifteenth and early sixteenth centuries, the period Machiavelli will focus on, and look back centuries or even a millennium or more, we cannot help but be astonished by the power of Christianity in ruling over men and women without any temporal power and sometimes even in conflict with temporal powers. How to explain the astonishing success of its unarmed prophet, who is portrayed throughout churches as Christ the King, sitting in judgment? How to explain the kingdom of true believers, or what Augustine called the "City of God," stretching across and beyond the boundaries of any temporal state and across time until judgment day? This "principality" does indeed have subjects without governing them in any ordinary manner, and does so despite how its princes proceed and live. In the *Discourses on Livy* Machiavelli treats Christianity as one "sect" among many. Discoursing on how states and sects require occasional reordering if they are to continue to exist, he writes:

But as to sects, these renewals are also seen to be necessary by the example of our religion, which would be altogether eliminated if it had not been drawn back toward its beginning by Saint Francis and Saint Dominick. For with poverty and with the example of the life of Christ they brought back into the minds of men what had already been eliminated there. Their new orders were so powerful that they are the cause that the dishonesty of the prelates and of the head of the religion do not ruin it. Living still in poverty and having so much credit with the peoples in confessions and sermons, they give them to understand that it is evil to say evil of evil, and that it is good to live under obedience to them and, if they make an error, to leave them for God to punish.

(III.1, 211–12)

"Our religion" is only one such "sect" in Machiavelli's analysis, and so ecclesiastical principalities in the plural may be his engagement with the spiritual power exercised by any religion, but principally the one reigning in his time.[7]

Having stated that he will not reason about ecclesiastical principalities since "they are ruled by superior causes that the human mind is unable to reach," Machiavelli satisfies the curious reader by putting his mind to explaining how the Church "has come to such greatness in temporal affairs." Its rise is all the more remarkable because of how quickly it happened, for Machiavelli explains that before Pope Alexander (elected pope in 1492) everyone, even the most petty baron and lord, "esteemed her little in temporal affairs," and now at the time of the writing of *The Prince* just a little more than twenty years later, the Church has grown powerful. His explanation of the rise of the temporal power of the Church takes the form of an analysis of the power dynamic in Italy that preceded this rise. He explains that before the French invasion of 1494 by Charles VIII the "province" of Italy was under the control of five major powers: the pope, the Venetians, the king of Naples, the duke of Milan, and the Florentines. These powers all had two principal concerns: not to allow an armed invasion from outside Italy and not to allow any state inside Italy to increase its power. Of particular concern to them were the pope and the Venetians. The Venetians were held in check by the combined power of the other states, while the power of the popes was constrained by the factious "barons" in Rome, principally the Orsini and Colonna families. These armed barons kept the pontiff "weak and unstable," and even if a "spirited" pope emerged, such as Sixtus IV (pope during 1471–84), the brevity of the popes' lives (their reigns lasting an average of ten years by Machiavelli's estimate) kept anyone from overcoming these factions. "This used to make it that the temporal powers of the pope were little valued in Italy," Machiavelli explains, thereby pointing to the factions in Rome as the principal cause of the weakness of the papacy in temporal affairs and also thereby indicating that the removal of these factions will be his explanation for a change in the situation.

"Then there arose Alexander VI ..." (*Surse di poi Alessandro VI* ...), Machiavelli dramatically commences his story. He explains: "With Duke Valentino as his instrument, and with the opportunity of the arrival of the French, he did all of those things that I discussed above concerning the actions of the duke." Now we finally have confirmation of what we suspected in chapter 7: Cesare Borgia was not only dependent on the fortune of his father, but was even his "instrument." "Although his intent was not to make the Church great, but the duke," Machiavelli explains, "nonetheless what he did resulted in the greatness of the Church, which after his death, when the duke was eliminated, was the heir to his labors." So far Machiavelli has discussed the motive behind the increased temporal power of the Church, namely the ambition of the popes, though not ambition on behalf of the Church, and the opportunity, namely the French invasion that disrupted the power dynamics in Italy, but he has not discussed what he has already indicated was the key factor that held the popes in check, namely the factions in Rome.

"Then came Pope Julius ..." (*Venne di poi papa Iulio* ...) he continues the story: "He found the Church great, since it possessed all the Romagna; and the barons of Rome were eliminated, since Alexander's blows had annihilated these factions." Strangely, Machiavelli did not mention the annihilation of the factions in Rome among Alexander's (or Cesare's) actions. In fact, the subjection of the Orsini in particular and the seizure of their states were among Alexander's principal objectives, partly in order to give these states to members of his family and partly to consolidate his power, and he was also not above murdering an Orsini cardinal or having Cesare eliminate other members of the family at Senigallia, as we have seen in chapter 7. At any rate, after a brief account of the continued military conquests of Julius, and remarking that his successes came with "so much greater honor for himself inasmuch as he did everything for the increase of the Church and not for any private person," Machiavelli returns to the all-important issue of the factions in Rome. Building on Alexander's success, Julius kept the Orsini and Colonna factions in check, first through sheer intimidation with the great power of the Church and second by preventing them from having any cardinals, "who are the origin of the tumults among them." Machiavelli has quietly introduced a new consideration into his explanation: the way in which the power dynamics within the Church, in the form of ambitious and fractious cardinals, relate to the power dynamics outside of the Church but inside Rome, namely the factions among the powerful barons there, which in turn are related to the larger power dynamics in Italy as a whole. "Nor will these factions ever be at peace whenever they have cardinals," he explains, "because their cardinals nourish the factions in Rome and outside, and their barons are forced to defend the factions, and thus from the ambition of the prelates are born the discords and tumults among the barons."

Machiavelli concludes his story of the rise of the temporal power of the Church by bringing it up to the time of the writing of *The Prince*. "Thus His Holiness Pope Leo has found this pontificate most powerful. One hopes, if the former popes made it great with their arms, this one will make it very great and venerable through his goodness and his other infinite virtues." Machiavelli's tone here is once again difficult to discern. Given what he has said, and also left unsaid, in his account of Alexander and Julius, it is perhaps difficult to believe that he thinks Pope Leo will rule through "goodness and his other infinite virtues" rather than to follow his predecessors by ruling through force and fraud. But perhaps he has other plans in mind. Before being elected to the papacy on March 11, 1514, an event that led to Machiavelli's release from prison, Pope Leo X was Cardinal Giovanni de' Medici, and the head of the Medici family. The dedicatee of *The Prince*,

Lorenzo de' Medici was his nephew (the original intended recipient of the work, Giuliano de' Medici, his younger brother). Lorenzo's "fortune" and "other qualities," as Machiavelli writes in the Dedicatory Letter, are paralleled by Leo's "goodness and his other infinite virtues." Given that in the rousing final chapter of *The Prince* exhorting someone to free Italy from the barbarians he refers to the fact that the Medici now control Florence and the papacy, as noted above at the end of my discussion of chapter 7, some interpreters have suggested that Machiavelli's intention was to urge Lorenzo with Leo's backing to solve Italy's political divisions by creating a unified state in at least northern Italy, perhaps in imitation of what Alexander VI and Cesare Borgia had intended to do.

Whatever Machiavelli's intentions in this regard, it is clear from chapter 11 that the temporal power of the Church is central for his analysis of the vulnerability of Italy due to its being divided. He hinted at this issue at the end of chapter 3 when he reported his conversation with Cardinal Rouen, responding to Rouen's remark that the Italians did not understand war by saying that the French did not understand politics since they had let the Church grow stronger, and he makes this growing strength the subject of chapter 11. He is much more blunt in the *Discourses on Livy*. As we saw above when discussing chapter 10, he remarks there that Italy has been corrupted by the wicked examples of the Papal Court and suggests a thought experiment of moving the papacy to Switzerland to see its effects, but more importantly and more interestingly for interpreting *The Prince* he argues:

> the church has kept and keeps this province divided. And truly no province has ever been united or happy unless it has all come under obedience to one republic or to one prince, as happened to France and to Spain. The cause that Italy is not in the same condition and does not also have one republic or one prince to govern it solely is the church. For although it has inhabited and held a temporal empire there, it has not been so powerful nor of such virtue as to be able to seize the tyranny of Italy and make itself prince of it. On the other hand, it has not been so weak that it has been unable to call in a

power to defend it against one that had become too powerful in Italy, for fear of losing dominion over its temporal things.

(I.12, 38)

Among other examples of bringing in "barbarian" powers, Machiavelli refers to the very French invasions he analyzed in chapter 3 when dissecting Louis XII's failure to conquer Italy, an invasion to which he points in the present chapter as the occasion that allowed the Church to increase its temporal power. When discussing chapter 3, I suggested that Machiavelli's seemingly unpatriotic advice about how to conquer Italy could be seen as a recipe for how to unite Italy, and now we see that the temporal power of the Church is a major obstacle to such unification. What remedy to this problem might Machiavelli be contemplating?[8]

NOTES

1 As Lefort (2012 [2005], 128) comments of the types of principalities and modes of acquisition Machiavelli treats in chapters 6–9: "But from one group to another the distance disappears when we want to specify their shapes and assess exactly what distinguishes them" (translation altered).

2 See Tarcov 2013b, 583.

3 E.g., Benner 2013 and Vatter 2013.

4 In the *Discourses on Livy*, within his discussion of the "cycle" of regimes, Machiavelli describes how a "popular state," by which he seems to mean the rule of the people or at least not the rule of "the great" alone, decays into a "licentious" one, with the result that a principality arises (I.2, 11–13).

5 Machiavelli also discusses the conspiracy against Nabis in the *Discourses on Livy* (III.6, 224–25).

6 For a hint on this point, see de Alvarez 1999, 49–50.

7 In the *Discourses on Livy* in a chapter titled "That the Various of Sects and Languages, Together with the Accident of Floods or Plague, Eliminates the Memories of Things," Machiavelli discusses "the Christian sect" and "the Gentile sect" and then estimates that sects vary two or three times in 5,000 or 6,000 years (II.5, 139). By Machiavelli's calculation, Christianity would be due to expire as early as the year 1667.

8 For one suggestion, see Scott and Sullivan 1994.

7

ARMS

At the beginning of chapter 12 Machiavelli makes an explicit transition to a new subject: "Since I have discussed point by point all of the qualities of those principalities that I proposed to reason about at the start, and since I have considered to some extent the causes for their well being or illness, and shown the ways in which many have tried to acquire and hold them, it remains for me now to discuss generally the offensive and defensive measures that may befall each of the aforementioned principalities." In other words, it seems, having treated how to acquire a principality now he will discuss how to use its arms offensively and defensively. This subject will occupy him for chapters 12–14 before he makes another explicit transition in chapter 15, turning from how the prince should deal with his enemies to how he ought to treat his subjects and friends or allies. Chapters 12–14 therefore comprise a separate section on arms.

His discussion of arms has paramount importance according to Machiavelli, who even states at the outset that arms are in fact more important than laws: "And because good laws cannot exist where there are not good arms, and where there are good arms there should be good laws, I shall leave out the reasoning of laws and I shall speak of arms." Through the whole tradition of political theory from Plato and Aristotle to Cicero and other Roman thinkers to Aquinas and other medieval writers, including the authors of the mirror-of-princes genre, the question of good laws and justice was the most important consideration and the question of military affairs a decidedly subordinate or secondary consideration. For example, in the *Politics* Aristotle criticized the Spartan regime for ordering its institutions and laws to aim at war, arguing that war was properly seen as a means to peace and that the Spartans had therefore misunderstood the proper aim of the political association.[1] Machiavelli therefore appears to upend the entire tradition with his intentionally bold statement. His claim that he will leave out any reasoning about laws in fact turns out to be an overstatement, for he does discuss laws. Yet his main point in making this statement about leaving out the argument concerning laws seems intended to suggest that his predecessors, with their focus on good laws—whether or not Machiavelli agrees with them about what good laws may be—had neglected to consider the necessary precondition or foundation for those laws. His reversal of emphasis on arms instead of laws may not necessarily mark an entire reversal of the tradition of political theory through glorification of militaristic states at the expense of justice, therefore, but rather a more "realistic" assessment of the necessary preconditions for law, justice, and the well-being of a state. That said, the word "justice" is notably nearly absent in *The Prince*. We shall have to see how Machiavelli's argument develops with regard to the proper use of military arms in relation to the state.

Finally, before turning to his discussion of arms, we should recall Machiavelli's own lengthy experience with military affairs in his official capacity in the Florentine government. In addition to directing military operations for the republic, including the prolonged siege of Pisa which he will discuss several times in *The Prince*, Machiavelli was particularly active in persuading the republic to establish its "own arms" in the form of a militia drawn from subjects of the Florentine Republic in the countryside. He met considerable resistance in this enterprise, largely from the powerful oligarchic family alliances that effectively controlled Florentine politics at this time who were hesitant to arm the Florentine populace, with whom they had long engaged in factional conflict, hence the decision to draw the militia from the subjects of the territory outside of the city itself. The views he advances on arms were therefore politically controversial in the context in which he was writing. Finally, we should also recall that the only major work Machiavelli published in his own lifetime was the *Art of War* (1521), so military arms is a subject on which Machiavelli did indeed have considerable experience and on which he considered himself an expert.

CHAPTER 12: HOW MANY KINDS OF MILITARY FORCES THERE ARE, AND CONCERNING MERCENARY SOLDIERS

As already noted, Machiavelli begins chapter 12 by announcing that he is making a transition to a new subject: how arms are to be used for attack and defense by the various types of principalities he has discussed. Having marked this transition, he then links this new topic to what he has previously written: "We have said above that it is necessary for a prince to have good foundations, otherwise of necessity he must be ruined. The principal foundations that all states must have, whether new or old or mixed, are good laws and good arms." The two principal points at which he had discussed the necessity of having good foundations were in chapters 7 and 9. In chapter 7 he discussed how difficult it is for a prince who acquires his principality through the arms and fortune of another to lay solid foundations since fortune has suddenly thrown his state in his lap without such foundations, and then claimed that his main example there, Cesare Borgia, had laid good foundations—or, rather, that it "appeared to him" that he had done so—by acquiring the good will of his people. In chapter 9 he reasoned about whether a prince who attains a civil principality should found himself on the great or the people, and argued that founding on the people is preferable. In both cases where he has previously discussed the necessity of good foundations, then, his focus has been on how a prince should found himself on the people. The relationship between his concern with founding on the people and his new topic of military arms will become clear across his treatment of arms in chapters 12–14, for he will argue that a prince must have his own arms drawn from his people.

Having made these introductory remarks, Machiavelli turns to his subject. "I say, therefore, that the arms with which a prince defends his state are either his own or they are mercenary, either auxiliary or mixed." He will focus on mercenary arms in chapter 12, turning to auxiliary, mixed, and one's own arms in chapter 13. The subject of mercenary arms deserves an entire chapter because it is Machiavelli's contention that reliance on mercenary arms is the principal reason for Italy's vulnerability. "Mercenary and auxiliary arms are useless and dangerous," he states bluntly, "and if a prince keeps his state founded on mercenary arms, he will never stand firm nor secure." After a scathing description of mercenary arms as disunited, ambitious, without discipline, and unfaithful, Machiavelli reveals the reason for their being such: "The reason for this is that they have no other love nor other reason that keeps them in the field save a small stipend, and this is not sufficient to make them want to die for you." We can already see why it is necessary to have one's "own arms," or subjects who are willing to fight and die for you.

"I should not expend much labor in persuasion on this point, because the ruin of Italy now is caused by nothing other than her having relied, for the space of many years, on mercenary arms." So Machiavelli now proclaims, and yet he will expend considerable labor making this point. Is Italy's ruin indeed caused by "nothing other" than her reliance on mercenary arms? Our analysis of Machiavelli's discussion in chapter 11 of the rise of the temporal power of the Church suggested another reason for Italy's disunion and vulnerability, and in fact Machiavelli now subtly links chapter 12 on mercenary arms to the previous chapter on ecclesiastical principalities. If mercenary arms seemed to put on a good show for a while, he explains, "when the foreigners came they showed what they really were, so that Charles, the king of France, was able to seize Italy with a piece of chalk." He refers here to the first French invasion of 1494 and the fact that Florence allowed Charles VIII to enter the city, lance on hip in the pose of a conqueror, and then billet his troops in houses designated with a mark of chalk. With this historical context noted, Machiavelli continues: "He who used to say that the cause of this was our sins was telling the truth, although the sins were not the ones he believed they were, but these I have narrated. And, since these were sins of the princes, they, too, have suffered the penalties for them." Machiavelli refers to Savonarola, the "unarmed prophet" of chapter 6, who preached that the French invasion of Italy was punishment for Italy's "sins," by which he meant its moral sins and irreligion. Although Savonarola famously inveighed against the sins of the Florentines and erected bonfires of the vanities in which he encouraged the citizens to burn their frivolous belongings such as decks of cards, lace, wigs, and such, the particular object of his ire was the corruption of the Church and especially Pope Alexander VI, the pontiff whom Machiavelli credits in chapter 11 with increasing the temporal power of the Church. As we have seen when analyzing chapter 11, in the *Discourses on Livy* Machiavelli points, like Savonarola, to the moral corruption of the Church as a source of Italy's woes, but more importantly, and unlike Savonarola, he offers an analysis of the problematic balance of political powers in Italy due to the Church's own temporal power there. Returning to the chapter under analysis, Machiavelli likewise points to different "sins" that are responsible for Italy's ruin: the sin of having relied on mercenary arms. "And, since these were sins of the princes, they, too, have suffered punishment for them." In sum, behind Machiavelli's discussion of mercenary arms and Italy's ruin is his analysis of the political dynamics in Italy thanks to the rise of the temporal power of the Church.

Machiavelli has characterized mercenary and auxiliary arms as "useless and dangerous" and now he explains the "infelicity" of these arms by arguing that excellent mercenary captains are dangerous, and especially dangerous to the prince who hires them, because of their ambition, and that bad mercenary captains are either useless or dangerous because of their very ineptitude. Having said this, he once again brings forward an imagined interlocutor who objects to what he has said: "And if it is answered that whoever has arms in his hands will do this, whether he is mercenary or not, I would reply that arms have to be employed either by a prince or by a republic." The imagined objection seems to be that military arms are always a threat to the existing political regime no matter who possesses these arms, whether from outside or from inside the state, a contention that history richly supports. If so, then the overarching question would be how to reconcile political authority with military forces given that all states need arms and even need arms as their "principal foundations," as Machiavelli states at the outset of this chapter.

As with his analysis of states in general, therefore, Machiavelli begins by subdividing states into principalities and republics, although this time he will not leave out the reasoning about republics. As for principalities, he argues: "The prince should go in person, and himself assume the office of captain." In other words, political and military power must be combined. As for republics: "The republic has to send its own citizens, and if it sends one who does not prove a worthy man, it should exchange him, and when he is worthy, it should restrain him with laws so that he does not cross the line." Once again, then, political and military power are combined, though there remains a threat to the republic from ambitious military captains such as Julius Caesar, who famously crossed the Rubicon with his army and effectively took power in Rome. Note also that although he began this chapter by stating that "good arms" are the basis for "good laws," Machiavelli's recommendation that republics should restrain potentially dangerous captains through laws suggests that "good laws" are also necessary for "good arms." He concludes his response to his imagined respondent with a sweeping claim. "From experience it is seen that very great strides are made by princes who are by themselves, and by armed republics, and never anything but harm is done by mercenary arms. And with more difficulty does a republic armed with its own arms fall into servitude under one of its own citizens than a republic armed with external arms." Given what he has said above about Italy's ruin, experience also reveals that unarmed republics, such as Florence, are vulnerable to falling into servitude either to an external power or to one of its own citizens. The implication of these remarks makes uncomfortable reading for the dedicatee of *The Prince*, Lorenzo de' Medici, whose family was expelled from power in 1494 due to the French invasion and restored to power through similar means in 1512, just before Machiavelli wrote his little treatise. At any rate, Machiavelli's focus here on armed republics and the conditions for their freedom with regard to both external and internal threats is notable in a book which supposedly leaves out the reasoning on republics.

In order to illustrate his thesis, Machiavelli turns to some examples. The Roman Republic and Sparta "stood armed and free for many centuries," he states, and then points to the Swiss in modern times as "highly armed and very free." Recall that in chapter 10 he brought forward the free German cities, of which the Swiss here would be included, as his only example in that chapter of well-fortified and free cities, and once again they seem to be the exception among the moderns. Yet apparently ancient republics also fell into the temptation of using mercenary arms, and Machiavelli points to Carthage and Thebes as examples of states that relied on such arms and lost their liberty. Among the moderns he points to the Milanese, who hired Francesco Sforza to fight for them only to have him join with Milan's enemies and "undo" the Milanese. Recall that Sforza was Machiavelli's example in chapter 1 of a "completely new" prince and again in chapter 7 as a brief example of a successful case of a new prince (as compared with the ultimately unsuccessful example of Cesare Borgia, who rose by arms and fortune of others), and now we know something more about how Sforza succeeded. Apparently such was the Sforza family business, for Machiavelli also points to Sforza's father, also a mercenary captain, who betrayed his own patron to her undoing. Machiavelli now admits that the Venetians and Florentines did successfully employ mercenary arms in the past to increase their empire, but he answers that they got lucky because the virtuous captains either did not have the opportunity to turn against their patrons or did not seize it. "But let us come to what happened a little while ago," he continues, and claims that the Florentines would have had no recourse against one of their more recently hired captains, Paolo Vitelli, who, had he succeeded in the enterprise for which Florence hired him, the capture of Pisa, would have had the Florentines at his mercy. What Machiavelli does not reveal here is that the Florentines suspected Vitelli of betraying them and had him arrested and executed, a successful anticipation of the potential danger the mercenary captain posed, and a success owing in part to Machiavelli himself, who was overseeing the military actions against Pisa at that time. As for the Venetians, Machiavelli states that while they fought with their own people and at sea they were successful, but when they turned to increase their dominion on land and employed mercenary arms they necessarily had to fear the men they hired if they won or if they lost, eventually losing all they had gained over 800 years "in one day's battle."

Having focused on these Italian examples in order to prove his main point that the ruin of Italy has been caused by reliance on mercenary arms, Machiavelli is now ready to ascend to a "higher perspective, so that having seen the origin and progresses of them, one may better correct them." From this "higher perspective" Machiavelli surveys the shift in political forces in Italy over the previous century or so. He explains that once the Holy Roman Empire lost its political influence in Italy and the pope then seized more reputation there in temporal affairs, Italy was divided into many states. Within many of these cities or states, the more popular elements with the encouragement of the Church took up arms against their nobles, who had previously enjoyed the support of the emperor. Once again we see the role of the Church in creating the ruin of Italy. If we combine his survey of these political developments in chapter 12 with his discussion in chapter 11 of how these political circumstances created the opportunity for the rise of the temporal power of the Church, we can glimpse the panoramic nature of Machiavelli's analysis.

The political scene Machiavelli is describing in this context to explain Italy's reliance on mercenary arms was the outcome of the centuries-old struggle in Italy between the Guelfs and the Ghibellines, with the Guelfs supporting the papacy's claims to authority and the Ghibellines allied with the Holy Roman Empire, a struggle that ended for the most part with the victory of the Guelfs although the repercussions of the struggle continued into Machiavelli's time. Since the defeat of the nobles or "great" in most cities meant the elimination or suppression of the military class, the result was that many cities found themselves without their own arms. In other cities, Machiavelli goes on to explain, the situation led to the rise of princes who now ruled over their cities, keeping their peoples unarmed. "Hence, since Italy had almost fallen into the hands of the Church and of a few republics, and since those priests and the other citizens customarily did not know about arms," he explains, "they began to hire outsiders." Furthermore, for their own purposes, these mercenary captains relied on cavalry rather than infantry. Here part of the thrust of Machiavelli's analysis is clear if we recall that the people are the traditional source of infantry forces, as in the Roman Republic for example, whereas the nobles or "great" are the traditional source of cavalry, given the cost of maintaining horses (hence the terms "cavalier," "caballero," etc., to designate nobles or gentlemen). At any rate, because of the series of events Machiavelli narrates from this "higher perspective," the republic and principalities of Italy found themselves without military arms of their own. All of this has led to the ruin of Italy by outsiders and these mercenary arms have, he concludes, "conducted Italy into slavery and shame."[2] He will return to this theme of Italian vulnerability in the concluding chapter of *The Prince*.

CHAPTER 13: ON AUXILIARY TROOPS, MIXED TROOPS, AND ONE'S OWN

Turning from mercenary arms to the other sorts of military forces he has promised to discuss, Machiavelli keeps his sights on the Italian scene. "Auxiliary arms, which are the other useless ones, are when one calls on a powerful person who with his arms comes to help and defend you, as Pope Julius did in recent times," he begins. Admitting that such arms may be useful, he nonetheless warns that they are almost always harmful: "For if they lose, you remain defeated, and if they win, you are left their prisoner." In order to illustrate his point, Machiavelli coyly states that the ancient histories are full of examples, but he nonetheless refuses to leave the "fresh example" of Pope Julius. What ancient examples might he have in mind? As we shall see, even though he claims that he refuses to leave his "fresh example" and the contemporary Italian scene, in fact through the course of this chapter he will sketch a historical landscape stretching from King David and the ancient Israelites to Philip of Macedon to the fall of the Roman Empire to the collapse of the eastern Roman Empire during the fourteenth and fifteenth centuries to his own times. Relying on the arms of others rather than one's own arms would appear to be another perennial issue of politics.

As for the "fresh example" of Pope Julius, strangely enough it does not prove Machiavelli's point. The specific example he chooses is the culminating battle of the War of the Holy League, at which time Julius was allied with the Venetians and Ferdinand of Aragon, who provided most of the troops, against the French, with Julius' aim being to recapture the cities in the Romagna which had gotten free of the domination of the Church after the death of Pope Alexander VI and fall of Cesare Borgia a decade earlier. The battle on which Machiavelli focuses is the Battle of Ravenna, fought on Easter Sunday 1512, in which the Spanish forces were severely defeated by the French, a crushing blow to Julius' aims. Unexpectedly, however, the Swiss mercenaries Julius had hired were able to drive off the French, who had lost their commander in the battle, and who were facing an English invasion back in France and shortly afterward withdrew from Italy. Machiavelli states that Julius' reliance on the arms of others "could not have been less considered," and yet he did not suffer the consequences because of his "good fortune." Given that he could have chosen numerous examples, ancient and modern, to prove his point, why does Machiavelli choose this one? We may get some help in answering this question by looking at his discussion of auxiliary arms in the *Discourses on Livy* (II.20), where Machiavelli refers his reader to his treatment of the subject in *The Prince*. For our purposes he helpfully remarks there: "If past things are read well and those of the present are reviewed, it will be found that for one who had a good end from [using auxiliary arms], infinite ones were left deceived by it" (II.20, 176). Similarly, in a letter written while he was following Pope Julius on his campaigns, in which he rehearses some of the themes that would later occupy him in *The Prince*, Machiavelli writes of the pontiff: "This pope, who has no scales or measuring stick in his house, obtains through chance—and disarmed—what ought to be difficult to attain even with organization and with weapons."[3] Perhaps Julius is the exception of success that proves the general rule of failure. Whatever the reasons for him choosing the apparently inapt example of Julius, his choice does have the effect of continuing his argument about the ruin of Italy owing to reliance on mercenary and auxiliary arms and his focus on the role of the Church in this regard.

To the "fresh example" of Julius he adds two more examples from recent times, only one of which supports his argument, once again oddly enough. First, he points to the Florentines, who turned to French troops in their attempt to retake Pisa (in 1498) and ran the dangers of the French turning on them, which did not in fact occur. Second, he mentions how the emperor of Constantinople sent Turkish troops into Greece (in 1353–54), with those troops remaining there after the war was over and establishing the first Turkish settlement there. "This was the beginning of the servitude of Greece to the infidels," he bluntly remarks, alluding to the growth of the Ottoman Empire in Greece and the Balkans and the eventual collapse of the Byzantine Empire with the Ottoman conquest of Constantinople in 1453. Earlier, in chapter 3, when he adduced "the Turk" as a positive example of how to hold a new dominion by going to live there, Machiavelli used no such pejorative language about "the infidels" he now employs when looking at the same events from the perspective of the defeated. At any rate, we now finally have an example that more or less proves Machiavelli's argument about the dangers of using auxiliary troops, although even here it must be admitted that the ultimate outcome in the case of the emperor of Constantinople employing the Turks as auxiliary arms took a full century to come to fruition. Are we meant to compare Machiavelli's analysis in chapter 12 of the century-long process of the vulnerability of Italy due to its political division and the rise of the temporal power of the Church, or what might be said to be the successor to the Roman Empire in the west, to the century-long fall of the Byzantine Empire, the successor to the Roman Empire in the east, to the Turks? Once again, we have to puzzle over why Machiavelli would choose examples that do not persuasively prove his point.

"Whoever, therefore, wants not to be able to win should avail himself of these arms, since they are much more dangerous than mercenary arms," Machiavelli now writes, with his "therefore" connecting this summary judgment to the preceding examples we have examined. He explains that auxiliary arms are more dangerous than mercenary arms because they are already united and directed by someone and thus ready to be turned against you. "A wise prince, therefore, has always avoided these arms and relied on his own; and he has wanted rather to lose with his own men than to win with others, judging it a not true victory if it was acquired with the arms of others." As we have anticipated, Machiavelli's overarching point is that a prince should rely on his own arms rather than the arms of others, whether mercenary or auxiliary.

In order to illustrate his main point he returns to the example of Cesare Borgia: "I shall never hesitate to cite Cesare Borgia and his actions." According to Machiavelli, Cesare began with auxiliary troops provided by the French, then turned to mercenary troops "since he judged there was less danger in them," and then found these mercenary arms to be "doubtful and faithless and dangerous to manage," and so finally "relied on his own." Yet as we saw in Machiavelli's account in chapter 7, Cesare in fact never succeeded in ridding himself of mercenary arms, so Machiavelli's analysis here would seem at best to praise Cesare's intentions rather than his actions.[4] As proof of the improving situation of Cesare in going from auxiliary arms to mercenary arms to his own arms, Machiavelli cites Cesare's growing "reputation." "And one will find that his reputation always increased, and he was never esteemed so much as when everyone saw that he was completely in possession of his own arms." Note that Machiavelli emphasizes Cesare's "reputation" rather than the results of his actions, in keeping with his implicit praise of his intentions rather than his actions. If he begins his account here of Cesare Borgia by declaring, "I shall never hesitate" (*Io non dubiterò mai ...*) to bring forward Cesare as an example, perhaps we are meant to doubt (*dubitere* = "hesitate" or "doubt") whether he is an apt example. Yet again Machiavelli's example does not fully support his argument.

Machiavelli now takes a sudden turn: "I did not want to depart from my examples, which are Italian and fresh, nevertheless, I do not want to leave out Hiero the Syracusan, since he was one of those who were named by me above." In writing this Machiavelli simultaneously emphasizes that he has thus far kept his sights on recent Italian examples while nevertheless shifting his gaze to an ancient example. Perhaps his ancient example will be more to the point. Machiavelli also reminds us that he named Hiero earlier, at the end of chapter 6, as an example of a new prince who rose to become "prince" of Syracuse through his own arms and virtue. He now gives us more information about how Hiero did so, relating that when he was made captain of the Syracusan forces he immediately saw that the mercenary military they were using was not useful, "because their commanders were made like our Italians," Machiavelli writes in order to emphasize the parallel to his own times, and therefore "had them all cut to pieces, and afterward he made war with his own arms, and not those of others." Unlike the case of Cesare Borgia, Hiero actually accomplished his goal and reigned successfully for over fifty years. Machiavelli's implied comparison of the two is reminiscent of the way in which he juxtaposed Agathocles the Sicilian, who was similarly successful, to Liverotto de Fermo, who was not successful for very long, in chapter 8. At any rate, the comparison to Hiero is not flattering for Cesare Borgia.

As if the successful example of Hiero were not enough, Machiavelli now unexpectedly brings forth a wildly successful new prince: David. "I want also to recall to memory a figure of the Old Testament suited to his purpose," he begins. The term "figure" (*figura*) means an example or parable that is called to memory as an exemplary case, or a "literary figure" of a kind, and the use of "figures" were common in sermons, for example in Savonarola's frequent appeals to Moses in his sermons. Recall that Machiavelli characterized his treatment in chapter 6 of Moses and the other exemplary princes as a "speech" (*parole*), or something akin to a sermon. In the present chapter, then, it seems that Machiavelli is preaching a sermon with David as his "figure": "When David offered himself to Saul to go to combat Goliath ... ." In his version of the story, Machiavelli states that Saul first gave David his own arms, "in order to give David spirit," but then David, having donned the arms, decided to refuse them, "saying that with those arms he could not acquit himself well, and for that reason he wanted to meet the enemy with his sling and his knife." Machiavelli then concludes the sermon with a moral: "In the end, the arms of others fall off your back, or they weigh you down, or they constrict you."

Comparison of Machiavelli's version of the story of David with the Old Testament original reveals a number of significant differences. First, David refuses Saul's armor, including his sword or knife, because he was not accustomed to wearing it, and so Machiavelli grants David considerably more initiative and independence than in the original. Second, Machiavelli has David go into battle with a sling and a knife whereas in the biblical account David meets Goliath with a sling alone. In fact, Scripture is adamant on this point: "So David prevailed over the Philistine with a sling and a stone, striking down the Philistine and killing him; there was no sword in David's hand. Then David ran and stood over the Philistine; he grasped his sword, drew it out of its sheath, and killed him; then he cut off his head with it" (1 Samuel 17:50–51 [RSV Bible]). In short, Machiavelli makes an armed prophet of David, a prophet who relies on his own arms, shockingly with no mention on Machiavelli's part of any divine assistance.[5]

Having called the "figure" of David to mind, Machiavelli now abruptly shifts his focus back to modern times with the example of another prince who saw the need to have his own arms. He recounts how King Charles VII of France (d. 1461), after freeing France from the English "with his fortune and virtue," "understood this necessity of arming oneself with one's own arms" and therefore formed an army drawn from men-at-arms and infantry. (He does not mention the role of Joan of Arc in these events.) Unfortunately, he continues, Charles VII's son Louis XI eliminated the infantry and instead hired Swiss mercenaries, and Machiavelli attributes the present dangers faced by the French (including a renewed English invasion at the time he was writing *The Prince*) to this error. France therefore came to have "mixed" forces, "part mercenary and part their own," which Machiavelli judges to be superior to either simple auxiliary or simple mercenary arms, but inferior to having one's own arms. He concludes the French example by opining that the military orders established by Charles VII would have made France "unconquerable," and then laments: "But the small prudence of men begins a thing because it tastes good for the time being, while it does not notice the poison that lies beneath, as I said above concerning consumptive fevers. Thus he who in a principality does not recognize evils when they arise is not truly wise, and this ability is given to few." This is not quite what he said about consumptive fevers in chapter 3. Instead, he explained that such diseases are difficult to recognize but easy to treat in the beginning, and easy to recognize but difficult to treat later on, likening the situation to political prudence that recognizes evils from afar and praising the Roman Republic in this regard. Interestingly, then, and to return to the present chapter, Machiavelli now criticizes the later Romans for lacking such prudence: "And if the first cause of the ruin of the Roman Empire is considered, it will be found that it was in the beginning to hire the Goths, for from that beginning the forces of the Roman Empire began to be enervated, and all of the virtue that was taken from it was given to the Goths." In other words, whereas the Roman Republic relied on its own arms in the form of a citizen army, the Roman Empire came to depend on mercenary arms, and so the republic was superior both in terms of prudence and relying on its own arms.

Machiavelli ends this chapter with an explicit conclusion: "Thus I conclude that unless it has its own arms, no principality is secure. Instead it is completely dependent on fortune, since it does not have the virtue reliably to defend itself in adversities." Unusually, Machiavelli buttresses his summary judgment with an authority: "And it was always the opinion and judgment of wise men 'that nothing is so weak and unstable as a reputation for power not founded on its own strength.'"[6] One's own strength in this context is one's own arms, and Machiavelli explains that these arms "are composed of your subjects, your citizens, or your dependents: all the others are either mercenary or auxiliary." Recall that at the beginning of his discussion of arms in chapter 12 Machiavelli referred back to his earlier discussions of founding on the people, and now we see that a prince should draw his own arms from his people. "And the way to order one's own arms is easy to find, if one goes over the orders of the four men named by me above," he explains, seemingly referring to the four examples he has given in the present chapter of Cesare Borgia, Hiero of Syracuse, David, and Charles VII of France. Or does he refer to the four exemplary new princes of chapter 6? At any rate, to these examples he now adds Philip of Macedon, the father of Alexander the Great, as well as "many republics and princes" who have properly "armed and ordered themselves." And then he concludes the chapter: "To these orders I entirely submit." Machiavelli is unusually deferential here, and one wishes that he would say more about the important subject of how to order one's own arms.

CHAPTER 14: WHAT THE PRINCE SHOULD DO CONCERNING THE MILITARY

Machiavelli frames chapter 14 as an explicit conclusion to the trio of chapters on arms by straightaway calling to mind his statement at the outset of chapter 12 that he will leave out the reasoning on laws and instead focus on arms: "Thus a prince must have no other object or thought, nor take anything as his art save warfare and its orders and training." This constant training is useful both for existing princes in maintaining their states as well as for private individuals who rise to the rank of prince, that is for new princes, and by saying this Machiavelli blurs the difference between acquiring and maintaining power. On the contrary, he tells us, those princes who have given more thought to "delicate things" than to arms have been seen to lose their states. Perhaps he means to remind us of what he said in the Dedicatory Letter about what things customarily delight princes: horses, arms, cloth of gold, precious stones, and similar adornments. As an example of an individual who acquired a state through his mastery of the art of war Machiavelli brings forward Francesco Sforza, his example in chapter 1 of a completely new prince, and notes that Sforza's successors lost their state because they did not similarly practice the art. In addition to the obvious reason why not knowing the art of war is detrimental to a prince, Machiavelli states that it is dangerous because it makes the prince "contemptible," commenting: "For between an armed and an unarmed man there is no harmony whatsoever, and it is not reasonable that a man who is armed should willingly obey a man who is unarmed, and that the unarmed should be secure among servants who are armed … ." How does this statement square with the success of ecclesiastical principalities and the Church, which have decidedly unarmed princes? Indeed, the success of these principalities as discussed in chapter 11 seems all the more remarkable given what Machiavelli writes in chapters 12 through 14 about the paramount necessity of arms and the art of war for "all states," as he proclaimed at the beginning of chapter 12.

Having given his lesson for princes instructing them to attend to the art of war, during war itself and especially during peace, Machiavelli now gives some pedagogical tips. "This he may do in two ways: one is with his deeds, the other is with his mind." As for deeds, apart from military exercises themselves, he recommends hunting. In addition to accustoming his body to hardship, hunting more importantly gives the prince knowledge of "the nature of terrains" such as mountains and plains. Doing so first of all familiarizes him with the terrain of his own dominion to better defend it, but secondly gives him knowledge of various terrains in general, thus enabling him to attack other states.[7] We should here recall the metaphor of mountains and plains in the Dedicatory Letter, with the prince there limited in his perspective and knowledge by remaining atop his mountain.

Although Machiavelli introduces hunting as a training of the body, it is more importantly a training of the mind. This realization helps explain the example he now gives of Philopoemen (d. 183 BCE), the Greek general and statesman who defeated Nabis the Spartan and put an end to an independent Sparta. "Among the other praises that writers have given Philopoemen, prince of the Achaeans, is that in times of peace he was ever thinking of the ways of war." Machiavelli then relates how Philopoemen would ride through the countryside with his friends (presumably hunting) and "reason with them" about the terrain and how they would attack or defend various sites. "He used to listen to their opinion, he used to say his own, and he used to strengthen it with his reasons, so that because of these continuous reasonings" he always had a remedy in all situations he faced in warfare. Two things should be noted about the way in which Machiavelli relates this example. First, although he is supposedly still discussing exercising the body for the art of war, his emphasis is on how Philopoemen reasoned in dialogue with his friends, or his "continuous reasonings." Second, he introduces the example by stating that Philopoemen was praised for doing so by "writers," Machiavelli's primary source here being the ancient historian Livy, although he is also undoubtedly referring to Plutarch and Polybius as well. Machiavelli himself is a writer, of course, and I suggest as readers of *The Prince* we should take as a model the way in which Philopoemen reasoned with his friends by questioning and challenging one another and providing reasons.[8]

From the supposed exercise of the body for war Machiavelli now turns to the exercise of the mind. He recommends that the prince read histories "and in them consider the actions of the excellent men." Here again, then, we see him raise the issue of writers and readers, and part of the crux of the matter is *how* these histories and other books should be read. By examining the conduct of these men in war the prince will learn how to avoid their losses and "imitate" their victories. In chapter 6 we saw him counseling the prince to imitate the greatest examples, and now he does so again. "And, above all, he must do as some excellent men did in the past, who chose some man from before their time who had been praised and glorified to imitate, and they always kept a book with his deeds and actions close by themselves," giving the examples of Alexander the Great imitating Achilles, Julius Caesar imitating Alexander, and Scipio imitating Cyrus. What books did they keep close by themselves for this purpose? Achilles is the hero of Homer's *Iliad*, and so Alexander was imitating a mythical hero. What book Julius Caesar might have read concerning Alexander is not clear since the major historical sources we now have about Alexander were written after Julius Caesar's death. Interestingly, however, the most famous story about Julius Caesar with regard to Alexander is that he supposedly wept at having accomplished so little when he reached the age at which Alexander died, a story which is more about a failure of imitation. As for Scipio and Cyrus, however, Machiavelli is very specific: "And whoever reads the life of Cyrus written by Xenophon recognizes afterward in the life of Scipio how much that imitation brought him glory, and how much, in his chastity, affability, humanity and liberality, Scipio conformed with those things that had been written by Xenophon about Cyrus."[9]

A few things are worth taking note of in this passage. First, Cyrus is the only example here who was also one of Machiavelli's examples in chapter 6 of exemplary new princes whom he urges a prince—or any reader—to imitate. The others he names there are Moses, Theseus, and Romulus, and so perhaps we are meant to think about where we would read about these princes and how we should read the books that speak of their deeds. Second, Machiavelli here once again emphasizes the relationship between a writer and a reader, here Xenophon and Scipio. But did Scipio properly imitate Cyrus, or what qualities and deeds enabled Cyrus to succeed militarily and otherwise? If he lists the supposedly virtuous qualities of Cyrus imitated by Scipio here (chastity, affability, humanity, and liberality), in the *Discourses on Livy* he is more revealing about Cyrus, as we saw above in discussing chapter 6 of *The Prince*. Cyrus is his example in the *Discourses on Livy* (II.13) of a prince who rises more through fraud than force, including through the fraud of appearing to be virtuous in the sense of being liberal, humane, etc., while in fact being ruthless. Similarly, he states there that the fact that Cyrus was "held to be virtuous" for his supposed affability, humanity, and mercy by his subjects, again citing Xenophon as his source, but reveals that this was Cyrus' successful management of appearances (III.22; see III.20). As for Scipio, as we shall see in chapter 17, his imitation of those qualities he admired in Cyrus in fact led him into considerable difficulties when his troops failed to obey him. Third, Xenophon is the only writer Machiavelli explicitly names as an author in *The Prince*, and so perhaps Xenophon is a model for Machiavelli. Finally, the question of Cyrus' actual versus apparent virtues and vices leads us directly to chapter 15, where Machiavelli begins his own discussion of the virtues and vices as a writer who "shall depart from the orders of others."

NOTES

1 See Aristotle, *Politics* II.9, 1279a–b.
2 Several interpreters and translators, including Connell in the translation I am using in this guide, have noted that Machiavelli here offers a grim pun: the arms of mercenary captains (*condottieri*) have "conducted" (*condotto*) Italy into slavery and shame thanks to those who have "hired" (*condotto*) them.
3 Machiavelli to Giovan Battista Soderini, September 13–21, 1506, in Machiavelli 2004, 135.
4 In a diplomatic report of November 13, 1502, Machiavelli recounts Cesare's realization that he would better maintain his acquisitions and gain new ones if he

had "his own arms" drawn from his subjects and neighbors, and specifies "this is his plan." He does not say that he succeeded in carrying out this plan.

5 Machiavelli would have been quite familiar with the image of David with a sling alone since he passed Michelangelo's famous statue of David every day when he entered his workplace, the Palazzo Vecchio, since the statue was then placed at the entrance. Given his official position at the time the statue was unveiled (1504), Machiavelli may have been involved in having Michelangelo's statue placed there, or at least he would have been well aware of the decision, especially since he was also personally acquainted with Michelangelo. In turn, Donatello's famous bronze statue of David (then placed in the courtyard of the Medici palace) does show him with a knife, although since he is shown standing over the severed head of Goliath the knife would be the one David took from Goliath and used to behead him. (Donatello's earlier marble statue of David, also placed in the Palazzo Vecchio, does not portray him with a knife.) Finally, another statue with which Machiavelli would have been familiar since it was displayed in the Palazzo Vecchio, a bronze by Andrea del Verrocchio, shows David with a knife, although, as with Donatello's version, it includes Goliath's head at David's feet. At any rate, given the desire by the Florentine Republic to be associated with David as evidenced by these statues, Machiavelli's contemporary readers would have been familiar with both the biblical story and the artistic representations of it.

6 The quotation is from Tacitus, *Annals* XIII.19, slightly altered. Tacitus puts this remark at the beginning of his account of the fall from power of the Emperor Nero's mother, Agrippina, and how her former followers abandoned her when they saw her loss of influence.

7 See Machiavelli's similar discussion in the *Discourses on Livy* (III.34).

8 In this light, it is interesting to note that Livy remarks that Philopoemen engaged in such debate both with himself when alone and with others when accompanied by them (*History of Rome* XXXV.28).

9 Machiavelli refers to Publius Cornelius Scipio Africanus (236–183 BCE), the general and statesman who defeated Hannibal in the Second Punic War. The source for the story of Scipio keeping Xenophon's book on Cyrus by him at all times is Cicero's *Tusculan Disputations* II.26. Cicero emphasizes that Xenophon was a pupil or follower of Socrates. The theme of the second dialogue of the *Tusculan Disputations* is how the study of philosophy enables one to attain a sound mind and body and thereby endure pain.

8

VIRTUE AND VICE

With chapter 15 and the following chapters we come to what might well be characterized as the heart of *The Prince*. It is only when the reader reaches chapter 15 that Machiavelli is ready to be forthcoming about his novelty and his break with what previous writers have written about virtue and vice. "I shall depart from the orders of the others," he declares. In this light, we should recall that in chapter 6 when discussing his exemplary new princes— Moses, Cyrus, Romulus, and Theseus—he wrote: "One should consider how there is nothing more difficult to treat, nor more doubtful to succeed in, nor more dangerous to manage than to make oneself a leader who introduces new orders" (chap. 6, 56). Machiavelli, too, will introduce new orders, and like his exemplary princes he will face enemies who adhere to the old orders and only lukewarm defenders of his new orders. The title of chapter 15 announces that Machiavelli will discuss "those things for which men and especially princes are praised or blamed." The fact that he begins with what is *said* or *believed* about the qualities of men and especially princes, praise and criticism, rather than announcing that his subject will be about those qualities and actions themselves, or *virtue* and *vice*, will turn out to be pregnant. For Machiavelli's novel teaching is, first of all, that there is an irresolvable conflict between what people believe are those qualities for which men and especially princes *should* be praised or criticized (namely, virtue and vice in the traditional sense) and what qualities and actions a prince must at least often have or take in order to secure their state (namely, what might be called political virtue and vice) and, second of all, that this conflict is a permanent feature of politics and even human life itself.

CHAPTER 15: ON THOSE THINGS FOR WHICH MEN AND ESPECIALLY PRINCES ARE PRAISED OR BLAMED

With his discussion of the prince's enemies and the art of war completed, Machiavelli makes another explicit transition at the outset of chapter 15: "It remains therefore to see what should be the ways and conduct of a prince, whether with his subjects or with his allies [or "friends"—*amici*]."[1] With this seemingly innocuous transition in place, he then pens one of the most important passages in *The Prince*:

> And because I know that many people have written about this, I worry in writing about it too that I shall be held presumptuous, especially since in debating this material I shall depart from the orders of the others. But since my intent is to write a thing that is useful for whoever understands it, it seemed to me more appropriate to go after the effectual truth of the thing than the imagination of it. And many have imagined republics and principalities that have never been seen or known to exist in truth.

Several points should be noted about this passage.

First, we saw in our discussion of the end of chapter 14 how Machiavelli wrote about writers and readers, suggesting that a prince should model himself after excellent men recounted in histories, pointing in particular to Xenophon's account of the life of Cyrus. Now in chapter 15 we see him drawing attention to the fact that he himself is a writer and that he addresses his work to "whoever understands it." We also saw how his example in chapter 14 of Philopoemen, who practiced the art of war by debating and reasoning with his friends about how they would attack and defend themselves in various situations, and now in chapter 15 Machiavelli announces that he will "debate" the material he is now going to discuss through an implicit dialogue with those who have written about it in the past. In short, at this important juncture we are reminded that we are readers of *The Prince* who should actively enter into the debate he takes up in his book.

Second, by saying that he worries that he will be "held presumptuous" in writing about how a prince should conduct himself, especially given that he will "depart" from what others have written on the subject, Machiavelli reminds us of the Dedicatory Letter, where he rebuffed the charge that he might be held presumptuous for daring to "discourse on and give rules for the conduct of princes" given that he was a man "of low and basest state." However, whereas the charge of presumption in the Dedicatory Letter regarded how a man of his low stature could dare address himself to a prince, now his presumption consists in daring to challenge what others have written about the conduct of princes or, more pointedly, in presuming to depart from the traditional or authoritative view of how men and especially princes should act.[2]

Third, as I also suggested when discussing the Dedicatory Letter, if the immediate addressee of *The Prince* is Lorenzo de' Medici, Machiavelli now reveals the ultimate or intended addressee of his work: "whoever understands it." Later on in his work, when discussing what sort of ministers or advisors a prince should have, he will explain that there are three sorts of "minds" (or, literally, "brains"): "one that understands by itself; another that discerns what others understand; and a third that understands neither itself nor others: the first is most excellent, the second is excellent, and the third useless" (chap. 22, 112). *The Prince* can be seen as a test of what sort of mind the reader has. Machiavelli most importantly addresses himself to the second type of mind, the one capable of discerning what another person—namely Machiavelli himself—understands and conveys through his book.

Fourth, and finally, Machiavelli declares that since his intention is to write something "useful" it is more appropriate for him to "go after the effectual truth of the thing than the imagination of it." The phrase "effectual truth" is an unusual formulation, in part because the word "effectual" (*effetuale*) is itself an unusual word, in Italian as in English. The root of the word is "effect" (*effeto*), as in "cause and effect," and has the sense of what actually occurs as an outcome of some action, or what is actually or factually the case, and as such Machiavelli contrasts the "effectual truth" about something to the "imagination" of it. The adjective "effectual" is also related to "effective" and means being capable of producing an intended effect, and so Machiavelli is claiming that the actual truth about the "thing" he is going to discuss is also effectual or effective in producing results, apparently unlike the "imagination of it." He therefore contrasts what he is going to write about the conduct of men and especially princes to what has been "imagined" about it by other writers: "And many have imagined republics and principalities that have never been seen or known to exist in truth." Machiavelli thereby suggests a relationship between the "effectual truth" (*verità effetuale*) and what is seen or known "in truth" (*in vero*).

What writers does he have in mind that have "imagined" republics and principalities that have never been seen or known to exist in truth? He does not say, but since his subject is the proper conduct of men and especially princes, or virtue and vice, works such as Plato's *Republic* with its imagined "city in speech" comes to mind, as do other works such as Xenophon's *Education of Cyrus*, Aristotle's *Politics* or *Ethics*, Augustine's *City of God*, as well as works in the mirror-of-princes genre which *The Prince* at least superficially resembles.[3] The only such work to which Machiavelli explicitly refers in *The Prince* is Xenophon's, as we have seen, and this fact should make us cautious about how to understand his appeal to the "effectual truth" rather than to the "imagination" of it. If Machiavelli were simply asking his reader to look at the cold hard truth of things rather than what is "imagined" about them, why would he suggest in the previous chapter that a prince, and we as readers, model ourselves on what Xenophon has written of Cyrus, that is, a largely fictional figure? Likewise, why would he have put forward in chapter 6 as examples to imitate princes who are mythical or semi-mythical, including Cyrus? As we noted in that context, although Machiavelli's statement that he will go to the "effectual truth" is often read as an appeal to cold-eyed realism about politics and other matters, this is an incomplete and misleading characterization of his thought, for he asks the prince—and the reader—to imagine a new world or at least to look at the world in a new way. In this regard, it is perhaps worthy of mention that chapter 15 is the only chapter in *The Prince* without any historical examples, ancient or modern, as though Machiavelli so indicates that his debate with those who have "written" about his subject or who (likewise?) "have imagined republics and principalities" transcends such examples.

Why should we look at the "effectual truth" concerning those things for which men and especially princes are praised or criticized rather than the "imagination of it"? Machiavelli offers an initial reason:

> For there is such a distance from how one lives to how one ought to live that he who abandons what is done for what ought to be done learns what will ruin him rather than what will save him, since a man who would wish to make a career of being good in every detail must come to ruin among so many who are not good. Hence it is necessary for a prince, if he wishes to maintain himself, to learn to be able to be not good, and to use this faculty and not to use it according to necessity.

This statement is often taken as the essence of how Machiavelli sees himself "departing" from what others have written of politics and morality. As Berlin remarks, however: "The fact that the wicked flourish ... has never been very remote from the consciousness of mankind."[4] Put more bluntly, everyone but the most naive person recognizes that always "being good" often leads "to ruin among so many who are not good." The question is rather whether one should keep being good despite the possible or even probable bad outcome. The classic argument on this point is the challenge posed to Socrates in Plato's *Republic* of proving that the just life is superior to the unjust life, even if someone were sure of getting away with injustice, for example by using the ring of Gyges to make himself invisible. Socrates makes this argument against the claim of Thrasymachus that the life of the unjust man, the successful tyrant, is the best way of life. By bringing forward Thrasymachus as a worthy opponent whose view must be seriously considered and refuted by Socrates, Plato demonstrates that he is well aware of the fact that injustice is often successful and justice unsuccessful, as he does in other dialogues. Countless other examples could be adduced, from the Melian Dialogue in Thucydides to the story of David and Uriah in the Old Testament, among many others, as witnesses to the sentiment Machiavelli here expounds.

Recognizing that Machiavelli's novelty cannot possibly consist in this simple realization that evil is often successful, other interpretations have been offered. Let us restrict ourselves to three influential alternatives. First, some scholars have argued that the essence of Machiavelli's novelty is that he separates politics from morality without rejecting the truth of the authoritative views about virtue and vice inherited from the classical or Christian traditions, and that he does so only reluctantly in the name of the ends of politics.[5] One initial stumbling block for this first line of interpretation is the title of chapter 15, where Machiavelli speaks of those qualities for which "men and especially princes" are praised or criticized, suggesting that his departure concerning virtue and vice reaches beyond just the political realm. Second, other scholars have instead claimed that Machiavelli confronts us with two separate and irreconcilable moralities, one traditional (and especially Christian) and the other political, and that he unhesitatingly opts for political morality for the sake of creating a stable and unified state, in particular in Italy, especially given that he regards traditional morality as unsuited to that task.[6] A third line of interpretation has Machiavelli go yet further, arguing that he rejects traditional notions of virtue and vice altogether as being merely what is "imagined" about politics and morals, and instead adopts a moral code, if it can even be called that, oriented toward the acquisition and maintenance of political power or, more generally, toward acquisition in all its forms. Under this interpretation, a prince (and perhaps anyone) would adhere to traditional virtues at best when it is necessary to do so for the sake of keeping up appearances.[7] Insofar as the qualities and actions needed for a prince to maintain his state are evil in the eyes of the traditional view, Machiavelli is a kind of "teacher of evil." This interpretation has a long pedigree, as witnessed by the prologue to Christopher Marlowe's play *The Jew of Malta* (1589–90), where, as we saw in the Introduction to this guide, he has Machiavelli himself address the audience and proclaim: "I count religion but a childish toy, and hold there is no sin but ignorance." Under any of the interpretations considered here, and there are many more, the crux of Machiavelli's originality is that what is traditionally written or said or imagined about virtue and vice is insufficient in one way or another for someone who wants to acquire and maintain political power.

These lines of interpretation regarding Machiavelli's novelty all have considerable appeal and textual support, but I believe that we can begin to glimpse a more comprehensive and satisfying answer concerning Machiavelli's departure from what others have written about virtue and vice from how he goes on to explain his turn to the "effectual truth of the thing." "Thus, leaving behind the things that have been imagined about a prince, and discussing those that are true, I say that all men, when they are spoken about, and especially princes, because they are placed higher, are noted for some of the following qualities, which bring them either blame or praise." First, then, men and especially princes are "spoken about" and certain things are "noted" or noticed about them, and, second, princes are "placed higher" or are more visible than other men. In other words, Machiavelli emphasizes how men and especially princes are *seen* and *spoken about* by others. But of course a prince may not in actually *be* how he *appears*, and likewise what others *say* about the prince might either be based on what they have seen, and therefore be inaccurate, or be grounded in common opinions or what is commonly said about how princes should and should not act. Put differently, how people see and assess the prince may be based on the "imagination of the thing" rather than the "effectual truth." If so, then the writers from whom Machiavelli departs have from his perspective made the same or at least a similar error. Machiavelli's challenge, therefore, is not merely to what has traditionally been written about the proper conduct of men and especially princes, but also to what is commonly thought about these matters. In short, he is challenging the reader.

In order to illustrate how men and especially princes are praised or blamed for certain qualities, Machiavelli turns to a list of such qualities: "That is to say, that one man is held liberal, one a miser (I use a Tuscan word because in our tongue an 'avaricious' man is still he who desires to take through robbery; we call a 'miser' the man who refrains excessively from using his own wealth); one is held a giver, one rapacious; one cruel, one compassionate ...," etc. A list of these pairs of qualities (as adjectives) will be easier to digest:

1	Liberal	Miserly
2	Giving	Rapacious
3	Cruel	Compassionate
4	Faithless	Faithful
5	Effeminate and Pusillanimous	Fierce and Spirited
6	Humane	Proud
7	Lascivious	Chaste
8	Honest	Crafty
9	Hard	Easygoing
10	Serious	Light
11	Religious	Unbelieving

And, for good measure: "and similar things." Again, several things should be noted about Machiavelli's presentation here.

First, Machiavelli is generally discussing how various individuals are "held" to be one thing or another, for example "held" to be liberal versus miserly. Again, then, his emphasis is on how the prince *appears* to others and is *spoken about* by them. We first saw the importance of how a prince is "held" to be in chapter 8 when Machiavelli discussed the case of Agathocles, where we were alternately told he was "virtuous" and then that "one cannot *call* it virtue" to have done the things he did (chap. 8, 65–66).

Second, in his list of eleven pairs of qualities he does not always place the praiseworthy quality first and then the blameworthy quality second (e.g., as he does with the first pair of "liberal" versus "miserly"), but instead sometimes reverses the order (e.g., "cruel" versus "compassionate"). By so doing, he may be indicating that what is commonly held to be praiseworthy or blameworthy may in fact actually sometimes not be worthy of praise or blame, or even that what is held to be the case about them is entirely opposite of what is actually the case. Indeed, when we get to chapter 17 we will see him argue that it is sometimes better to be cruel than compassionate, an argument he already foreshadowed in chapter 8 when discussing Agathocles and cruelty that is "badly used" versus "well used."

Third, his parenthetical remark about the Tuscan words for these qualities may suggest at least two things. First, like language itself, these qualities are at least in part a matter of convention. Second, since "liberal" has two possible opposites, "miserly" and "rapacious," the world of virtues and vices is not so neatly arranged into opposed qualities after all. This latter suggestion brings us to the comparison Machiavelli invites between his list of paired qualities and Aristotle's list of the virtues and vices, a subject I will discuss in more detail when we turn to chapter 16. For now it suffices to remark that Machiavelli's list of eleven pairs of praiseworthy and blameworthy qualities, or twelve if we count his addition of "and similar things," calls to mind Aristotle's list of twelve sets of virtues and vices. Machiavelli thereby evokes at least one major writer from whom he departs and may also indicate some of the reasons for his departure, notably that Aristotle's moral philosophy suffers from the same deficiencies as what is commonly imagined about virtue and vice.

The crux of what I suggest is Machiavelli's actual departure from what has previously been written about virtue and vice, and thus his novelty, comes to light now that he has raised the issue of appearance versus reality and what is commonly said about the actions of men and especially princes. "And I know that everyone will admit that it would be a most praiseworthy thing, among all the qualities listed above, for there to be found in a prince those that are held to be good." His phrasing here is revealing given that he has just subtly raised our doubts about what is actually praiseworthy versus what is held or said to be such. If common opinion—"everyone"—holds certain qualities to be praiseworthy, and therefore holds that a prince who possesses them is "most praiseworthy," are these qualities and that prince in reality to be praised or is he truly virtuous? Machiavelli himself "admits" the common opinion about the matter not necessarily because he agrees with it, but because "everyone" believes it to be the case. In other words, what is commonly held to be the case about praise and blame is itself a factor the prince (and the teacher of princes) has to take into account when acting (or writing). This realization brings us closer to his novelty.

Having stated what everyone admits to be the case, then, he immediately raises a problem:

> But because they cannot be had, nor wholly observed, since human conditions do not allow it, it is necessary for the prince to be so prudent that he knows how to flee the infamy of those vices that might take the state away from him. And as for those that would not take the state away from him, he should guard himself against them if possible, but, if he cannot, here he may let himself proceed with less caution. Indeed, let him not worry about incurring the infamy of those vices without which it is difficult for him to save the state.

Once again, several things should be noted about this very important passage.

First, Machiavelli identifies the reason why a prince (and perhaps anyone else) cannot have or wholly observe those qualities that are held to be good, because "human conditions do not allow it," apparently referring back to what he said near the beginning of the chapter about there being "such a distance from how one lives to how one ought to live" that acting in accordance with how one ought to live leads to ruin. What if "human conditions" were different? For Machiavelli, it seems, this would be to imagine republics or principalities that "have never been seen or known to exist in truth," and thus not worth considering except insofar as the "imagination" of the thing is itself a factor in determining how the prince should act to achieve his ends.

Second, his emphasis in this passage is once again on how a prince appears or is spoken about, for he urges the prince to know how to avoid the "infamy" of certain vices, that is, a bad reputation. Yet this is critical: a reputation for vice, whether or not what is held to be a vice is in reality a vice, may lead to a prince losing his state; and conversely a reputation for virtue, once again whether what is held to be a virtue is in reality a virtue, may help him maintain his state. In this light, as we saw in discussing chapter 8, Agathocles' blatant immorality led to success, but not "glory," that is a good reputation.

Third, having so far spoken of qualities that are praised or blamed, Machiavelli now finally uses the term "vice" and will shortly speak of "virtue" as well. On the level of what is held to be the case, the term "vice" clearly refers to qualities that are blamed, but what about what is actually or effectually the case? He does not state whether "vice" is equivalent to qualities that are blamed, much less whether "virtue" is equivalent to qualities that are praised. He neither affirms nor denies that those qualities ordinarily blamed are in fact vices or that those qualities ordinarily praised are in fact virtues. Rather, his emphasis is on the need for a prince to exercise "prudence" in managing his actions and reputation in order to maintain his state, for both the appearance and the reality of virtue and vice are critical for acquiring and maintaining power.

Machiavelli ends this chapter by offering a pithy summary conclusion: "For, if everything be well considered, something will be found that will appear a virtue, but will lead to his ruin if adopted; and something else that will appear a vice, if adopted, will result in his security and well-being." This passage seems to imply that what appears to be a virtue is in actuality often a vice, and likewise that what appears to be a vice is in actuality often a virtue. In this case, the standard for whether a quality or action is in actuality virtuous is whether it results in a prince's "security and well-being," and likewise the standard for whether it is in actuality a vice is whether it leads "to his ruin." The "effectual truth" of the thing is determined by the results, and, although he never quite states this conclusion, the ends justify the means.[8]

If Machiavelli now appears to equate virtue with the qualities and actions necessary for acquiring and maintaining power, this seemingly straightforward conclusion to his argument turns out not to be so simple. First, as noted above, he has never denied that what are ordinarily held to be virtues and vices are in fact virtues and vices, and he has never counseled the prince simply to ignore them. As we have seen above, the fact that he does not outright deny traditional moral standards has therefore led interpreters to suggest that he is arguing that what might be called "political virtue" and "political vice," which are measured by success or failure in maintaining one's state, are often different from what might be called "traditional virtue" and "traditional vice," which are perhaps to be observed outside of the political realm or inside the political realm when possible. On the other hand, other interpreters note that it is unlikely that Machiavelli would simply outright declare traditional moral standards to be false, and further argue that since he gives us no other standard than political success or failure, he must be rejecting traditional moral standards. Once again, these alternative interpretations are attractive in many respects.

Nonetheless, also once again, I suggest that Machiavelli's novelty consists in his teaching that both kinds of virtue and vice, or what we have termed "political" and "traditional," are, first, irreducible features of politics (and perhaps human life altogether) and, second, often in conflict with one another. These two types of virtue and vice are irreducible features of politics because, however much Machiavelli or anyone else may argue that traditional virtue is not truly virtue when considered from the perspective of political virtue, almost all people—or "everyone," as he states—will nonetheless persist in holding that traditional virtue is virtue, period. For example, everyone will persist in calling justice, moderation, liberality, courage, etc., virtues and will praise the person who possesses these qualities, and vice versa for what is held to be vice, despite what Machiavelli or anyone else may argue. Because traditional virtue and vice is an irreducible feature of political and moral life, men and especially princes must take traditional virtue and vice, or at least their appearance, into account in their actions because the appearance or actuality of traditional virtue helps the prince maintain his state and the appearance or actuality of traditional vice can lead him to lose it. Yet, as Machiavelli more obviously argues, whoever simply follows traditional virtue and avoids traditional vice will also often find that he is ruined. Second, because "traditional" and "political" virtue and vice are often in conflict, following Machiavelli's advice unhesitatingly to depart from traditional virtue and turn to political virtue, leads to a dilemma since this political virtue often looks like—or, in fact, is—traditional vice. In short, if the prince acts in accordance with political virtue in order to maintain his state, the "infamy" he incurs for appearing to follow traditional vice ironically endangers his hold on the state. The prince is often, perhaps very often, in a position where there is no simple solution to the conflict between political virtue and traditional virtue. The dilemma might be schematically represented, as it is in Figure 8.1.

In this diagram of the dilemma facing the prince, political virtue and political vice are assumed never to overlap, for they are each defined by whether or not the quality or action leads to political success or failure, and likewise traditional virtue and traditional vice are assumed never to overlap, with the assumption being that although we may disagree over whether a given quality or action is a virtue or vice in a certain circumstance, we do not disagree about the difference between traditional virtue or vice per se. There are therefore two types of overlap: first, where political

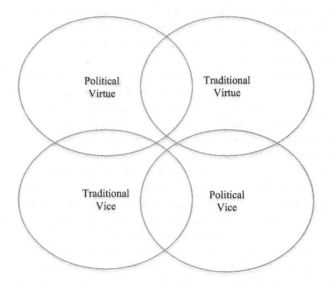

Figure 8.1 The Overlap of Traditional and Political Virtue and Vice

virtue overlaps with traditional virtue (and political vice overlaps with traditional vice) and, second, where political virtue overlaps with traditional vice (and political vice overlaps with traditional virtue). In the case of the first type of overlap, there is no conflict: by doing what is politically virtuous the prince is simultaneously doing what is traditionally virtuous (and likewise for political and traditional vice). These are the easy cases, perhaps the cases hoped for by those who have imagined republics and principalities that have never been seen or known to exist. In the case of the second type of overlap, there is a conflict: if the prince does what is politically virtuous, and thereby maintains his state, he will also be doing what is traditionally held to be vicious, and will thereby suffer from the reputation for vice if he is detected and thus endanger his state. Likewise, if the prince does what is traditionally held to be virtuous, and thereby gains a good reputation that will help him maintain his state, he will be doing what is politically vicious, thereby potentially losing his state. In the second type of conflict, then, the prince is always between a rock and a hard place, so to speak.

What is a prince to do given these potential conflicts? We might rank order his choices as follows:

1   Political virtue + traditional virtue: no conflict
2   If (1) is not possible, political virtue + traditional vice: conflict

    a   But appear to have traditional virtue: conflict resolved
    b   If (a) is not possible, then live with reputation for traditional vice: conflict (and hope that the advantages of having political virtue outweigh the disadvantages of a reputation for traditional vice)

3   Traditional virtue + political vice: conflict (and hope that the advantages of having the reputation for traditional virtue outweigh the disadvantages of having political vice)
4   Traditional vice + political vice: no conflict, but ruinous.

The upshot of the dilemma facing the prince is that the primary virtue of a prince consists in prudence, a prudence that navigates the often inevitable and irresolvable conflicts between "political" and "traditional" virtue and vice. In fact, prudence is the only Aristotelian virtue Machiavelli wholly embraces, although he divorces prudence from its necessary orientation toward (traditional) virtue in Aristotle's understanding.[9] As Machiavelli writes later in *The Prince*: "Nor let any state ever believe that it can always make safe choices. On the contrary, let it think that it has to take them all as doubtful. Because we find this, in the order of things, that one never tries to avoid one inconvenience without incurring another one. But prudence consists in knowing how to recognize the qualities of the inconveniences and choosing the less bad as if it were good" (chap. 21, 111). There is no absolute good as believed by those who have imagined republics and principalities that have never been seen or known to exist, but only lesser and greater evils among which one must choose.

With his general chapter on the qualities for which men and especially princes are praised or criticized in place, then, Machiavelli turns in the next few chapters to elucidate his novel teaching.

CHAPTER 16: ON LIBERALITY AND PARSIMONY

In chapter 15 Machiavelli provides a list of pairs of qualities that are praised and blamed, and in chapter 16 he turns to an analysis of the first pair, liberality and miserliness or, more kindly, "parsimony." Since he does not present an exhaustive treatment of all the paired qualities he listed, we should view this chapter as a model for examining the problems concerning "political" and "traditional" virtues and vices.

"If I am to begin, therefore, with the first of the qualities stated above, I say that it would be good to be held liberal," he begins, but then immediately raises a problem: "Nonetheless, liberality, used in such a way that you are held to be liberal, harms you, for if it is used virtuously and as it ought to be used, it will not be recognized, and you will not shed the infamy of its contrary." The first step of Machiavelli's analysis is that he states that it would be good "to be held liberal." He does not specify whether the person who is held to be liberal or generous is actually liberal or only appears to be so, but at any rate his emphasis is on how the person is viewed and spoken of. The second step is his claim that if one is actually liberal in the "traditional" sense of the virtue, or if liberality is "used virtuously" as Machiavelli phrases it in a nod to the "traditional" understanding, then he will in fact not get recognized for his liberality, that is he will not appear to be liberal even though he actually is. Still worse, even though he is in reality liberal in the "traditional" sense, he will appear or have the reputation for the "contrary" quality. Which "contrary" quality? In chapter 15 Machiavelli explained that liberality has two contrary qualities: miserliness and rapaciousness. Both of these contrary qualities will turn out to be important in his analysis of the dilemma now facing the liberal prince. Now for the third step in the analysis. In order to avoid the reputation for being the contrary of liberal, therefore, the prince must become even more liberal to the point of being prodigal or lavish. "And for this reason, out of wanting to retain among men the name of a liberal man, it is necessary not to leave out any quality of sumptuousness, so that always a prince of this kind will consume all of his means in works such as these." In order to keep up appearances and a name for being liberal, therefore, the prince will be forced to tax and otherwise burden his people, making himself hateful to them. This leads to the fourth step of the analysis. Recognizing this, the prince now stops attempting to be prodigal or lavish so as to maintain the reputation for liberality and instead goes to the other extreme of being miserly. Machiavelli concludes his account of the dilemma facing his prince: "Thus, since a prince cannot use this virtue of the liberal man in such a way that it is recognized without harm to himself, he ought, if he is prudent, not to worry about the name of the miser." Although he explains why this course is best, that is because he at least seems liberal in the eyes of the many whom he no longer burdens and only seems miserly in the eyes of the few who had anticipated his liberality, Machiavelli nonetheless leaves us with the problem that the reputation for miserliness can endanger the prince's hold on his state.

The vicious circle facing the prince who wants to have the name for being liberal can be read as a parody of Aristotle's doctrine of the virtues, and therefore as part of Machiavelli's departure from those who have written on the subject before him.[10] In his discussion in the *Nicomachean Ethics* of the virtues and vices, to which Machiavelli seems to allude with his list in chapter 15 of the qualities deemed to be worthy of praise and blame, Aristotle defines a virtue as a mean between two contrary extremes. For example, liberality is a mean between the deficient extreme of miserliness on the one side and the excessive extreme of prodigality on the other side. Likewise, courage is a mean between the excessive extreme of rashness on the one side and the deficient extreme of cowardice on the other. Machiavelli's discussion of liberality mirrors and shatters Aristotle's treatment. Even if liberality is indeed the mean between miserliness and prodigality, when it is "used virtuously," as he says, the "effectual truth" is that others do not "recognize" the prince's behavior as liberal but instead hold it to be miserly, and so in this instance the traditional virtue appears to be a traditional vice. Only by going to the excessive extreme of prodigality can the prince appear to be liberal, and so the appearance of having a traditional virtue now requires adopting what is considered the other extreme of a traditional vice. But the exercise of the traditional vice of prodigality in order to have the appearance of the traditional virtue of liberality exhausts the possibility of being either liberal or prodigal, because the prince now runs out of resources and must either burden his subjects to keep being liberal or prodigal, incurring their hatred, or no longer appear liberal, earning their contempt. The only solution, it seems to this point, is to become miserly, or to adopt a traditional vice. In short, in Machiavelli's analysis, liberality is a self-defeating virtue in terms of its political consequences.[11]

Machiavelli has recommended that a prince should not fear incurring the reputation of being a miser given the self-defeating character of liberality, and now he gives some examples to prove his point. "In our times we have not seen great things done except by those who have been thought misers; the others were eliminated," he claims, pointing to the examples of Pope Julius, the present French king (Louis XII as of the writing of *The Prince*),[12] and the present king of Spain (Ferdinand). Machiavelli admits that Julius had the name of being a liberal man since he spent freely in order to obtain the papacy, but notes that he was miserly once he had attained it. "Therefore," he concludes his argument, "a prince ought to care little—if he wishes not to have to rob his subjects, to be able to defend himself, not to become poor and contemptible, and not be forced to become rapacious—about incurring the name of miser. For this is one of those vices that let him rule." To return to the analysis of "traditional" versus "political" virtues and vices, it therefore seems that miserliness, a traditional vice, is in fact often a political virtue because it helps the prince maintain his state.

With this conclusion stated, Machiavelli now entertains two consecutive objections from an imaginary reader. First: "And if someone should say, 'Caesar arrived at the empire through liberality, and many others, because they were, and were held, liberal, achieved the highest ranks,' ... ." Before listening to Machiavelli's reply, note that the challenger thrusts at Machiavelli's first assumption in his analysis of liberality: that it is impossible to both *be* liberal and *appear* to be such. Caesar was liberal and was also held to be such, claims his interlocutor. Machiavelli's response is that one must distinguish, as he did just above with regard to Pope Julius, between actions required when one is on the way to acquiring a principality and those once one has acquired it and "you" are a prince. When you are a prince, liberality is harmful; when you are trying to become a prince, liberality is useful. If Caesar had continued to be liberal once having attained the empire, Machiavelli suggests, he would have destroyed his state, the assumption being that he would have suffered the same vicious circle of liberality Machiavelli has just analyzed.[13]

Machiavelli's response to this first objection brings on another, and this time he reveals a solution to the problem of liberality, regardless of whether one is becoming a prince or already is a prince. "And if someone should reply, 'Many have been princes and have done great things with their armies who were held very liberal.'" Machiavelli's response is shocking once we absorb it: "I respond to you that either the prince spends what belongs to himself and his subjects, or what belongs to others. In the first case, he ought to be very sparing. In the other, he ought not leave out any part of liberality." In other words, the prince should be rapacious with regard to other peoples so that he can be liberal with his own, all the while himself being miserly with his own resources. Now we see how the two possible qualities opposed to liberality Machiavelli casually noted in chapter 15 when discussing Tuscan usage—miserliness and rapaciousness—come to the rescue of the vicious circle of liberality. The prince can (1) maintain a reputation for the traditional virtue of liberality by (2) exercising the traditional vice of prodigality successfully if he (3) exercises another traditional vice opposed to liberality, namely rapaciousness, thereby (4) earning the reputation of another traditional virtue, being a "giver," while (5) simultaneously adhering to another traditional vice, miserliness, without (6) incurring reputation for being a miser.

Machiavelli now summarizes the lesson and gives some examples. "And of what is not yours and your subjects' one may give more broadly, as did Cyrus, Caesar, and Alexander. For spending what belongs to others does not strip you of reputation but adds to it; the spending of what is yours is what hurts you." Curiously, Cyrus, Caesar, and Alexander were three of the princes Machiavelli cited at the end of chapter 14 when discussing how excellent men of the past have imitated what they have read about another excellent man of the past, with Alexander the Great imitating Achilles, Caesar imitating Alexander, and Scipio imitating Cyrus as written about by Xenophon. The suggestion would seem to be that Caesar imitated Alexander with regard to being liberal with other people's property in order to come to power. What about Cyrus' imitator, Scipio? Machiavelli will in fact address Scipio in the next chapter, so he here sets up the question of whether Scipio correctly imitated Cyrus. To return to the present chapter, Machiavelli states that liberality is self-consuming, and the dilemma facing the prince with regard to liberality either forces him to be poor and contemptible or rapacious and hateful. Quietly putting his shocking solution behind him, he concludes the chapter by once again recommending to the prince that he not be concerned with having the name as a miser, which is perhaps the next best option if he does not have the option of being liberal with other peoples' things.

CHAPTER 17: ON CRUELTY AND COMPASSION, AND WHETHER IT IS BETTER TO BE LOVED THAN TO BE FEARED, OR THE CONTRARY

Cruelty and compassion are the next pair of qualities that are praised or criticized listed by Machiavelli in chapter 15. The term "compassion" requires some explanation. The Latin term in the chapter title, *pietate*, and the Italian term used in the body of the chapter, *pietoso* as an adjective and *pietà* as a noun, each have a wide range of meanings that include "compassion," "mercy," and "piety." Given the potentially religious overtones of the word, and especially given the close association of compassion, mercy, and piety with Christianity, some scholars have suggested that chapter 17 is concerned with Machiavelli's engagement with Christian views concerning virtue and vice just as chapter 16 was concerned with his engagement with ancient, and particularly Aristotelian, moral ideas.[14] In this light, his general argument in the chapter that it is necessary sometimes to be cruel rather than merciful, and that it is better to be feared than loved, can be seen as a criticism of Christian views to the contrary or a diagnosis of how following such views leads to poor political results.[15]

"Descending next to the other qualities mentioned before," Machiavelli begins, "I say that each prince ought to desire to be held compassionate and not cruel, nonetheless he must be alert not to use this compassion badly." We already saw in chapter 8 in his discussion of Agathocles that cruelty can be "badly used" and "well used," and we also saw Machiavelli almost apologize for saying so: "Cruelties may be called 'well used,' if it is permissible to speak well of evil ..." (chap. 8, 67–68). Machiavelli thereby signals his departure from traditional, and especially Christian, conceptions of virtue and vice. Now we learn that compassion (or mercy or piety) can likewise be used "badly." In order to prove his point, Machiavelli explains that Cesare Borgia was "held to be cruel," but his cruelty "restored the Romagna, unified it, and restored it to peace and to faith." Our minds are thus cast back to chapter 7 and Machiavelli's account of how Cesare rendered the Romagna peaceful and obedient and especially the story he tells there of the stupefying execution of Remirro de Orco at the hands of Cesare. To return to the present chapter, Machiavelli writes: "If one considers this well, one will see that he was much more compassionate than the Florentine people, who, to avoid the name of cruelty, allowed the destruction of Pistoia." What seems at first appearance to be cruel turns out to be compassionate, and vice versa, at least if one "considers this well" as opposed to considering it superficially.

Machiavelli draws a lesson for a prince from these examples: "A prince, therefore, must not care about the infamy of cruelty in keeping his subjects united and faithful, because if he makes a very few examples, he will be more compassionate than those who, through too much compassion, allow disorders to occur from which arise killings or robberies." One must be cruel in order to be kind it seems. This lesson is particularly apt for new princes, he argues, for "it is impossible for the new prince to avoid the reputation of cruelty because new states are full of perils." In order to buttress this statement Machiavelli calls on the authority of Virgil, whom he interestingly treats as a writer advising princes since he characterizes the poet as putting his own words of advice into the mouth of one of his characters, Dido. The quotation from the *Aeneid* (I.563–4) has Dido defending the initially inhospitable welcome given to Aeneas and his Trojan men: "'The harshness and newness of my kingdom drive me to make such exertions, and to protect my borders far and wide with guards.'" This quotation is odd support for Machiavelli's point for several reasons. First, the newness of her kingdom and the harsh conditions under which it is founded does not lead her to be cruel to her own people in order to keep them united and faithful, which is Machiavelli's argument for cruelties well used, but at most cruel or at least inhospitable to foreigners. Second, Dido is renowned not for her cruelty but rather for her love. The quotation from the *Aeneid* Machiavelli cites comes just before Dido, busy building the new city of Carthage, meets and falls in love with Aeneas, who has escaped the fall of Troy and is in search of a new fatherland that will turn out to be Rome. Despite his love for Dido, the dutiful Aeneas, who is characteristically referred to as "pious Aeneas," an interesting detail given the subject of Machiavelli's chapter, leaves Carthage and the abandoned Dido builds a great pyre and burns herself to death for love of Aeneas. Far from being a story of the necessary cruelty of a new prince, the example of Dido would seem to be a warning against the dangers of love in politics. Be that as it may, after quoting Virgil, Machiavelli urges the prince to be cautious in creating fear too readily and to proceed "in a manner tempered with prudence and humanity." How can a prince simultaneously commit the necessary cruelties, thus gaining the potentially dangerous "infamy" of or reputation for cruelty, not thereby create fear of himself and yet also temper his actions with humanity? Machiavelli seems to ask the impossible of the prince. Will he provide a solution to this new dilemma as he did with the dilemma of liberality?

The debate over cruelty and compassion strangely unresolved, Machiavelli turns to a related debate: "From the above a debate arises whether it is better to be loved than feared or the contrary."[16] Machiavelli also here turns from the prince's actions, cruel or compassionate, to his subjects' feelings toward him, love and fear, with the supposed parallel being that the compassionate prince will be loved and the cruel prince feared. This change of perspective helps explain why debate arises at this point, for we have learned that even though "each prince ought to desire to be held compassionate and not cruel," as Machiavelli states at the outset of the chapter, a prince cannot always be compassionate and thus loved, but must sometimes be cruel and thus feared (or even hated), and therefore faces a dilemma.[17] "The answer is that one would want to be both the one and the other," Machiavelli readily responds, but then complicates matters: "but because it is difficult to join them together, it is much safer to be feared than loved, if one has to do without one of the two." In order to explain his reasoning, he offers one of the most general statements he ever does in *The Prince* concerning human nature. "For the following may be said generally about men: that they are ungrateful, changeable, pretenders and dissemblers, avoiders of dangers, and desirous of gain, and while you do them good they are wholly yours, offering you their blood, their property, their life, and their children, as I said above, when the need is far off, but when it comes close to you they revolt."[18]

In referring the reader to what he had said above, Machiavelli alludes to his discussion in chapter 9 of how a prince should found himself on the people, and specifically his remark there that in peaceful times the people adhere to the prince "when death is far off" but are nowhere to be found when he has need of them in adverse times, which therefore leads him to recommend that "a wise prince must think of a way by which his citizens, always and in every circumstance, have need of his state and of himself, and then they will always be faithful to him" (chap. 9, 71). Returning to chapter 17, having presented his rather dim view of human nature, Machiavelli states that the prince "who has founded himself wholly on their words, because he finds himself naked of other preparations, is ruined." The mere words of men are unreliable, and so, as Machiavelli already suggested in chapter 9, the prince must ensure that the people are properly motivated to keep their word or, to use the language he employs here concerning the friendships purchased by the prince, they must be "possessed." Returning to the theme of love and fear, he pronounces: "Men have less fear of offending one who makes himself loved than one who makes himself feared, since love is held in place by a bond of obligation which, because men are wretched, is broken at every opportunity for utility to oneself, but fear is held in place by a fear of punishment that never abandons you." In short, being feared depends on the prince whereas being loved depends on the people, a conclusion that suggests that cruelties "well used" are more dependable in their effects than compassion, even when it is "well used."

"Nonetheless," Machiavelli now qualifies his point, "the prince must make himself feared in such a way that, although he does not acquire love, he avoids hatred. For being feared and being not hated may exist together very well." How easy is it to be feared without also being hated? In order to avoid becoming hated, Machiavelli states that the prince must merely abstain from the citizens' property and their women. (In this light, we should recall that in Machiavelli's time the honor of women was central to a family's and especially the head of a family's own honor and standing.) Note that Machiavelli is not arguing that a prince should abstain from harming property or persons because to do so would be a violation of natural rights, a conception that first arose and took root well over a century after he was writing, or because doing so would violate the rule of law, a conception that was available to him through a long tradition, but rather as a prudential calculation by the prince to avoid becoming hated. In the same light, Machiavelli now advises the prince to proceed against someone's life only if there is "appropriate justification and manifest cause," another counsel of prudence and not because of any concern he voices for the rule of law per se. Indeed, Machiavelli's reasons are shockingly frank: "But above all he should abstain from the property of others, for men sooner forget the death of their father than the loss of their patrimony," that is their inheritance from their father. In sum, when the prince is at home with his people, he should resist the temptation to become rapacious with regard to their property, whether to be able to be liberal with it, as we saw in the previous chapter, or otherwise, and he should keep bloodshed rare.

Yet things are quite different when the prince is abroad, just as we saw in Machiavelli's treatment in chapter 16 of liberality, where he cautioned the prince not to be rapacious with regard to his own subjects and instead counseled him to be rapacious toward others so that he could be liberal to his own people without paying the price. "But when the prince is with his armies, and has command of a multitude of soldiers, then it is wholly necessary not to care about the reputation of cruelty, because without this reputation no army ever was kept united and disposed to any feat of arms." In order to illustrate his point, Machiavelli draws a comparison between two ancient generals, Hannibal and Scipio, a comparison he also makes at greater length in his *Discourses on Livy*.

Of Hannibal Machiavelli writes: "Numbered among the admirable actions of Hannibal is the following," namely that he led a very large army composed of troops from various countries and yet "there never arose any dissension, neither among themselves, nor against the prince, in bad as well as his good fortune." How did Hannibal keep his men in line in such unfavorable circumstances? Machiavelli's answer is blunt: "This could not have arisen from anything other than his inhuman cruelty, which, together with his other infinite virtues, made him always venerable and terrible in the sight of his soldiers; and without it, his other virtues would not have sufficed for him to achieve that effect." We are reminded of Agathocles, who was also said to be cruel, although Machiavelli did not dare at that point to number his cruelty among his virtues as he now does by including Hannibal's "inhuman cruelty" among his "other infinite virtues." That he knows he is departing from what others have written concerning virtue and vice is obvious from what he writes next: "In this regard the writers have understood little, for on the one hand they have admired this action of his, and on the other they condemned the principal cause of it." In other words, they have admired the end Hannibal achieved but condemned the means necessary for achieving it. Who are "the writers" Machiavelli has in mind? He refers first and foremost to Livy's initial summary view of Hannibal where, after describing his great courage and fortitude as a general, he writes: "But with these great virtues came great vices: inhuman cruelty, a perfidy worse than Punic, no truthfulness, no reverence, no fear of the gods, no respect for oaths, no religion."[19] It seems that both writers and their readers can misunderstand the very events they relate or read, and part of properly understanding and thus properly imitating excellent men of the past requires reading these works with the proper "sense" or "flavor," as he states in the *Discourses on Livy*. [20]

In order to confirm his view about the reasons for Hannibal's success, Machiavelli turns to a comparison with Scipio: "And that it is true that Hannibal's other virtues would not have sufficed may be understood in Scipio, who was exceedingly rare, not only in his own times but in all the memory of things that are known." Machiavelli refers to Publius Cornelius Scipio Africanus (236–183 BCE), the Roman general and statesman who first conquered Spain and then turned his sights on Africa and defeated Hannibal. Machiavelli may call Scipio "exceedingly rare, not only in his own times but in all the memory of things that are known," either because his military virtue was so outstanding or because somehow his example is pertinent beyond his own time. At any rate, he pairs two of the greatest generals of antiquity and finds Hannibal preferable to Scipio, the man who defeated him, due to a quality Scipio lacked: "inhuman cruelty."

In order to make his case, Machiavelli first points to the fact that Scipio's armies rebelled against him in Spain. "This did not arise from anything other than his compassion, which had given more license to his soldiers than is appropriate to military discipline." His account here is broadly consistent with Livy, who also notes Scipio's merciful character and well-known clemency, but he leaves out two major points. First, Livy suggests that Scipio's very success in beating the Spaniards meant that the soldiers no longer had the opportunity for plunder and became restless. Perhaps we are to infer that Scipio should have been more liberal with other people's things. Second, and more importantly, he fails to note that the mutiny took place when Scipio was gravely ill and rumored to be near death.[21] This fact would be in direct contrast to what Machiavelli has written of Hannibal, for while he emphasizes that Hannibal's "inhuman cruelty ... made him always venerable and terrible in the sight of his soldiers," Scipio, the general who ruled through love, no longer held the loyalty of his troops once he was out of sight. Machiavelli goes on to relate that Fabius Maximus called Scipio "the corrupter of the Roman military" due to his compassion. The specific instance when Fabius made this charge regarded the next story Machiavelli relates, of Scipio's failure to punish a subordinate for his sacrilegious plundering of the Locrians, although Fabius also referred back in this context to Scipio's earlier leniency toward his troops in Spain. Here Machiavelli fails to mention that Fabius also criticized Scipio for his cruelty in putting down the revolt of his troops by having the ringleaders savagely slaughtered in front of the troops, and in fact Fabius' criticism was that Scipio indulged his troops and then had to be cruel to them due to his indulgence.[22] "And it all arose from his easy nature," Machiavelli comments: "so much so that when someone wanted to excuse him in the Senate, he said that there were many men who knew better how not to err than to correct errors."[23] In sum, Machiavelli concludes of Scipio that his nature would have dishonored the fame and glory he gained, but this "harmful quality of his not only was hidden, indeed it brought him glory," since he exercised his command (*imperio*) under the direction of the Senate. What Machiavelli means by this last comment is unclear, but he may be suggesting that Scipio if unchecked may have posed a threat like Julius Caesar later did when he overstepped the bounds of the command (*imperio*) he was granted by the Senate and his ambition came fully to light.[24]

As mentioned already, Machiavelli pursues the parallel of Hannibal and Scipio in the *Discourses on Livy* as well. His discussion there is part of a group of chapters discussing whether humanity or cruelty is more effective in both domestic and military contexts, with him tackling the question of why it seems that either mode can be effective. He appears to argue that it is in fact another quality that enables a prince or captain to succeed through either mode: "Therefore it is of little import to a captain whichever of these ways he walks, provided that he is a virtuous man and that the virtue makes him reputed among men. For when it is great, as it was in Hannibal and in Scipio, it cancels all those errors that are made so as to make oneself loved too much or to make oneself feared too much." Great virtue, and especially the reputation for virtue, enables a prince or captain to succeed through using various modes, although as he goes on to explain it is important that he stick to one mode and not alternate between being cruel and humane (III.21, 263). This was precisely Fabius' criticism of Scipio, so Machiavelli's more critical treatment of Scipio in *The Prince* seems to be that he is an example of how compassion "badly used" leads to cruelty, perhaps also "badly used."

One further feature that his discussion in the *Discourses on Livy* of Hannibal and Scipio sheds light on in *The Prince*, both with regard to his treatment of Scipio and more generally with regard to the theme of the appearance versus reality of the virtues and vices, is the hovering presence of Xenophon's Cyrus there. When he first introduces the example of Scipio in the *Discourses on Livy*, Machiavelli compares his humane modes of acting to what is written by Xenophon of Cyrus. "One sees too how much this part," that is, humanity, "is desired in great men by peoples, and how much it is praised by writers, and by those who describe the lives of princes, and by those who order how they ought to live. Among them Xenophon toils very much to demonstrate how many honors, how many victories, how much good fame being humane and affable brought to Cyrus ..." (III.20, 262). The reason Xenophon has to "toil very much" to demonstrate Cyrus' humanity and affability, as Machiavelli reveals earlier in the *Discourses on Livy* and as we saw when discussing the example of Cyrus as an exemplary new prince in chapter 6 of *The Prince*, is that Cyrus' success was in fact due to his use of fraud and his ability to maintain the appearance of being virtuous in the traditional sense (see II.13, 155). Recall from our discussion of chapter 14 that Machiavelli gives the example of Scipio imitating Cyrus as written about by Xenophon when he discusses how princes should imitate the actions of exemplary princes they read about in works of history. The question I raised there was whether Scipio read Xenophon properly, and therefore whether he imitated the actual as opposed to apparent modes used by Cyrus to gain and maintain power. We now see from his discussion of Xenophon in the *Discourses on Livy* that the apparent virtues of Cyrus—his humanity and affability—are the qualities praised by "writers, and by those who describe the life of princes, and by those who order how they ought to live." Like Scipio, these writers have misread Xenophon's work on Cyrus and have been taken in by appearances. To return to chapter 17 of *The Prince*, then, Machiavelli's critical account of Scipio being too compassionate or humane as against Hannibal's successful cruelty is an example of how a prince can misunderstand the qualities needed to acquire and maintain power, in this case from misreading what a writer, here Xenophon, has written about the virtues and vices necessary for ruling.

Ending this chapter, Machiavelli offers an explicit conclusion: "I conclude, therefore, returning to being feared and loved, that since men love at their own pleasure, but fear at the pleasure of the prince, a wise prince must found himself on that which is his, and not on that which belongs to others: he must only contrive to avoid hatred, as was said." By stating that he is "returning" to the question of whether it is better to be feared or loved, he effectively treats his comparison of Hannibal and Scipio as a digression. In one sense it was, for his point was that a prince or captain has to proceed differently with his army than his people, embracing the reputation for being cruel with his troops while making himself feared by the people but avoiding being hated by them. Insofar as his recommendation to be feared without being hated leaves the prince with something of a dilemma, however, perhaps the digression on Hannibal and Scipio offers something of a solution in an indirect manner. Namely, if Scipio is a cautionary example of being too compassionate and of relying too much on being loved, and if Hannibal's cruelty toward his troops would have turned fear into dangerous hatred if used on his people, then the prince Scipio inaccurately imitated, Cyrus, would offer a solution insofar as he was able to appear compassionate and humane, thus exercising compassion "well used," while simultaneously using force and fraud, thus perhaps also exercising cruelty "well used." In short, Cyrus may be an example of how to be loved and feared at the same time, with the appearance of compassion preventing fear of him from turning into hatred. If so, the last words of the chapter, "as was said," ironically invite the reader to wonder what was left unsaid by Machiavelli in this context, and instead ask the reader to recall the apparently positive mention in chapter 14 of how Scipio imitated Xenophon's Cyrus and compare it with the critical assessment of Scipio he now provides.

CHAPTER 18: IN WHAT WAY FAITH SHOULD BE KEPT BY PRINCES

In chapter 15 Machiavelli wrote that "everyone" will admit that it would be a praiseworthy thing for a prince to have those qualities "that are held to be good," and in opening chapter 18 he once again cites what "everyone" knows: "How laudable it is in a prince to maintain faith and to live with integrity and not cleverness, everyone understands." And we should therefore not be surprised that this statement is immediately followed by Machiavelli's signature word: "Nonetheless." Rather than contradicting what "everyone" believes by recommending that a prince should break faith, at least not yet, however, Machiavelli points out that "one sees from experience in our own times" that what actually occurs goes against what is held to be praiseworthy. Specifically, experience reveals that princes who have accomplished great things have "held faith of small account," even surpassing those who acted with "sincerity" by instead acting through "cleverness." In other words, Machiavelli is revealing a conflict between what "everyone" believes and what probably "everyone" observes, or a conflict between "ought" and "is." Unlike cruelty and compassion, for example, he does not have to work very hard to show that things are not as they appear. He is not revealing the hidden tricks of the prince's trade, or what is known as the *arcana imperii*, but instead stating the obvious. How can it be that we hold on to believing that keeping faith is praiseworthy when we are confronted with a world in which honesty is clearly not the best policy?[25]

With this observation about the conflict between "ought" and "is" in place, then, Machiavelli addresses himself to his audience: "You should know, therefore, that there are two kinds of combat: one with laws, the other with force. The first one is proper to man, the second is proper to beasts. But because many times the first is not enough, one must have recourse to the second. For a prince, therefore, it is necessary to know well how to use both the beast and the man." How does this statement address the conflict between "ought" and "is"? The parallel he establishes appears to be between keeping faith and doing "combat" through laws, on the one hand, and breaking faith and doing "combat" through force, on the other. If treaties or other such agreements are considered to be a form of law, then being faithful to the promises made in such treaties or agreements could be understood as following the law. Likewise, the prince ruling over his own subjects through laws and adhering to the rule of law could also be understood as a kind of keeping faith. Interestingly, however, Machiavelli characterizes even ruling through law as a form of "combat," presumably not only between the prince and other states but also between the prince and his own people. At any rate, his point is that the "combat" proper to man, laws, is not always sufficient and a prince must have recourse to the form of "combat" proper to beasts: force.

When remarking what is seen from experience "in our own times" concerning how those princes who have not been faithful have been more successful Machiavelli stated the obvious, but now he tells us what was hidden by "ancient writers." Speaking of how a prince must "know well how to use both the beast and the man," he explains: "This point has been taught covertly to princes by the ancient writers, who write how Achilles and many others of those ancient princes were given to Chiron the centaur to raise, so that under his instruction he would look after them. This having as a preceptor a half-beast and half-man means nothing other than that it is necessary for a prince to use the one and the other nature; and the one without the other does not endure."[26] Machiavelli makes overt what was previously covert. What about ancient times made such a lesson necessarily covert and what about "our own times" makes it timely to reveal?

We might begin to answer this question by observing that what Machiavelli claims these unnamed "ancient writers" taught about the need to use the nature of the beast as well as the nature of man conflicts with the more obvious or more authoritative teaching of most of the ancient philosophers—Plato, Aristotle, Cicero, et al.— concerning politics and morals. Namely, these ancient writers uniformly argued that the beastly or animal part of us, the body and the passions, must be ruled by what is distinctly a part of human nature and the highest part, the soul and reason. Related, they further argued that ruling through law as opposed to force was also distinctly and properly human (though, contrary to Machiavelli's implication, they never thought force would also not be necessary, in part due to the fact that most people are not ruled by reason). If these authors are among those Machiavelli charges with having "imagined republics and principalities that have never been seen or known to exist in truth," then either he is charging them with being mistaken that princes can rule through laws alone or he is suggesting that at least some of these writers actually had a "covert" teaching concerning the need to rule like a beast that contradicts what they overtly taught. Interestingly, however, he challenges what the ancient writers overtly taught based on what supposedly at least some of these writers covertly taught, thus appealing to tradition in order to combat tradition. Or perhaps Machiavelli is attributing a covert teaching to them that they did not in fact have, and thus hiding his own novelty while seeming to appeal to an ancient teaching.

Since the prince must know how to use the nature of the beast as well as the nature of man, Machiavelli recommends that among the beasts he choose the fox and the lion, explaining: "for the lion does not defend himself from traps, and the fox does not defend himself from wolves. He must, therefore, be a fox to recognize traps, and a lion to awe the wolves." In saying this, Machiavelli refers to a discussion in the most widely read moral treatise of his time, Cicero's *On Duties* (*De Officiis*), and thus indicates a great departure he is making from what others have written on his subject. Cicero writes: "There are two ways in which injustice may be done, either through force or through deceit; and deceit seems to belong to a little fox, force to a lion. Both of them seem most alien to a human being; but deceit deserves a greater hatred. And out of all injustice, nothing deserves punishment more than that of men who, just at the time when they are most betraying trust, act in such a way that they might appear to be good men."[27]

Now, in Machiavelli's Aesopian tale, lions (force) awe wolves (rapacious appetite), but foxes (cleverness) recognize traps or snares, which suggests a method of hunting used by humans with their own cleverness. Humans are therefore also foxlike, but according to Machiavelli many princes "simply stick with the methods of the lion" to awe the wolves and do not understand that they also need to use the methods of the fox to avoid the traps set by clever men. Lions do not seem to be aware of such traps or think that their awesome force is sufficient. Foxes in turn are aware of deceit and the need to use deceit, and are therefore the exemplars of knowing when to break faith, the subject of this chapter. Machiavelli now draws the moral of his fable: "Therefore, a prudent lord cannot, nor should he, observe faith when such observance turns against himself, and when the reasons that made him promise it are eliminated." He then explains why this is the case: "And if men were all good, this precept would not be good; but because they are wicked, and they would not observe faith for you, you too do not have to observe it for them." When claiming that ancient writers covertly taught the need to use both the beast and the man through the image of the half-man and half-beast Chiron Machiavelli called the centaur a "preceptor" (*precettore*), and now he himself offers a bestial image that is half lion and half fox and draws a "precept" (*precetto*) from his fable. Machiavelli emerges as a new preceptor who teaches princes that they need not, indeed cannot, observe faith given that men are not "all good" and are in fact "wicked."[28]

At the outset of this chapter Machiavelli characterized the actions of faith-breaking princes "in our own times" as being blatantly obvious to everyone, and now he justifies this faith-breaking as "legitimate" given the state of human affairs, but he also counsels the prince to "color" or "paint over" his inobservance of faith. He claims that he could provide "infinite modern examples" of such behavior and states that those who have known how to "use the fox" have succeeded better. His characterization of these "infinite modern examples" might seem simply to repeat what he stated at the outset of the chapter about the actions of princes "in our own times," unless it is the case that those who know best how to "use the fox" have not been so blatant about breaking faith and have instead successfully "colored" their actions to appear otherwise. This suggestion perhaps makes sense of what Machiavelli next writes: "But it is necessary to know how to color this nature well, and to be a great pretender and dissembler, and men are so very simple, and they so well obey present necessities, that he who deceives will always find someone who will allow himself to be deceived." The foxlike prince uses his foresight and cleverness to overcome those who are shortsighted and "so very simple."

While he has claimed that he could provide "infinite modern examples" of such behavior, Machiavelli does "not want to be silent about" one of the "fresh" examples: Pope Alexander VI. (Recall that Pope Julius II was his "fresh example" in chapter 13.) His portrait of the pontiff is shocking: "Alexander VI never did anything, never thought about anything, other than deceiving men, and he always found a subject to whom he could do it." Alexander succeeded in his deceit, Machiavelli comments, "because he knew well this aspect of the world." Are we meant to be surprised that the prince of the Church, who inculcates and relies on the faith of his flock for their obedience, is so ready to abuse that faith, or so successful at doing so? Is there something about faith that makes men more credulous in modern times despite what they observe all around them?

The announced subject of this chapter is in what way faith should be kept by princes, but Machiavelli abruptly broadens his scope to take up a general discussion of the qualities that are praised and blamed. "Thus it is not necessary for a prince actually to have all the above written qualities, but it is very necessary to seem to have them." As he has progressed in his discussion, Machiavelli has moved from stating that it would be praiseworthy or laudable for a prince to have all of the qualities that are held to be good, to then qualifying that statement that he cannot always observe them, to the point where he now more bluntly argues that the important thing is to "seem to have them." The reader is now prepared for an even more daring lesson. "Indeed, I shall dare to say the following: that when these qualities are possessed and always observed they are harmful. And when they seem to be possessed, they are useful." If these qualities are harmful when they are "always" possessed and observed, Machiavelli does not deny that they are sometimes useful. What he does state is that it is always useful to *seem* to possess them. This observation helps us understand what he next writes: "So that it is useful to seem compassionate, faithful, humane, honest, and religious—and to be so, but to stay so constructed in your spirit that if it is necessary not to be these things, you are able and know how to become the contrary." Sometimes, it seems, it is useful both to "seem" to have these qualities as well as to actually possess them ("and to be so"), but other times one must "become the contrary," in the best case maintaining the appearance of seeming to have them. Is possessing these qualities sometimes good because the qualities themselves are truly virtues, or are they only virtues when it is "useful" to possess them? Machiavelli does not say.

Instead, he proceeds to give his daring lesson added emphasis: "And one must understand the following: that a prince, and especially a new prince, cannot observe all of those things for which men are believed good, since to maintain his state" the prince must "often" act in a contrary way. "And for this reason he needs to have a spirit disposed to change as the winds of fortune and the variation of things command him, and, as I said above, not to depart from the good if he is able, but to know how to enter into evil when he needs to." Machiavelli has never quite said above what he claims to have said, for among other things he has not yet used the terminology of "good" and "evil." At the end of chapter 15 he argued that some things "appear a virtue" but lead to the prince's ruin while other things "appear a vice" but result "in his security and well being," thus at least coming close to equating virtue and vice with (political) success and failure. Now he plainly states that a prince must know how to "enter into evil" when necessary in order to "maintain his state." In short, Machiavelli maintains a studied ambiguity about whether "traditional" virtues and vices, or good and evil, are indeed actually virtues and vices, and must regrettably be violated due to political necessity, or whether political necessity and success define what is virtuous or vicious or that the "effectual truth" is that the true virtues and vices are "political" virtues and vices. The only lesson he has unambiguously offered is that it is always best to seem to possess and observe "traditional" virtues.

Without addressing the riddle of what are truly virtues and vices, Machiavelli instead presses his unambiguous lesson concerning the utility of appearance. "Thus a prince must take great care that nothing ever leave his mouth that is not full of the five qualities stated above, and that he appear, to hear him and to look at him, all compassion, all faith, all integrity, all humaneness, all religion— and there is nothing more necessary to appear to have than this last quality." His emphasis on the paramount importance of appearing religious is somewhat surprising, for why devote chapters to liberality, compassion, and keeping faith and not focus on religiosity if it is so important? Yet all but one of the five qualities he mentions concern religion. As noted already, "compassion" translates *pietà*, which also means "piety," "faith" (*fede*) means faith in the religious sense as well as "faithful" in keeping promises, and "humanity" (*humanità*) is opposed by Machiavelli in chapter 15 to "prideful" (*superbo*) and therefore relates to the Christian virtue of humility. Perhaps his focus on modern examples in this chapter is meant to signal to us that he is departing in particular from what Christian writers have said about these qualities.

In order to explain why a prince should take great care concerning appearances or, as he states, concerning what others hear coming out of his mouth or see when looking at him, Machiavelli writes: "And men in general judge more with their eyes than their hands, because everyone sees what you seem to be, few feel what you are—and those few do not dare to oppose the opinion of the many, who have the majesty of the state that defends them."

The emphasis he puts on sensory experience here is striking. As we anticipated when analyzing the metaphor he employs in the Dedicatory Letter of an artist placing himself in the plain so that he can "consider" the mountain (or princes) and atop the mountain in order to "consider" the plain (or peoples), reliance upon sight alone is potentially deceptive because appearances themselves can be deceptive, sometimes intentionally so. Machiavelli here aligns what we see with our eyes to opinion, which leads to mistaken judgments, and what we touch with our hands to what truly is ("what you are"). If "those few" who "feel what you are" do not "dare" to oppose the opinion of the many, Machiavelli himself dares to do so, for as he stated just above: "Indeed, I shall dare say the following: that when these qualities are possessed and always observed they are harmful. And when they seem to be possessed, they are useful." If the prince must take great care "that nothing ever leave his mouth that is not full" of those qualities held to be virtuous, Machiavelli dares to speak differently.

Given what he has said about men not being all good and about most men judging by what they see as opposed to feel, Machiavelli offers the prince some concluding advice. "And in the actions of all men, and especially of princes (where there is no judge to whom to protest), one looks to the end. Therefore let a prince act so as to win and maintain his state; the means will always be judged honorable and praised by everyone. For the masses are always captivated by appearances, and by the outcome of the thing, and in the world there are only the masses, and the few have no standing when the many have someone to support them." The "end" (*fine*) of princes is to acquire and maintain their states, and Machiavelli claims that if they succeed the "means" will be judged honorable and praised by "everyone." If we are tempted to conclude he is arguing that the ends justify the means, there is nonetheless a complication: the praise accorded to those means is given by "everyone," or the "masses" (*vulgo*), who are taken in by appearances and by the "outcome" (*evento*), and who are therefore poor judges. Perhaps one solution is that the "end" of the prince is different from the "outcome" as judged by the vulgar. For example, the prince's "end" of acquiring and maintaining power may lead him to use certain "means" such as favoring the people over the great or not being rapacious with their goods and women, not because these "means" are somehow good or "ends" in themselves but because they help him attain his "end," whereas the "masses" praise the "outcome" they perceive of the prince favoring them instead of the great or not plundering their property and are therefore mistaken about the prince's true "end."[29] Alternatively, but not in contradiction to what has been suggested, perhaps "everyone" or "the masses" allow themselves to be duped concerning the prince's true nature and ends. As Lefort suggests: "They would like to believe in his virtue, in a good image, and it is enough for them that he not make that belief impossible for them to be satisfied. In sum, if it is not difficult for him to mystify them, it is because that is their wish."[30]

If Machiavelli "dares" to let things come out of his mouth that others dare not say, he ends the chapter with curious caution. "A certain prince of present times, whom it is best not to name, never preaches anything but peace and faith, and he is a great enemy of both; and if he had observed both, either his reputation or his state would have been taken from him many times." Most interpreters take "a certain prince" to refer to Ferdinand of Spain, whom Machiavelli unhesitatingly names in chapter 21 and characterizes as making use of religion as a pretext for acts of "pious cruelty." As we have seen, Machiavelli's discussion of keeping faith in this chapter, and of compassion or mercy or piety in the previous chapter, have significant religious overtones, so perhaps his caution in concluding this chapter has less to do with "a certain prince" than with the uses and abuses of religion "in our own times."

CHAPTER 19: ON AVOIDING CONTEMPT AND HATRED

Chapter 19 is the longest chapter in *The Prince*, and also somewhat anomalous in other respects. Part of its anomalous character derives from its uncertain place among the series of chapters beginning in chapter 15 concerning the qualities for which men and especially princes are praised or criticized. As we have seen, at the end of chapter 18 Machiavelli broadens his treatment of one of the qualities held to be praiseworthy, keeping faith, to a more general discussion of the need to appear to have "all the above written qualities" and particularly certain ones he names. Chapter 18 and its concluding discussion might therefore seem to be a logical finale to the analysis he began in chapter 15. Yet he commences chapter 19 in a way that suggests that it is the concluding chapter to this series of chapters: "But because I have spoken concerning the most important of the qualities that are mentioned above, I want briefly to discuss the others ... ." Since chapter 20 clearly begins a new set of chapters, chapter 19 therefore seems to be the conclusion to the set of chapters on virtue and vice. Also anomalously, his "brief" discussion in chapter 19 actually contains what seems to be a lengthy digression on conspiracy and on a number of Roman emperors.

Let us begin with what "other" qualities there were remaining to be discussed in chapter 19. In chapter 15 he named eleven pairs of qualities for which men and especially princes are praised or blamed, and in chapters 16–18 he has thematically treated three pairs—liberality versus miserliness (chapter 16, pair 1), cruelty versus compassion (chapter 17, pair 3), and being faithful versus faithless (chapter 18, pair 4)—and he has also more or less incidentally taken up four more pairs—giving versus rapacious (pair 2), humane versus proud (pair 6), honest versus crafty (pair 8), and religious versus unbelieving (pair 11). Thus, if we take Machiavelli at his word, four more pairs remain to be discussed: effeminate and pusillanimous versus fierce and spirited (pair 5), lascivious versus chaste (pair 7), hard versus easygoing (pair 9), and serious versus light (pair 10). When he introduces chapter 19, Machiavelli announces that he wants to discuss the other qualities "... under the following general terms: that the prince should think, as is said in part above, to avoid those things that could make him hateful and contemptible, and whenever he will avoid this thing, he will have fulfilled his duties and he will not find any peril at all in the other infamies."[31] The qualities he has not so far discussed do in fact seem to be those that might make a prince either particularly hated or held in contempt. What is remarkable about his statement, however, is how strong it is: as long as the prince avoids being hated or held in contempt, he can get away with all the other infamous things, even apparently without regard to appearances. Avoiding the negative extremes of being hateful or contemptible, it seems, is more important than cultivating any positive qualities.

In referring to what he has "said in part above" on the subject of the prince being hated, Machiavelli alludes to his discussion in chapter 17 of cruelty versus compassion and of love, fear, and hatred, and he also thereby indicates that there was something incomplete about that discussion. He further alludes to his earlier discussion when he repeats that what makes a prince particularly hateful is when he is rapacious with the property and women of his subjects, and he now adds that the "generality of men" live content if the prince abstains from doing so. Further, he adds another consideration: "One has only to combat the ambition of the few, which is checked in many ways and with facility." Recall his discussion in chapter 9 of the people and the great, with the great wanting to oppress and the people wanting not to be oppressed, and how the prince should if possible found himself on the people. The question of whether and how to found on the people versus the great has returned for our consideration, and this reconsideration will shortly lead Machiavelli to digress on certain Roman emperors.

As for what makes the prince contemptible, Machiavelli lists his being held to be effeminate, pusillanimous, and irresolute, and cautions the prince "to guard himself as from a reef" against such appearances. The prince should contrive to make himself seen as great, spirited, weighty, and strong. These negative and positive qualities correspond more or less to the qualities still remaining to be discussed. In sum, he urges the prince to be resolute in his pronouncements to his subjects and to cultivate such a reputation that no one thinks of deceiving him. The issue of deception immediately leads him to the other apparent digression in chapter 19, on conspiracies.

The great reputation the prince creates concerning himself turns out to be all-important, for such a reputation makes it difficult to conspire against him. Conspiracy now surprisingly becomes a dominant theme of chapter 19, and it is perhaps worth noting that if the longest chapter of *The Prince* is concerned with conspiracies, so too is the longest chapter of the *Discourses on Livy* (III.6). Interestingly, in this regard, Machiavelli's discussion of conspiracies in chapter 19 of *The Prince* leads him to what he terms a "discourse" on certain Roman emperors, further evoking his other major political writing. At any rate, having raised the issue of conspiracies, Machiavelli explains that a prince must have two "fears": "one inside, on account of his subjects, the other outside, on account of external powers." As for external threats, he explains that the prince can defend himself with good arms and good allies, and that good arms will bring him good allies. This statement is reminiscent of what he said at the outset of chapter 12 about good arms being the condition for good laws, so apparently good arms are the condition for both internal and external security. Recalling this earlier statement helps prepare us for what Machiavelli next writes: "And internal things will always stand firm when external ones stand firm, unless they have already been disturbed by a conspiracy." Back to the problem of conspiracy. Oddly, as supposed proof that a prince can survive the motions caused by external things if he stands firm, Machiavelli returns to the example of Nabis the Spartan, whom we saw in chapter 9 as a supposed instance of a prince who successfully founded himself on the people and was able to withstand attack from outside. The example is odd here because Nabis was in fact killed through conspiracy. How can a prince guard himself against conspiracy?

The prince has to be concerned about conspiracies from his subjects even when "external things are not in motion," Machiavelli explains, but a prince can secure himself against these conspiracies by avoiding being hated and despised and by keeping the people satisfied, and Machiavelli here explicitly refers the reader back to his discussion in chapter 9 of a prince founding himself on the people. "And one of the most powerful remedies a prince has against conspiracies is to be not hated by his people." Being "not hated" by the people—he does not say being loved by them—deters would-be conspirators, who have to worry about being betrayed by their fellow conspirators, an issue Machiavelli discusses at length in his treatment of conspiracies in the *Discourses on Livy*. "And to reduce the thing to brief terms, I say that on the side of the conspirator there is only fear, apprehension and worry about a punishment that frightens them; but on the side of the prince there is the majesty of the principality, the laws, the defenses of his friends and of his state that defend him. So that when popular benevolence is added to all these things, it is impossible that anyone should be so foolhardy as to conspire ... since he has the people as his enemy, and for this reason he can hope for no refuge whatsoever."

Of the "infinite examples" he could give "of this matter," Machiavelli will content himself with one instance that happened in recent memory (in 1445). What "this matter" may be is unclear, but given the story he recounts it appears to relate to what he has said about the "impossibility" of a conspiracy when the prince has "popular good will." If so, his example is extremely inapt, and so we will have to wonder why he chooses it. He relates how Messer Annibale Bentivoglio of Bologna, whom he specifies was the grandfather of the "present" Messer Annibale, was assassinated in a conspiracy led by a rival family with only his infant son surviving him, whereupon the people of Bologna rose up and killed the conspirators out of "popular good will." "This benevolence was so great," he continues, that they found the son of a blacksmith in Florence who was rumored to be a member of the Bentivoglio family and gave him the government of the city until the infant who survived the conspiracy came of age.[32] While it is true that the story demonstrates the "popular good will" toward the Bentivoglio family given that the people killed the conspirators, that good will did not after all prevent Messer Annibale the elder from being killed in a conspiracy. Moreover, by specifying that the assassinated prince was the grandfather of the "present" Messer Annibale, Machiavelli would be drawing the attention of his contemporary reader to recent affairs in Bologna: the fact that the infant son of Messer Annibale the elder, who came to power when his former blacksmith cousin died, was ousted from power in 1506 and that his son, the present Messer Annibale the younger, regained power in 1511 only to lose it the next year. What are we to make of this example, chosen among "infinite" possible examples, which seems to illustrate that a prince is vulnerable to conspiracies even when he has "popular good will" on his side, contrary to Machiavelli's thesis? This is the kind of thing Machiavelli does that makes some readers suspect that *The Prince* is less a book of advice for a prince than either a parody of princes or a trap for them.[33] As for the possibility that he is setting a trap for a prince, and even the prince to whom he dedicates the book, it is worth recalling that just prior to writing *The Prince* Machiavelli himself was imprisoned and tortured by the Medici on suspicion that he was involved in a conspiracy against them.

With this inapt example offered, Machiavelli doubles down on his thesis: "I conclude therefore that a prince must hold conspiracies of little account, if the people are benevolent to him. But if they are his enemy, and they have hatred for him, he must fear everything and everyone." Perhaps his real point is that the prince who is hated by the people knows he has enemies and must be alert to conspiracies whereas a prince who has a people benevolent toward him is lulled into a false sense of security. In this chapter Machiavelli has returned to the issue he discussed earlier in the work, especially in chapter 9, concerning founding on the people as opposed to on the great, and now he raises it again. "And well-ordered states and wise princes have with all diligence taken care not to make the great desperate and to satisfy the people and keep them content, because this is one of the most important matters that concern a prince." How this is related to the danger of conspiracies he does not say, but one element of the story about the Bentivoglio he did not underscore was that the dissatisfaction of the "great," a rival family, was the source of the conspiracy despite "popular benevolence" toward the ruling family. How can a prince manage the conflict between the great and the people in such a way as to avoid conspiracy?

Having signaled that "well-ordered states and wise princes" have managed this conflict, Machiavelli gives an example from "our times": the Kingdom of France. "In it," he explains, "are found infinite good institutions on which the liberty and the security of the king depend, of which the first is the Parlement and its authority." Note that these institutions give the king "liberty and security," by which Machiavelli seems to mean freedom of action and security from conspiracies, among other things, and he does not here claim that these institutions give anyone else liberty. In chapter 4 Machiavelli gave France as an example of the kind of state that is easy to enter but difficult to hold for a prince who wished to acquire it, explaining that the barons in the state hold their own states not due to the favor of the king but due to their ancient bloodlines. The barons therefore pose a problem for the king of France, "for always one finds some malcontents and some who want to revolt" (chap. 4, 52). To return to chapter 19, Machiavelli writes: "For the person who ordered that kingdom," apparently referring to King Louis IX, who ruled in the thirteenth century, "recognized the ambition of the powerful and their insolence, and he judged that a bit in their mouth was necessary to correct them; and, on the other hand, he recognized that the hatred of the populace against the great was founded on fear." In order not to seem to favor either the great or the populace, and thereby bring on himself anyone's hatred, the king hit on the idea of creating the Parlement, beginning with the Parlement of Paris but with more parlements being added later. The Parlement was a judicial court, not a legislative body, and through this third party the king could "beat down the great and favor the lesser folk" without drawing any blame on himself. "And this order could not have been better or more prudent, nor could there be a greater cause for the security of the king and the kingdom." If hatred engenders conspiracies, then the institutional solution of erecting the Parlement kept the king from being hated, and thus conspired against, while allowing him to manage the conflict between the great and the people. Machiavelli draws a conclusion: "Again I conclude that a prince must esteem the great, but not make himself hated by the people." But hasn't he just shown that the greater threat to the king of France, not to mention to the Bentivoglio, came from the disgruntled great rather than from the people?

Machiavelli now imagines "many" readers coming forward to object to "this opinion of mine" concerning a prince not making himself hated by the people: "It would appear perhaps to many, if the life and death of some Roman emperors is considered, that these emperors were examples contrary to this opinion of mine, since they could find some emperor who always lived excellently and showed great virtue of spirit, but nonetheless lost his empire, or indeed was killed by his own men who had plotted against him." Machiavelli answers that he wants to respond to these counterexamples, and will do so by discussing the qualities of certain emperors, "showing that the causes of their ruin were not dissimilar to what has been advanced by me; and, on the other hand, I shall put under consideration those things that are notable to whoever reads the actions of those times."[34] By stating that he will do more than respond to the apparent counterexamples by also considering other "notable" things from the period of Roman history he will examine, Machiavelli prepares us for what he all but announces is a digression from his subject.

Commencing his digression, Machiavelli explains that the period of about a century from Marcus Aurelius (121–180 CE) and Maximinus (c.173–238 CE), or about sixty years counting from Marcus' death, will "suffice" for his purposes. This period followed a century of relative peace and prosperity, with orderly succession of emperors who died in their sleep, ending with Marcus Aurelius, and was a period of tumult and disorderly succession, ending with the division and near collapse of the Roman Empire following the assassination of Maximinus. What is perhaps most notable, if not unique, about the period under examination was the power of the Praetorian Guard and the army more generally. Originally formed by the first emperor, Augustus, the Praetorian Guard was the emperor's personal guard, but it eventually gained enough power to make and unmake emperors. As Machiavelli therefore explains, in addition to the problem in other principalities of contending with "the ambition of the great and the insolence of the people," the Roman emperors faced "a third difficulty": "to have to endure the cruelty and avarice of their soldiers." If the modern example of the Kingdom of France shows how the ambition of the great and insolence of the people can be managed by a third party, the Parlement, the ancient example of the Roman emperors also essentially managed the conflict between the people and the great by making that conflict irrelevant due to an even more dangerous third party, the army. Perhaps we should also recall in this regard the praise Machiavelli gave in chapter 13 to a French king who "understood the necessity of arming oneself with one's own arms" and thus created an army composed both of men-at-arms (barons) and infantry (people) (chap. 13, 83). If the French also solved the problem of how to use "one's own arms," the Roman army in the time of the emperors seems more like mercenary troops, or at least they were no longer the emperor's "own arms."

The presence and strength of the soldiers in the period of the Roman Empire Machiavelli will discuss complicated the emperors' ability to found on the people and not be hated by them, that is, their ability to follow Machiavelli's advice on the subject. Whereas the Roman people "loved quiet" and therefore "loved modest princes," the army loved "the prince of military spirit" and wanted him to be "insolent, cruel, and rapacious" so that they could satisfy their own "avarice and cruelty." He explains that this situation made it so that those emperors who, "whether by nature or by art, did not have a great reputation" in order to hold both the people and the army in check, were "always ruined." Most of them, and especially those who came to the principate as "new men," that is with the aid of the Praetorian Guard or other troops, recognized that they could not satisfy "two different humors" and therefore turned to satisfying their troops at the expense of the people. In chapter 9 Machiavelli diagnosed every city as having two "humors," the great and the people, with their different appetites for oppressing and not being oppressed, but in Rome it seems that the body of soldiers replaces the great as the second "humor," although the soldiers share the great's appetite for oppressing. Machiavelli does not blame the emperors for siding with the soldiers, for he explains that it is necessary to avoid the hatred of the more powerful group or "collective" (*università*), a term used in medieval legal and political thought to denote a collectivity with a shared, recognized interest, including the collectivity of the people itself. The Praetorian Guard and the army comprised such a "collective" during this period of the Roman Empire. The emperor's decision to favor the troops, he comments, "turned out to be useful or not for them depending on whether that prince knew how to maintain his reputation with them."

With this lengthy prologue at an end, Machiavelli turns to an even lengthier analysis of the various emperors and their fates. It will be useful to summarize these emperors, how they attained the empire, and how they died, in Table 8.1.

Rather than following Machiavelli step by step through his discussion of these emperors, I will try to bring together what he says in such a way as to illuminate his main points.

Table 8.1 Roman Emperors Discussed in Chapter 19 of *The Prince*

Emperor	How Attained the Empire	How Died (Year CE)
Marcus Aurelius	Adopted son of predecessor	Died of natural causes (180)
Commodus	Son of Marcus Aurelius	Assassinated (192)
Pertinax	Proclaimed by Praetorian Guard	Murdered by Praetorian Guard (193)
Julianus	Proclaimed by Praetorian Guard	Executed by Senate (193)
Septimus Severus	Seized control with troops	Died of natural causes (211)
Antoninus Caracalla	Son of Septimus Severus	Murdered by soldiers (217)
Macrinus	Proclaimed by Praetorian Guard	Executed (218)
Heliogabalus	Proclaimed by troops	Murdered by Praetorian Guard (222)
Severus Alexander	Adoptive heir of Heliogabalus	Murdered by army (235)
Maximinus	Proclaimed by troops	Murdered by Praetorian Guard (238)

Machiavelli begins his analysis of these emperors by stating that all of those who were "of modest life, lovers of justice, enemies to cruelty, humane and benign" (namely, Marcus Aurelius, Pertinax, and Severus Alexander) had a bad end with the exception of Marcus Aurelius. (Incidentally, the sentence just quoted contains one of the very few uses of the word "justice" in *The Prince*.) The reason he gives for the exception of Marcus is that he succeeded to the empire by hereditary right and did not have to acknowledge his power from either the soldiers or the people. He characterizes Marcus as having "many virtues that made him venerable" and that enabled him to keep the soldiers and the people in check while becoming neither "hated nor despised." Was Marcus' success due to the fact that he was a hereditary prince, or due to his virtues, or due to avoiding becoming hated or despised? Recall in this light that Marcus was the last emperor in a line of rulers stretching back nearly a century who succeeded to the empire in an orderly manner through hereditary succession (either as the natural heir or more often the adopted heir of the previous emperor). At any rate, Marcus reigns as the exception to the general rule of what befell these emperors.

The relevant comparison to Marcus, therefore, would be his son Commodus, who also succeeded to the empire by hereditary right. Machiavelli briefly mentions Commodus in the following paragraph as an emperor who came to a bad end due to being "most cruel and rapacious," but takes up Commodus a few paragraphs later: "But let us come to Commodus, who had great facility in holding his empire because he had it by hereditary right … . And he needed only to follow in the footsteps of his father, and he would have satisfied both the soldiers and the people." Instead, he explains, Commodus had "a cruel and bestial spirit" who practiced his "rapacity" on the people by indulging his troops. However, it was less the hatred of the people that led to his downfall than the fact that he undermined his dignity (unlike his father) by fighting with gladiators and other such actions unworthy of an emperor and thereby became contemptible in the eyes of the soldiers. "And since he was hated by one side and despised by the other, there was a conspiracy against him and he was killed." Could Commodus have succeeded, in part due to his hereditary right, if he had not become contemptible to the soldiers despite being hated by the people? At any rate, it is clear from the example of Commodus that being a hereditary prince is not sufficient, and therefore we can infer that Marcus Aurelius' success and good end depended either on his virtue or his avoiding being hated or despised.

The other two emperors Machiavelli mentions along with Marcus Aurelius as what we might call "good emperors" are Pertinax and Alexander Severus. As for Pertinax, Machiavelli explains that he was created emperor against the will of the soldiers and tried to bring the troops back to an "honest life" since they had grown licentious under Commodus. His actions toward the soldiers made him hated, and he was also despised by them because of his old age. He was therefore "ruined," a polite way of saying that he was assassinated by the Praetorian Guard. Based on the example of Pertinax Machiavelli notes that hatred can be acquired "by means of good works as well as wicked ones," and refers his reader back to his earlier discussions, in chapters 15 and 18, concerning the need for a prince who wants to maintain his state "to be not good." Is he suggesting that Pertinax should have learned "to be not good"? Should he have continued to indulge the troops and thereby incurred the hatred of the people? As for Alexander Severus, Machiavelli explains that this "good emperor" who observed the rule of law was "held to be effeminate" and was therefore disdained by the army, which conspired against him and killed him. In both cases, then, these "good emperors" fell prey to their troops because they were hated or held in contempt. Once again, the exception among the "good emperors" was Marcus Aurelius, and perhaps we can now conclude that he succeeded less because of his virtue than because he avoided being hated or disdained, which is after all the title of the present chapter: "On Avoiding Contempt and Hatred."

From the "good emperors" who suffered a bad end Machiavelli turns to the "most cruel and rapacious" emperors (namely, Commodus, Septimus Severus, Antoninus Caracalla, and Maximinus), all of whom also had a bad end, with the exception of Septimus Severus. These emperors satisfied the soldiers at the expense of the people, that is, they employed the strategy Machiavelli perhaps hinted could have been used by Pertinax. Why did they all come to a bad end, again with the exception of Septimus Severus? We have already discussed Commodus, who was hated by the people and despised by the army, which killed him. As for Antoninus Caracalla, who succeeded to the empire by hereditary right from Septimus Severus and who is therefore parallel to Commodus, Machiavelli explains that, like his father, he was "a man of excellent parts, which made him marvelous in the sight of the people and welcome to the soldiers." Nonetheless, "his ferocity and cruelty were so great and so unheard of ... that he became most hateful to all the world." Antoninus was therefore killed by one of his own centurions, whose brother the emperor had disgraced and killed, a story that leads Machiavelli to comment on the fact that an "obstinate spirit" of this sort is unstoppable in his revenge. If Commodus erred by becoming contemptible in the eyes of his soldiers, Antoninus seems to have erred by becoming hateful to them, or at least to some of them. As for Maximinus, the last emperor in terms of the time period being covered, Machiavelli states that he too was a warlike man who gained the favor of the army, which elected him to the empire. Nonetheless, he explains, Maximinus soon lost his state by becoming both hateful and contemptible: contemptible because of his lowly origins and hateful because of the reputation he gained as "a very cruel man." As a result, the Senate conspired with "all the people of Rome and all of Italy," and the army ultimately killed him not only because they were "disgusted with his cruelty," but, perhaps more so, because he was failing in a siege he was conducting (and, by implication, therefore unable to satisfy the troops' rapacity). Could Maximinus have succeeded if he had been able to satisfy the army despite being hated by the people? In several cases we have seen that the real danger to "good" and "bad" emperors alike arose from being hated or held in contempt by the army, whether or not they were hated by the people. If so, then the existence of the separate "humor" of the group of soldiers during the period of Roman history Machiavelli is examining is the critical factor in explaining the fates, and especially the bad fates, of these emperors.

What about the exceptional case of Septimus Severus, the "bad emperor" who nonetheless succeeded and died in his bed? Having noted that these "cruel and rapacious" emperors all met a "wretched end" except Severus, Machiavelli offers an initial explanation for this exception: "For in Severus there was such virtue that, by maintaining the soldiers as his friends, although the people were burdened by him, he was able always to rule happily. For these virtues of his made him so marvelous in the sight of the soldiers and the people that the latter remained somehow stupefied and astonished, and the former reverent and satisfied." Machiavelli's language here echoes what he wrote earlier in *The Prince* concerning the effect Cesare Borgia's spectacular execution of Remirro de Orco had on the people of the Romagna, leaving them "at once satisfied and stupefied" (chap. 7, 62). What were Severus' astonishing virtues? Machiavelli writes: "And because the actions of that man were great and noteworthy in a new prince, I want briefly to show to what extent he knew well how to use the person [*persona*] of the lion and of the fox, whose natures, I say above, are necessary for a prince to imitate." If we look back to his discussion in chapter 18 of the lion and the fox we see that he did not counsel a prince to "imitate" them, as he writes here, but rather to "use" the nature of man and beast, and among the beasts to "choose" the lion and the fox. In addition to now instead speaking of imitation, Machiavelli interestingly writes that a prince must know how to use the "person" (*persona*) of the lion and of the fox. The term "person" or "persona" originally referred to a mask worn by an actor, hence our use of "persona" to refer to a kind of role someone takes on in certain circumstances that is not identical to their true character. Using the "person" or "persona" of the lion and of the fox therefore means to take on these bestial roles as needed. Machiavelli therefore explains that Severus' "virtues" made him "so marvelous" "in the sight" of both the soldiers and the people; it seems that Severus played his parts well.[35]

To show how Severus used the "person" of the lion and of the fox, Machiavelli relates how he persuaded his troops to avenge the death of Pertinax by killing Pertinax's short-lived successor, Julianus. "And under this color, without showing that he aspired to the empire," he made his way to Rome, was elected emperor, and killed Julianus. Since he wanted to become "lord of all the state," that is sole lord, Severus then used the nature of the fox to trick his rivals in the eastern and western portions of the empire, Niger and Albinus. Summing up, Machiavelli writes: "And whoever will examine minutely the actions of this man will discover him a most ferocious lion and a most clever fox, and he will see him feared and revered by everyone, and by the army not hated, and he will not marvel that Severus, a new man, will have been able to hold so great an empire, because his very great reputation always defended him from that hatred which, on account of his robberies, people could have been able to conceive." In keeping with the language of appearance and play-acting he has used with regard to Severus, Machiavelli's emphasis in explaining his success is on Severus' ability to maintain "his very great reputation" in order to instill fear and awe, but not hatred, and especially not to become hated (or held in contempt) by the army. In sum, Severus' success and happy end is the flip side of those emperors, "good" or "bad," who met a less happy end: he avoided the reputation of being hated or held in contempt, particularly with regard to the soldiers.

Machiavelli concludes his analysis of these Roman emperors by quickly dispatching of Heliogabalus, Macrinus, and Julianus, saying that he will not reason about them since they were "entirely contemptible" and were immediately eliminated. We might wonder why he even mentioned them in the first place if he was not going to reason about them, except perhaps for the sake of completeness. Perhaps by his very dismissal of these emperors because they were "entirely contemptible" Machiavelli underscores the problem faced by all of the emperors he discusses due to their reputation with the soldiers. What about the two exceptional emperors who died in their beds: Marcus Aurelius and Septimus Severus? We have seen that Marcus' success does not seem to have depended critically on his attaining the empire by hereditary right, but instead seems to have been due to the other two factors Machiavelli names: his "many virtues" and especially his avoiding being hated or held in contempt. As for Severus, he is also said to have possessed considerable "virtues," though different virtues from those of Marcus, and these virtues likewise allowed him to avoid being hated or held in contempt. Let us return to the metaphor of chapter 18 of the centaur as teaching princes "to use both the beast and the man" (93–94), mentioned above with regard to Severus. Given that Machiavelli uses Severus to illustrate how a prince might successfully use or imitate the beastly natures of the lion and the fox, we might consider Marcus, whom he first introduces as "Marcus the philosopher," as a prince who successfully "used" the man. Marcus and Severus seem to represent the two halves of Machiavelli's model of a half-man and half-beast teacher of the art of ruling.

Why has Machiavelli led us through this seeming digression on certain Roman emperors? Has he thereby accomplished what he claimed he wanted to do at the outset, namely defend "this opinion of mine" concerning the need to avoid being hated by the people as well as consider "those things that are notable to whoever reads of the actions of those times"? As for the issue of hatred, we have noted that his treatment of these Roman emperors focused on how being hated or held in contempt led to the downfall of most of them, in keeping with the subject announced in the chapter title: "On Avoiding Contempt and Hatred." However, in the case of these emperors, it was less the hatred or contempt of the people than of the army that proved problematic. This leads us to what is most "notable" about the time he is examining, namely that the existence of a body of soldiers became a "humor" with which the emperors had to contend along with the "humor" of the people.

In concluding his digression on Rome, Machiavelli in essence once again underscores its digressive character by saying that the princes "of our own times" do not have the same worry, or at least "have less of this difficulty of satisfying their soldiers extra-ordinarily." He explains that none of these modern princes "keeps together armies that are experienced in the government and administration of provinces, as were the armies of the Roman empire." He alludes to a consideration he has not explicitly raised: the sheer extent of the Roman Empire meant that its far-flung provinces required administration by powerful generals with their armies and prolonged commands that made their troops loyal to their generals and a threat to Rome. In the *Discourses on Livy* (III.24) Machiavelli argues that these prolonged commands were among the main causes for the collapse of the republic.

Having said that modern princes do not face the same difficulty the Romans did with regard to the army, Machiavelli draws an extremely curious parallel to modern times: "And for this reason, if then it was more necessary to satisfy the soldiers than the people, because the soldiers could do more than the people, today, for all princes except for the Turk and the Sultan, it is more necessary to satisfy the people than the soldiers, because the people can do more than the soldiers." He excepts the Turk, that is the Ottoman Sultan, because the security and strength of his kingdom depend on his army. Similarly, he explains the kingdom of the Sultan, that is the Mamluk sultanate in Egypt, is entirely dependent on the soldiers. Then he makes a curious comparison: "And you should notice that this state of the Sultan is unlike all the other princi-palities, because it is similar to the Christian pontificate, which cannot be called either a hereditary principality or a new princi-pality." He explains that the children of the Sultan are not his heirs, but a new Sultan is elected. "And since this order is ancient, it cannot be called a new principality, since there are not any of those difficulties in it that there are in new ones. For even if the prince is new, the orders of the state are old, and they are established to welcome him as though he were their hereditary lord." One aspect of the Mamluk sultanate, especially in the latter part of the fifteenth and early sixteenth century when Machiavelli lived, he does not mention here is that it was rather similar to the Roman Empire during the period he has earlier discussed in terms of the conspiracies and assassinations against the sultans, especially by their armies. What are we supposed to learn about the Christian pontificate from either the comparison to the Mamluk sultanate or, by extension, to the period of the Roman Empire he has analyzed? Does the Christian pontiff have to satisfy his own "army," perhaps the College of Cardinals, or perhaps the factious barons in Rome he discussed in chapter 11, without regard to his people? In this light, we should recall his description in chapter 11 of ecclesiastical principalities and how they are attained either through virtue or fortune but maintained with neither and how they fail to govern, and perhaps satisfy, the people.

"But let us return to our matter," Machiavelli writes, abruptly cutting off our consideration of the surprising parallel he has drawn. "I say that whoever will consider the above-written discourse will see that either hatred or contempt has been the cause of the ruin of those emperors named above," he states, failing to mention the critical role of the soldiers. Instead, he blames the failed emperors for making a mistake in imitating a successful emperor: Pertinax and Severus Alexander as "new" princes should not have imitated Marcus Aurelius, a hereditary prince, and likewise Caracalla, Commodus, and Maximinus should not have imitated Septimus Severus because they did not possess sufficient virtue to do so.[36] We have already seen the problem with imitating the wrong type of exemplary prince, or the wrong aspects of some exemplary prince, with the case of Scipio's mistaken imitation of Xenophon's Cyrus. In his discussion of these emperors Machiavelli had not mentioned that they were imitating successful emperors, and so the question of imitation seems to be Machiavelli's own emphasis. At least one thing is peculiar about his claim here:

Commodus could not have imitated Septimus Severus because Severus reigned *after* Commodus. The only emperor discussed who Commodus could have imitated was his own father, Marcus Aurelius, especially given that he too was a hereditary prince. As Machiavelli wrote above of Commodus: "And he needed only to follow in the footsteps of his father, and he would have satisfied both the soldiers and the people." Commodus' error was in not imitating Marcus. The only way in which it seems he would have more properly been an imitator of Severus, if that were chronologically possible, is in that they shared a cruel nature, and if so his error would be that he did not, like Severus, play the fox as well as the lion. If it was chronologically impossible for Commodus to imitate Severus, it is not impossible for the would-be prince who is reading Machiavelli's work. This consideration helps explain how Machiavelli concludes his discourse: "Therefore a new prince in a new principality cannot imitate the actions of Marcus, nor again is it necessary for him to follow those of Severus. But he must choose from Severus those parts that are necessary to found his state, and from Marcus those that are appropriate and glorious for preserving a state that is already established and firm." Or, to recall what was suggested above, this prince should "use" the man, as did Marcus, and "use" the beast, as did Severus.

NOTES

1 The term *amici* was traditionally used to refer to what might be termed the partisan allies of a prince in the regime, as opposed to the subjects over whom the prince simply ruled. For example, the Medici relied upon a close network of supporters during their effectively princely rule in Florence during the fifteenth century. See Hörnqvist 2004, 39.

2 Machiavelli makes an even more audacious claim to novelty at the outset of the *Discourses on Livy* by writing: "Although the envious nature of men has always made it no less dangerous to find new modes and orders than to seek unknown waters and lands, because men are more ready to blame than to praise the actions of others, nonetheless, driven by that natural desire that has always been in me to work, without any respect for those things I believe will bring common benefit to everyone, I have decided to take a path as yet untrodden by anyone" (I Preface, 5).

3 In his "Discourse on Remodeling the State of Florence" (1520), written at the request of the Medici rulers of Florence and speaking of the opportunity to

remodel the laws and orders of the city, Machiavelli writes: "And so much has this glory been esteemed by men seeking for nothing other than glory that when unable to form a republic in reality [*in atto*], they have done it in writing [*in scritto*], as Aristotle, Plato, and many others ..." (quoted in Viroli 2013, 40).

4 Berlin 1979 [1972], 26.

5 The classic example of such an interpretation is Croce (1925).

6 The classic example of such an interpretation is Berlin (1979 [1972], esp. 44–45). See also Wolin 1960.

7 Some examples of this line of interpretation include Strauss 1958; Orwin 1978; Mansfield 1996.

8 In the *Discourses on Livy*, when discussing Romulus' fratricide, Machiavelli writes: "It is very suitable that when the deed accuses him, the effect [*effetto*] excuses him; and when the effect is good, as was that of Romulus, it will always excuse the deed" (I.9, 29).

9 Orwin 1978, 1219.

10 See Orwin 1978, 1220–22.

11 Interestingly, in his own treatment of liberality Aristotle also recognizes the danger that exercising the virtue would deplete the resources necessary for liberality, and the possibility that this situation would lead to the temptation to be unjust in order to continue being liberal. Aside from arguing that the turn to injustice is not permissible, unlike Machiavelli Aristotle does not discuss the problem of the reality versus appearance of being virtuous. See *Nicomachean Ethics* IV.1, 1121a–b.

12 Since Louis XII died on the night of December 31, 1514–January 1, 1515, this passage has been critical in attempts to date when Machiavelli completed writing *The Prince*, with the fact that he refers to Louis XII as the current king of France suggesting that he completed *The Prince* or the bulk of it by the end of 1514.

13 Julius Ceasar is Cicero's primary example of injustice being used on behalf of liberality (*On Duties* I.42).

14 See Orwin 1978, 1222–23.

15 The question of cruelty versus compassion is also central to Seneca's *On Clemency* (*De clementia*), a forerunner of the mirror-of-princes genre. Most notably, when distinguishing between a king and a tyrant, Seneca characterizes the tyrant as relying on cruelty and adopting as his motto, "Let them hate, as long as they fear" (*On Clemency* I.12).

16 Such debates can be found in a number of books in the mirror-of-princes genre. See Gilbert 1938. See also Cicero, *On Duties* II.23: "But there is nothing more suited to protecting and retaining influence than to be loved, and nothing less suited than to be feared."

17 Orwin 1978, 1224.

18 In the *Discourses on Livy* Machiavelli writes: "As all those demonstrate who reason on a civil way of life, and as every history is full of examples, it is necessary to whoever disposes a republic and orders laws in it to presuppose that all men are bad, and that they always have to use the malignity of their spirit whenever they have a free opportunity for it ... . Men never work any good

unless through necessity, but where choice abounds and one can make use of license, at once everything is full of confusion and disorder. Therefore it is said that hunger and poverty make men industrious, and the laws make them good" (I.3, 15). Note that Machiavelli does not claim that all men are bad, but only that one should take the worst case scenario of presupposing them to be bad when ordering laws.

19 Livy, *History of Rome* XXI.4.

20 Speaking of how his contemporaries do not think of imitating what they read about ancient republics and kingdoms, Machiavelli explains: "This arises, I believe, not so much from the weakness into which the present religion has led the world, or from the evil that an ambitious idleness has done to many Christian provinces and cities, as from not having a true knowledge of histories, through not getting from reading them that sense [*senso*] nor tasting that flavor that they have in themselves" (I Preface, 6). See also *Discourses on Livy* III.30 (280) where Machiavelli writes of reading the Bible "judiciously" (*sensatamente*).

21 See Livy, *History of Rome* XXVIII.24.

22 See Livy, *History of Rome* XXIX.19.

23 Actually, this characterization of Scipio as being unable to correct wrongdoers owing to his compassionate or lenient character was said not by someone in the Roman Senate, but by the Locrians themselves when they agreed to have Scipio's subordinate punished for the sacrilege without allowing Scipio himself to go unpunished. See Livy, *History of Rome* XXIX.21.

24 Livy emphasizes Scipio's great ambition for glory. See esp. *History of Rome* XXVIII.17.

25 Machiavelli evidently considered his discussion in *The Prince* of breaking faith important enough to explicitly refer the reader of the *Discourses on Livy* to it (see III.42).

26 What writers Machiavelli has in mind is not clear, but one clear possibility is Xenophon, who describes Chiron in the *Cyropaedia* (IV.3.17) as possessing a man's intelligence but the speed and strength of a horse.

27 Cicero, *On Duties* I.41.

28 The term "wicked" is perhaps too strong as a translation for the Italian *triste*, which means "wretched" or "sad," including as in the sense of "a sad state of affairs," as opposed to "evil" (*malvagio*) or "bad" (*cattivo*). Importantly, Machiavelli does not appear here to be appealing to the doctrine of original sin in his characterization of human nature.

29 Compare Machiavelli's discussion in the *Discourses on Livy* of Romulus. Having claimed that Romulus' fratricide can be justified if we consider the "end" (*fine*) he had in doing so, Machiavelli writes: "So a prudent orderer of a republic, who has the intent to wish to help not himself but the common good ... should contrive to have authority alone ... . It is very suitable that when the deed accuses him, the effect [*effetto*] excuses him; and when the effect is good, as was that of Romulus, it will always excuse the deed" (I.9, 29). See Warner and Scott 2011.

30 Lefort 2012 (2005), 170.

31 Aristotle argues that hatred and contempt are the primary reasons why tyrannies are overthrown (*Politics* V.10, 1312b).

32 See Machiavelli's account of these same events in his *Florentine Histories* (VI.9–10), where he emphasizes not so much the "popular benevolence" toward the Bentivoglio as the strong partisan conflict in Bologna.

33 See, for example, Dietz 1986.

34 The primary source Machiavelli has in mind for reading about these times is Herodian, whose *History of the Roman Empire from the Death of Marcus Aurelius* covers this very period.

35 In the *Discourses on Livy* Machiavelli writes of the emperors from Julius Caesar (who was not in fact an emperor) to Maximinus: "And if there was any criminal among those who died ordinarily, such as Severus, it arose from his very great fortune and virtue, two things that accompany few men" (I.10, 32).

36 Herodian, Machiavelli's principal historical source, notes Pertinax's "consistent and deliberate imitation of Marcus's reign" (*History* II.4). More interesting, he relates how Septimus Severus told the Senate that he had come to avenge the death of Pertinax and intended to imitate Marcus Aurelius' reign in every respect (*History* II.14).

9

PRUDENCE

The group consisting of chapters 20–23 feels like a pause after his discussion of virtue and vice in chapters 15–19 and before the concluding crescendo of *The Prince* in chapters 24–26. Machiavelli takes up a series of seemingly unrelated topics in these chapters— whether fortresses and "many other things" are useful or useless, what a prince should do to be thought outstanding, the prince's private counselors, and how to avoid flatterers. Yet these subjects can be seen as a continuation of what he stated at the outset of chapter 15 remained for him to discuss, namely how a prince should conduct himself with regard to his subjects and allies.

What seems to unify these chapters and connect them to the preceding discussion of virtue and vice is the question of prudence. Near the end of chapter 21, Machiavelli writes: "Because we find this, in the order of things, that one never tries to avoid one inconvenience without incurring another one. But prudence consists in knowing how to recognize the qualities of the inconveniences and choosing the less bad as if it were good" (111). In what is perhaps the paradigmatic account of prudence, Aristotle defines it as an intellectual virtue that deliberates about the means to achieve a given end, namely a given good or virtue. For Aristotle, prudence (*phronêsis*) necessarily aims at the good and at virtue, and for example he will not call someone "prudent" if the end he aims at is evil or vicious, but rather terms that quality a certain "cleverness," so that a successful thief might be called "clever" but not properly "prudent."[1] For Machiavelli, in turn, his novel teaching concerning virtue and vice requires a novel account of prudence. In the sentence quoted above, then, he characterizes prudence as "choosing the less bad as if it were good." He seems to thereby suggest that there is no "good" simply speaking, just as he earlier seemed to suggest that there is no "virtue" or "vice" simply speaking. If so, then what it is prudent for a prince or perhaps anyone to do depends on the circumstances, and this would help explain the unusually tentative character of much of the advice he will offer in chapters 20–23.

CHAPTER 20: WHETHER FORTRESSES AND MANY OTHER THINGS MADE OR DONE BY PRINCES EVERY DAY ARE USEFUL OR USELESS

Machiavelli begins chapter 20 with a list of topics concerning the various things princes have done to hold their states securely, and he mostly presents them in an "on the one hand, on the other hand" manner that prepares us for much of the advice he seems to offer: "it depends." Specifically, he lists six topics concerning what princes have done: (1) disarmed their subjects; (2) kept subject towns divided; (3) fed hatreds against themselves; (4) won over initially suspect subjects; (5) built fortresses; (6) ruined and destroyed fortresses. After listing them, he takes up his role as a judge on the subject only to say that he cannot yet judge: "And although on all of these things I cannot pass definitive sentence without coming to the particulars of those states where any decision like this has to be made, nonetheless I shall speak in the broad way that the matter by itself allows."

Yet the very first thing Machiavelli does after this rather indecisive introduction is to make a decisive judgment and, moreover, with regard to a topic he did not say he was going to discuss. "Thus it never happened that a new prince disarmed his subjects; on the contrary, when he has found them unarmed he has always armed them. For in arming them those arms become yours; those who are suspect to you become faithful, and those who were faithful remain so, and from subjects they are all made into your partisans." On the contrary, he says, disarming these subjects offends them: "you show them that you have diffidence toward them, whether for cowardice or lack of faith, and the one and the other of those opinions generate hatred against you." Far from founding himself on the people, the prince who disarms them makes himself hated by them. Such a prince must thus turn to mercenary arms, and Machiavelli sends his reader back to what he has said about such arms, especially in chapter 12. "For this reason, as I have said, a new prince in a new principality has always ordered the arms there." Machiavelli specifies that he is speaking of "a new prince in a new principality," or of the kind of entirely new prince and principality he discussed in chapter 6. He states that "the histories" are filled with such examples, but strangely he does not provide any examples. Perhaps he is now revealing in what sense Moses, Cyrus, Romulus, and Theseus founded their states using their "own arms": they armed their peoples.

Matters are otherwise, it seems, with a state that is not entirely new. "But when a prince acquires a new state, which like a limb is attached to his old state, then it is necessary to disarm that state, except for those who were your partisans in acquiring it," although they too must be rendered "soft and effeminate" so that "you" ultimately rely on your own soldiers from your old state. The kind of state Machiavelli is discussing is what he termed "mixed" in chapter 3. Yet the lesson he offered in chapter 3 seems to have been forgotten now, for earlier he said that malcontented subjects in such a state help bring the prince into the state but are soon disappointed. Would it be safe to arm these future malcontents? Oddly, Machiavelli will shortly recall his earlier advice when he discusses how an acquiring prince can turn those subjects whom he initially suspects to be hostile into his friends. It seems that a "mixed" state, or perhaps anything other than a new state or a state that is effectively made anew, poses a problem for a prince who wants to rely on his "own arms," because the state is made up of groups that are some of them friendly and some of them hostile.

From one topic on his list Machiavelli turns to the next, namely holding subject towns by keeping them divided. "Our own ancients, including those who were esteemed wise," he writes, referring in particular to the Medici, "used to say that it was necessary to hold Pistoia with factions and Pisa with fortresses." We have already seen Machiavelli criticize Florence's policies toward Pistoia, stating in chapter 17 that Florence allowed the factional conflict there to ruin Pistoia. Apparently "our own ancients" were not so "wise" in nourishing factions in subject towns. "This, in those times when Italy was in a certain way balanced, must have been a good feat," he writes with apparent irony, "but indeed I do not believe it can be given as a precept today." Recall that in chapter 12 Machiavelli discussed the change in the balance of power in Italy over the previous century due to the waning influence of the Holy Roman Emperor (and his Ghibelline allies) and waxing influence of the Church (and its Guelf allies), a situation that for complicated reasons discussed above led Italy to become reliant on mercenary arms and vulnerable to foreign invasion. To return to chapter 20, Machiavelli seems to allude to his earlier analysis when he writes: "On the contrary, divided cities, when the enemy approaches, are necessarily lost, because the weaker party always joins with the outside forces and the other will not be able to stay in power." What he writes here could apply equally to a specific subject town kept divided by factions, such as Pistoia, or to Italy as a whole. Machiavelli's other example of mistaken reliance on fomenting faction also evokes his earlier discussion. He relates that the Venetians also nourished the Guelf and Ghibelline "sects" in the cities subject to them, and these factions became bold after their defeat at Vailate (in 1509) and revolted. "Measures like these are therefore evidence of weakness in the prince," he concludes, "because in a strong principality such divisions will never be permitted." Even if they are profitable in peacetime, he adds, the error in relying on them becomes manifest during wartime. We might add that since the prince must think of nothing more than of war, as Machiavelli proclaimed in chapter 12, the conclusion must be that sowing divisions in subject cities is never a good strategy.

Next on his list of topics are princes who have fed hatreds against themselves, but he tackles it in a somewhat different way than one might expect. "Without doubt princes become great when they overcome the difficulties and oppositions that are made against them," he begins, and so "fortune" seems to aid them in this by making enemies arise for them to overcome, "most of all when she wants to make a new prince great." As he remarked in chapter 6, fortune provides the opportunity for a prince, and especially a completely new prince, to demonstrate his virtue. "For this reason, many judge that a wise prince, when he has the opportunity, must cleverly nourish some enmity, so that, when it is defeated, his greatness comes out increased." Machiavelli offers no judgment on what "many" judge would be a good idea for a "wise prince." Would a "wise prince" tempt fortune in this manner?

After this brief and inconclusive treatment of tempting fortune, Machiavelli moves to a lengthier treatment of princes, and especially new princes, who win over subjects whom they initially held in suspicion, finding them more faithful and more useful than those in whom they initially had confidence. Earlier in this chapter he recommended arming one's partisans in a newly acquired state, but what he now writes seems to contradict that earlier advice, which itself was in tension with what he had written in chapter 3. Machiavelli gives one example of a prince who ruled through those who were suspect to him: Pandolfo Petrucci of Siena.[2] But then he quickly adds: "But of this thing one cannot speak broadly, because it varies according to the subject." What he is willing to affirm is that princes can always easily win over those who were enemies at the beginning of their principate, at least those that must rely on someone and who are "forced" to serve him faithfully. If such initially suspect men are found to have "more faith and more usefulness," as Machiavelli stated at the outset of his treatment of this topic, it is because they have to be so. What about those in whom the prince initially had confidence? Given what he has stated in chapter 17 about what can be said "generally" about men, namely that they are unreliable in their promises, and his statement in chapter 18 about men being "wretched" or "wicked" and not observing faith, the implication here would be that the prince must not depend on the continued faithfulness of those in whom he might have confidence, and should instead also ensure that they too have a reason to rely on him.

In chapter 3 Machiavelli addresses the difficulties facing a new prince with regard to those who initially favored him, and that earlier discussion now comes to the fore in this chapter. "And since this matter requires it, I do not want to neglect to remind the princes who have taken a state anew, by means of favors from within it, that they should consider well what cause moved those who favored him to favor him." Again, in chapter 3 he explained that those who are discontented with their present rulers favor new princes, but their expectations of the new prince are disappointed. He now expands on this problem: "And, if there is not natural affection toward him, but if it was only because those men were not content with the former state, he will be able to maintain them as friends only with hardship and great difficulty, because it would be impossible for him to be able to content them." A review of examples drawn from ancient and modern affairs, he writes without providing any such examples, will show that it is actually easier to win over those who were content with the previous state, whom the prince might otherwise reasonably think he should suspect.

Finally, Machiavelli turns to fortresses and whether to build them or tear them down. The custom has been for princes to build fortresses as the "bridle and the bit of those who design to act against them" or as refuge, including refuge from their own people. "I praise this mode, because it has been practiced since ancient times," Machiavelli claims. To what extent does he praise things just because they are ancient, given that in the very first sentences of *The Prince* he implies that he will not follow custom and given his proclamation in chapter 15 that he will depart from the modes of others? We should therefore not be surprised to next see his favorite word: "Nonetheless … ." He gives several examples "in our own times" of princes who tore down their fortresses in order to hold their states. "Fortresses, therefore, are useful or not according to the times; and if in one respect they do well for you, in another they harm you." Most importantly, he goes on to explain, princes who fear their people more than outsiders should build fortresses, but those who fear outsiders more than their own people should do without them. After remarking that the fortress restored by the Sforza family in Milan has brought them great harm, probably because having it made them less concerned with the support of the people, Machiavelli offers a pithy lesson: "For this reason the best fortress there is, is not to be hated by the people." Once again, the prince must found on the people. Fortresses have never profited princes in "our own times," he claims, with the exception of the Countess of Forlì, but Machiavelli immediately takes back that exception as well, for if having a fortress in the first instance enabled her to withstand a popular revolt, in the second instance it did not. She ought not to have been hated by her people, Machiavelli advises, advice too late for the countess. Machiavelli ends this chapter with an unusual amount of praise to hand around. "Therefore, having considered all of these things, I shall praise whoever will make fortresses, and whoever will not make them, and I shall blame anyone who, because he trusts in fortresses, will think little of being hated by the people." Nonetheless, we might now add, the clear thrust of Machiavelli's lesson is that founding on the people is the most important consideration, enabling one to do without fortresses.[3]

CHAPTER 21: WHAT THE PRINCE SHOULD DO TO BE THOUGHT OUTSTANDING

"Nothing makes a prince so greatly esteemed as do great campaigns and giving rare examples of himself," so begins chapter 21, and then Machiavelli promptly gives an example: Ferdinand of Aragon, the present king of Spain. Beginning as almost a "new prince" given that he began as a weak king, Ferdinand has risen to be "the first king of the Christians" through his great and sometimes extraordinary actions. Beginning with his attack on Granada, which culminated in driving the Moors out of Spain in 1492, Ferdinand gained power in Spain and abroad, including in Italy. Having already called him "the first king of the Christians," Machiavelli notes that he always made use of religion in his undertakings, notably in "an act of pious cruelty" in chasing the Marranos, that is Jews and Muslims who converted (sincerely or not) to Christianity, out of Spain and "despoiling" them, an act Machiavelli characterizes with a rare editorial comment: "nor could this example be more wretched or more rare." Ferdinand made similar attacks on Africa, Italy, and France "under this same cloak" of religion, Machiavelli continues: "And so he has always done and ordered great things, which have always kept the spirits of his subjects suspended and wondering and occupied with their outcome." Machiavelli's description of Ferdinand is reminiscent of what he wrote about Septimus Severus, the Roman emperor who imitated the fox and the lion, though with the notable addition of Ferdinand's cloak of Christian piety. Recall also that Machiavelli appeared to allude to Ferdinand without naming him at the end of chapter 18 as a prince who "never preaches anything but peace and faith, and he is a great enemy of both" (chap. 18, 96). But are we supposed to esteem Ferdinand, especially given his act of "pious cruelty"? Machiavelli does not say. Instead, he recommends that a prince also gain esteem by doing great things within his state, a remark that perhaps silently accuses Ferdinand of not doing so, and to "give himself the fame of a great man and of an excellent talent."

Machiavelli moves on to say that a prince is esteemed "when he is a true friend and a true enemy," taking sides in foreign affairs unhesitatingly with one side or the other in a dispute (something Ferdinand conspicuously did not do). Having said this, he divides the question to explore the different possible scenarios: "For if two powerful neighbors of yours come to blows, either they are of a quality that if one of them wins you have to fear the victor, or not. In each of these two cases, it will always be more useful for you to reveal yourself and wage open war," rather than trying to remain neutral. He then takes up the first case, namely when you do have to fear either of the victors, presumably because they are both more powerful than you. In order to defend this portion of the argument, Machiavelli brings forward the example of Antiochus III, king of the Seleucid Empire, one of the states created out of the breakup of Alexander the Great's conquests in the area stretching from what is now Syria, Iraq, and Iran into Pakistan and India. The events Machiavelli relates occurred in 193 BCE. Antiochus had come into Greece and was elected general of the Aetolian League, a confederation of cities in central Greece, in order to repel the Romans. Machiavelli tells how Antiochus sent orators to the Achaeans, who were leagued with the Romans, in order to encourage them to remain neutral. In the assembly of the Achaeans the Roman legate replied to the argument that they should remain neutral: "'As to what they say, moreover, about your not intervening in the war, nothing is further from your interests: you will be the prize of the victor, without thanks and without dignity.'"[4] In other words, the Romans gave the Achaeans the same argument Machiavelli gives the reader of *The Prince* concerning the dangers of being neutral. What Machiavelli does not discuss here, but did discuss in chapter 3, is that the Romans ultimately seized control of all of these provinces in Greece because they recognized dangers from afar (see chap. 3, 46–47). To return to chapter 21, Machiavelli caps the story with a general lesson: "Irresolute princes, to avoid present dangers, follow the neutral way most of the time, and most of the time they are ruined." What if you decide not to remain neutral and the side you favor wins, again given the case that it is stronger than you and you therefore have to fear it? According to Machiavelli, "he is obliged to you, and there is a contract of love; and men are never so dishonest that in a very great example of ingratitude they would oppress you" and will, in addition, "have some regard, and for justice most of all." (This is another of the very few times Machiavelli uses the term "justice" in *The Prince*.) The example of the Achaeans, and all of Greece, losing their freedom to Rome over the next fifty years after the event Machiavelli recounts does not support such fond hopes.

With this unsettling analysis of the first case, where you do have to fear either of the victors, Machiavelli turns to the second case, when you do not have to fear them because you are strong enough. In this case, he writes, it is "even greater prudence" to ally oneself with one party or the other and not try to remain neutral. Essentially, in justifying this prudence Machiavelli outlines the policy of "divide and conquer" used by the Romans. Having done so, he tacitly criticizes those who thought that allying with Rome was a good idea: "And here it should be noted that a prince must be careful never to make a partnership with one who is more powerful than himself in order to harm others, unless necessity compels him," for you remain "his prisoner" and at the "discretion of others." Sometimes states could have avoided such an imprudent choice, as with the Venetians allying themselves with France, and sometimes they have no choice, as with the Florentines. Having said this, Machiavelli offers a general and important lesson concerning prudence in a world were everything is doubtful and there are often no "safe choices." "Because we find this, in the order of things, that one never tries to avoid one inconvenience without incurring another one. But prudence consists in knowing how to recognize the qualities of the inconveniences and choosing the less bad as if it were good."[5]

Machiavelli concludes the chapter by turning back to what the prince can do to be held in esteem with regard to his own subjects. A prince should show himself to be a lover of the virtues by giving hospitality to virtuous men (especially those who are excellent in an art), should encourage his subjects to practice their trades, offer rewards for those who succeed in doing so, keep his people occupied with feast days and spectacles, and meet regularly with guilds and other associations.[6] What is perhaps most remarkable about this advice is how brief it is. Subjects that other writers, for example in the mirror-of-princes genre, might linger over scarcely detain our author.

CHAPTER 22: ON THOSE WHOM PRINCES KEEP IN THEIR SERVICE FOR SECRET MATTERS

If Lorenzo de' Medici had persisted this far in reading Machiavelli's "small gift," his job application, he would have found this chapter particularly interesting. "The choice of ministers is not of small importance to a prince," Machiavelli explains, and these ministers are good or not good depending on the prudence of the prince. Rather than beginning with the ministers and their counsel, however, Machiavelli begins with appearances: people judge the "mind" of the prince by seeing the men he has around him. If they are "capable and faithful," then people reckon that the prince is wise, and otherwise not. Note that these ministers must be judged both capable and faithful, for Machiavelli will soon reveal what happens if they are capable but not faithful.

As an example of how a prince is judged by way of his choice of minister, Machiavelli offers Pandolfo Petrucci, prince of Siena, whom he says had to be judged a worthy man due to the qualities of his minister, Messer Antonio of Venafro. (We briefly encountered Pandolfo in chapter 20 as an example of a prince who ruled his state through those who were suspect to him.) As an introduction to his example, Machiavelli makes a general statement: "And because minds are of three kinds—one that understands by itself; another that discerns what others understand; and a third that understands neither itself nor others: the first is most excellent, the second is excellent, and the third useless ... ." As for Pandolfo, Machiavelli explains that "of necessity" if he was not in the first rank he must have been in the second. Why is this outcome so "necessary," as Machiavelli emphasizes here, for couldn't it be the case that Pandolfo's mind was of the third rank and that he simply got lucky in his choice of minister? In any case, perhaps Machiavelli does not make a firm decision about which rank in which to place Pandolfo's mind because he is not judging the matter directly, but instead based on a choice made by Pandolfo, for as he explained in chapter 18, "men as a whole judge more with their eyes than their hands" (95). At any rate, he explains that even if someone does not have "inventiveness" himself, he may be able to recognize good or evil in what those around him do and say, in such a way that "the minister cannot hope to deceive him, and he remains good." Machiavelli once again subtly raises the possibility that a minister, and especially a minister with a more excellent mind, may not be faithful. What would Lorenzo de' Medici have made of this?

How can a prince know his minister? Machiavelli offers a rule of thumb that "never fails": "when you see the minister think more of himself than of you, and that in all of his actions he seeks some profit for himself, a man of this kind, made in this way, will never make a good minister, and never will you be able to trust him." On the other hand, if a prince finds a minister who thinks not of himself but of the prince, then he must be honored, enriched, and made to share in the prince's honors and offices, but for a reason that is, so to speak, Machiavellian: "so that he sees that he cannot stand without him." Just as the prince cannot rely on the love or faithfulness of his people but must instead bind the people to him by more reliable motives, so too with the prince's ministers. "Thus when ministers and princes are made in this way, they are able to trust one another; and when otherwise, the end will always be harmful, either for one or for the other." And Machiavelli ends the chapter on this ominous note.

CHAPTER 23: BY WHAT MEANS FLATTERERS ARE TO BE AVOIDED

"I do not want to leave out one important point," Machiavelli begins chapter 23, "and an error from which princes defend themselves with difficulty, if they are not very prudent, or if they do not make good choices." This chapter seems to be a continuation of the previous chapter and the discussion there of prudent princes making good choices of advisers. The important point Machiavelli wants to discuss is the problem of flatterers, of which the courts of princes are full. The real problem, however, seems to be princes themselves, for like all men they are prone to self-deceit and thus vulnerable to this "plague." The remedy for this disease is to make men understand that they do not offend you when they tell you the truth, but this remedy produces another disease, namely that if everyone can tell you the truth you lose their "reverence" and run the danger of becoming "contemptible." What is a prince to do?

A "prudent prince" must take a third way, Machiavelli explains, by choosing "wise men" in his state and allowing only them to have "free access to speak the truth to him, and only concerning those things that he asks, and nothing else." If most princes, like most men, are prone to self-deceit and therefore to flattery and falsehood, then the "prudent prince" must possess a great deal of self-knowledge as well as prudence to choose such wise men and know what to ask them. As such, Machiavelli explains that this "prudent prince" should ask about everything and listen to the opinions given by his counselors, but then "choose by himself, in his own way" and then stick to his choice. If the prince begins to listen to others he runs the risk of again becoming vulnerable to flatterers and vacillating in his decisions and thereby becoming contemptible.

In order to illustrate his point Machiavelli will bring forth one "modern example." He relates how Priest Luca (*Pre' Luca*) spoke of his prince, Maximilian, the present Roman emperor, saying how Maximilian never took counsel with anyone and, yet, "used never to do anything in his own way." In a new sentence in which it is not clear whether he is continuing to relate what Priest Luca said, apparently to Machiavelli himself,[7] or whether he is giving his own judgment, he continues: "This arose from his holding to a pattern contrary to the one stated above." Namely, because Maximilian is a secretive man he does not confer with anyone or communicate his plans, but once he begins to act he listens to the contradictory opinions of those around him and, "like a simpleton," discards his original plans. "From here it arises that the things that he does in one day he destroys the next, it is never understood what he wants, or what he plans to do, and one cannot found oneself on his decisions." This is an unusually unflattering judgment on Machiavelli's part, especially for a prince still reigning at the time. It is also an unusually frank, perhaps too frank, statement by a minister concerning his prince.

With the cautionary tale of Maximilian concluded, Machiavelli advises: "A prince therefore must always take counsel, but when he wants, and not when others want," and in fact he should discourage anyone from offering him advice unless he asks. But when he does ask advice, he must be a broad questioner and patient listener to the truth. Having said this, Machiavelli makes a remark that seems to contradict what he said at the beginning of chapter 22, namely that people conjecture about what sort of mind the prince has by seeing the men he has around him as advisors. Instead, he writes: "And because many reckon that any prince who creates for himself a reputation as prudent is held thus, not because of his nature, but because of the good counselors he has about him, I say without doubt they are deceived. For the following is a general rule that never fails: a prince who is not wise by himself cannot be counseled well, unless by chance he has already entrusted himself to one person alone, who is a most prudent man, to govern him in everything. In this case it could even happen that he would be counseled well, but it would not last long, because that governor, in a brief time, would take his state away from him." Which is the general rule that "never fails": that a prince who is not himself wise cannot be counseled well, or that a prince who is apparently not wise and happens to have a prudent counselor will soon lose his state to him? If instead of entrusting himself to one prudent counselor the unwise prince listens to several, he will not get unified advice or have faithful advisers. The unwise prince is in peril whichever way he turns.

Machiavelli ends this chapter by returning to an issue that arose at the end of the previous chapter concerning the need for a prince to keep a good advisor always dependent on him in order to keep the advisor faithful. Having told what happens to an unwise prince with regard to his counselors, he ends the chapter with one of his pithy and frank statements about human nature: "For men will always turn out wicked for you if they are not made by some necessity to be good. For this reason one concludes that good counsels, wherever they come from, must arise out of the prudence of the prince, and not the prudence of the prince from good counsels."

NOTES

1 Aristotle, *Nicomachean Ethics* VI.8–12.
2 What he does not reveal is that Pandolfo Petrucci narrowly avoided being assassinated in a conspiracy that included his friends, and even his father-in-law, an example he does discuss in his chapter on conspiracies in the *Discourses on Livy* (III.6).
3 See Machiavelli's similar discussion of the inutility of fortresses, with some of the same examples he uses here, in the *Discourses on Livy* (II.24).
4 Machiavelli loosely quotes Livy, *History of Rome* XXXV.41. Immediately before the passage quoted, the Roman legate asks the Achaeans to have faith in the Romans.
5 Similarly, in the *Discourses on Livy* he explains: "In all human things he who examines well sees this: that one inconvenience can never be suppressed without another's cropping up ... . And so, in every decision of ours, we should consider where are the fewer inconveniences and take that for the best policy" (I.6, 21–22).
6 As Connell remarks in an editorial note to this passage in his translation, Machiavelli's advice here reads like a description of Lorenzo de' Medici "the Magnificent" (grandfather of the Lorenzo to whom Machiavelli dedicates *The Prince*), and he refers to Machiavelli's *Florentine Histories* (VIII.36) for a similar description. This is the very end of the *Florentine Histories*, which Machiavelli concludes by writing that after Lorenzo's death (in 1492) Italy's ruin shortly began.
7 Machiavelli met "Priest Luca" (Luca Rinaldi, bishop of Trieste), who served as an ambassador to Maximilian, in 1507–8 when he was sent by the Florentine Republic to the emperor's court on a diplomatic mission.

10

VIRTUE, FORTUNE, AND THE REDEMPTION OF ITALY

The Prince concludes with a trio of chapters in which Machiavelli takes up the great question of the relationship between virtue and fortune, of how fortune or chance can be opposed by virtue, and applies this analysis to the contemporary situation in Italy. Machiavelli begins by first diagnosing why the Italians are vulnerable to foreign invasion, because their princes have not opposed fortune with virtue and their own arms, then takes up a more abstract treatment of the relationship between virtue and fortune, and finally returns to the Italian scene and exhorts a prince—perhaps the dedicatee of his book, Lorenzo de' Medici—to remedy the disease by uniting Italy.

CHAPTER 24: WHY THE PRINCES OF ITALY HAVE LOST THEIR KINGDOM

In the beginning of *The Prince* Machiavelli began, as is customary, with hereditary princes whose ancient bloodlines made them seem to be "natural princes" to their peoples, but now at the end of the work the new prince has all but replaced the hereditary prince. "The things set forth above, if observed prudently make a new prince appear ancient, and they make him immediately more secure and more firm in his state, as though he had grown old in it," he now tells us: "For a new prince is observed with much more interest in his actions than a hereditary one; and when these actions are recognized to be virtuous, they grip men much more, and they obligate them much more than does ancient blood." Virtue, or rather being recognized as virtuous, turns out to be more powerful than "ancient blood" or any other claim to authority. He explains that this is the case because men are more concerned with present things than past ones. "In this way he will have doubled his glory, by having given a beginning to a principality, and by having adorned it and strengthened it with good laws, with good arms and good examples; just as a man has doubled shame if, although born a prince, he has lost his principality through his lack of prudence." Machiavelli thus points back to the title of the chapter, which announces that he will discuss why the princes of Italy have lost their "kingdom" (or, in another manuscript version, their "states"). Perhaps he makes an unusual choice of the word "kingdom" (*regnum*) here because the Italian states share common defects, or perhaps he is commencing his concluding appeal to a prince to unite Italy and secure the entire province from foreign invasion, an appeal that comes to a head in chapter 26. In any case, he now offers this new prince a "double glory" for his deeds.

Turning to his analysis of why these Italian princes have failed, he argues, first of all, that they share "a common defect as regards their arms," and points us back to his lengthy discussion of this issue beginning in chapter 12. Second, he explains that they either have their peoples as their enemies, and therefore did not follow his repeated advice to found on the people, or, even if they do have their peoples as their friends, they have not known how to assure themselves with regard to the great, so perhaps they again failed to follow his advice concerning the need to choose one or the other of the two humors that are found in every state. Machiavelli thus once again connects two themes in his work, having one's own arms and founding on the people, and applies them to Italy's current woes.

Without these defects as to arms and the people, he explains, if states have "enough sinews" (*tanto nervo*), a phrase that evokes the traditional image of the state as a body with its prince as the head, they can field a successful army. As an example of a state with "enough sinews," Machiavelli evokes Philip of Macedon, immediately specifying that he does not mean the father of Alexander the Great, but instead the prince who was defeated by Titus Quinctius, namely Philip V of Macedon. Why does he provoke us to think of the other Philip of Macedon, the father of Alexander the Great? At the end of chapter 13 he mentioned the other Philip, specifically naming him as the father of Alexander the Great, as an example of a prince who successfully relied on his "own arms." Does he suggest that we should compare the two Philips? As for Philip V of Macedon, he attempted to resist Roman expansion into Greece following the defeat of Hannibal (201 BCE), with Rome claiming that it was protecting the freedom of the Greek cities from the Macedonians, events to which Machiavelli referred in chapter 21 with regard to Antiochus and his attempt to persuade the Achaean League to remain neutral in his war with the Romans. Philip V of Macedon was decisively defeated by the Romans (in 197 BCE) under the command of Titus Quinctius Flamininus, who happens to be the Roman legate whom Machiavelli quotes in chapter 21 as warning the Achaeans not to remain neutral. Philip V's dominion was henceforth confined to the Kingdom of Macedon, which would fall prey to the Romans soon after his death. Despite Philip's loss to the Romans, Machiavelli praises him: "Nonetheless, because he was a military man, and one who knew how to please the people and to assure himself of the great, he supported a war for many years against them; and if, in the end, he lost his dominion over certain cities, nonetheless he kept his kingdom." What are we to make of this example? The other Philip of Macedon and his son Alexander would be examples of successful conquerors of the free cities of Greece, and far beyond, whereas this Philip of Macedon is an example of an unsuccessful conqueror of these same free cities against the overwhelming power of Rome, which did succeed in conquering these cities, and also far beyond. Throughout *The Prince* we have seen Machiavelli repeatedly concern himself with the conquest of Greece, whether by the

Romans in ancient times or by the Ottoman Turk in modern times. Perhaps the disunity of the states of ancient Greece and other factors that made them vulnerable to the Romans serves as a parallel to the situation of Italy in Machiavelli's own time. Be that as it may, even the lesser example of Philip V of Macedon seems beyond reach to the princes of Italy, to whom Machiavelli now turns.

"Therefore these princes of ours, who were in their principalities for many years, ought not to accuse fortune for having lost them, but their own laziness," he states. The abrupt "therefore" with which Machiavelli begins this paragraph seems to indicate a contrast: unlike Philip V of Macedon, who had "enough sinews" in his state and *therefore* was able to hold it against the Romans, "these princes of ours" failed to have the arms and support of the people and *therefore* were unable to withstand the foreign invasions of the past twenty years. Then, preparing the famous simile of the next chapter likening fortune to a river, he explains that these lazy princes did not consider during quiet times that the times could change, "which is a common defect of men, to not think of storms during a calm." When adverse times came, he writes, referring principally of the French invasion of 1494, these princes fled rather than defending themselves, a painful reminder to Lorenzo de' Medici given that his Medici forbearers fled Florence with the French invasion and lost their state. Instead, these princes put their faith in "hope"—hope that their peoples would call them back—or in "belief"—belief that "you will find someone to catch you." Such hope and belief are good only when there is no other remedy. "For that defense was cowardly, and it did not depend on you," he concludes, "and the only defenses that are good, certain, and enduring are those that depend upon yourself and your own virtue." And in this way Machiavelli prepares us for the famous discussion of to what extent fortune can be mastered by virtue.

CHAPTER 25: HOW MUCH FORTUNE IS ABLE TO DO IN HUMAN THINGS, AND BY WHAT MEANS SHE MAY BE OPPOSED

Fortune (*fortuna*) was conceived of as a capricious goddess from ancient times onward. The Romans built temples to Fortuna and hoped to propitiate the goddess and make her favorable to them. Images of the wheel of fortune were common in medieval and Renaissance iconography, with stories of a sudden reversal of fortune when the goddess decided to overturn things with a turn of the wheel. The notion of the divine or occult forces of fortune continued to exist in some tension with Christian beliefs in divine providence, with preachers such as Savonarola inveighing against astrologers and others who thought they could read the fortunes of men and especially princes.[1] With this backdrop, then, Machiavelli takes up the questions announced in the chapter title: how much fortune is able to do in human things, and by what means she may be opposed.

"It is not unknown to me that many persons have held, and hold, the opinion that the things of the world are governed by fortune and by God, that men, with their prudence, cannot correct them, and that instead they have no remedy for them whatsoever. For this reason they might judge that there would be no point in sweating much in the things of this world, but let themselves be governed by chance." Machiavelli thus begins his discussion from the position of utter resignation to what fortune—and God—ordain for "the things of the world." In the chapter title, Machiavelli spoke only of fortune and not God, but in the first sentence of the chapter he writes of both fortune and God. Is he equating fortune and God, or are they distinct? As we shall see, he will immediately drop any further mention of God. Likewise, in the chapter title he spoke of what fortune does in "human things," and now he writes of how fortune and God govern "the things of the world," or what appears to be a more comprehensive category than "human things" alone. He also speaks of "the things of this world," a formulation that evokes the world beyond, with those who are of this opinion concerning how the world is governed by fortune and by God not "sweating" too much about this world because it is the next world that concerns them. How are "human things" related to "the things of the world"? If "the things of the world" are equivalent to nature, then does Machiavelli's professed knowledge of how to govern states rest on a more comprehensive understanding of nature that he only just permits us to glimpse here?[2] In any case, the opening paragraph of this chapter is uncharacteristically philosophical in tone for Machiavelli.

With regard to the resigned stance toward a world in which fortune and God govern everything Machiavelli explains that this opinion has been "more believed" in "our own times" because of "the great variety of things"—or great "variation" (*variazione*) of things—"that have been seen, and are seen every day, beyond all human conjecture." Given the context of these final chapters, Machiavelli would appear to refer in particular to the French invasion of 1494 and subsequent events. Having experienced this great variety or variation of things himself, Machiavelli claims that he too is sometimes of this opinion, but once again we then encounter his favorite word: "Nonetheless, so that our free will may not be eliminated, I judge that it may be true that fortune is the arbiter of half of our actions, but that she indeed allows us to govern the other half of them, or almost that much." This is Machiavelli's sole reference in *The Prince* to "free will." Yet the philosophical and theological issues surrounding free will seem to be of little interest to him, and perhaps for this reason he drops God and speaks now only of fortune. Rather, he is concerned with exhorting us to exercise our freedom to govern the world to the greatest extent possible. Being able to govern more or less half of our actions is a significant improvement upon where he began, with the opinion that the things of the world are completely beyond our control, or nearly so. If the opinion held by "many persons" leads to passivity, Machiavelli's judgment concerning what men may govern is a call to action.

In order to illustrate his judgment concerning what fortune leaves to men to govern, Machiavelli employs a simile that should make us recall the title to the chapter, where he wrote of "by what means she may be opposed." Not content with our half of dominion over the things of the world, his simile suggests that we should actively oppose fortune.

> And I liken her to one of these ruinous rivers that, when they become angry, flood the plains, ruin the trees and the buildings, and lift earth from one side and place it on the other. Each person flees before them; everyone surrenders to their attack without being able, under

these circumstances, to block them at any point. Although they really happen this way, it does not follow from this that men, when there are quiet times, are not able to make provision for it with both dikes and embankments, so that, if later the rivers rise, either they would go into a canal, or their attack would be neither so boundless nor so harmful.

This famous image evokes what Machiavelli wrote in the previous chapter about lazy Italian princes who flee rather than fight and who do not think in quiet times of preparing for the storm. These princes have allowed themselves to be governed by chance rather than themselves governing. Perhaps the reason for their inaction is that they are among the "many persons" who hold the opinion with which Machiavelli began this chapter concerning the extent to which fortune and God govern the world. From the image of the river, Machiavelli pursues his simile by turning back to fortune: "It happens similarly with fortune. She shows her power where virtue is not prepared to resist her; and she turns her rushing current here where she knows that embankments and dikes have not been made to hold her." What are these "embankments" and "dikes" with regard to governing states? He gives us some indication by applying his simile of fortune being like a river to Italy: "And if you will consider Italy, which is the seat of these changes and the one who has put them in motion, you will see that this is a landscape without embankments and without any dikes. For, if she had been diked by appropriate virtue, like Germany, Spain and France, either this flood would not have made the great changes that it has, or it would not have come here. And, in general terms, I want it to suffice to have said this concerning opposing fortune."

Let us pause over Machiavelli's analysis of the Italian scene. What does he mean by stating that Italy is "the seat [*sedia*] of these changes and the one who has put them in motion"? Recall that in chapter 12 Machiavelli discussed the Italian reliance on mercenary arms "from a higher perspective," and from that perspective he provided an analysis of the historical changes that occurred in Italy over the previous century or more, explaining how the Holy Roman Emperor lost authority there and the

Church, traditionally the emperor's rival, gained power. With disarmed peoples and priests, the Italians turned to mercenary arms, with Machiavelli concluding acerbically: "And the result of their virtue was that Italy was overrun by Charles, plundered by Louis, forced by Ferdinand, and insulted by the Swiss" (chap. 12, 80). The primary player in this drama, as is also evident from chapter 11 on ecclesiastical principalities, was the Church. To return to the present chapter, in characterizing Italy as the "seat" (*sedia*) of the changes experienced in his times Machiavelli calls to mind the Latin phrase for the "Holy See," or the ecclesiastical jurisdiction of the Pope in his role as bishop of Rome: the *Sancta Sedes*. In part because of the role of the Church, the Italian "landscape" is without embankments and dikes, and if we take Machiavelli's remark that Germany, Spain, and France have "been diked by appropriate virtues" to mean that he is equating "dikes" with laws, then "embankments" might be equated with arms, thus once again pointing to the ruinous role of the Church in Italy with regard to lacking proper arms.

With his discussion concerning opposing fortune "in general terms" complete, Machiavelli turns to "the particulars," by which he seems to mean how particular individuals grapple with fortune. He remarks how a certain prince is happy one day and ruined the next without him changing in "nature or any quality." How could that be? "This I believe arises first from the causes that are reviewed at length earlier, that is, that the prince who relies completely on fortune is ruined when she changes." To which earlier discussion does he refer? If he is referring to chapter 7 and his discussion of new princes who attain a state through the arms and fortune of others, then he is offering a new indictment of Cesare Borgia, whom he at that point excused for failing because he suffered "an extraordinary and extreme malignity of fortune" (chap. 7, 59), but whom he now characterizes as having relied "completely" on fortune and thereby as having been ruined when fortune changed.

Having dropped any mention of God and speaking now only of fortune, Machiavelli formulates his explanation for the varying fortunes of princes as a "belief": "This I believe ... ." His own belief now replaces what he said at the outset of the chapter is "more believed" in his own time than any other, namely that fortune and God entirely govern the world.[3] As he continues his explanation he professes another belief: "I believe, too, that the man who conforms his way of proceeding to the quality of the times is happy, and similarly that he whose proceedings the times disagree with is unhappy."[4] Note that the actor changes in this sentence: whereas the man who "conforms" to the times is the actor in the first case, "the times" become the actor in the second case by "disagreeing" with the "proceedings" of the man. Is the first man exercising his virtue to combat or at least cooperate with fortune whereas the second man is not doing so and thereby allows fortune to combat him? If so, then we may have a means of solving the dilemma with which Machiavelli now presents us.

After noting how varying modes of proceeding lead to varying outcomes, with some men proceeding with caution and others with impetuosity, and so on, but coming to different ends depending on whether the way in which they proceed agrees with the times or not, Machiavelli confronts us with a dilemma: "Nor is a man to be found who is so prudent that he knows how to accommodate himself to this: both because he cannot deviate from that toward which his nature inclines him, and, moreover, because when a man has always prospered by walking in one path, he cannot be persuaded to depart from it." The second reason, that a man continues in the path to which he is accustomed, seems to be a problem that can be overcome, but what about deviating from what a given man's "nature," or we might say character, inclines him to? Machiavelli seems to suggest that our control over our own natures is limited, and therefore prudence in resisting fortune is also limited. Yet at the end of this paragraph he offers the possibility that it can be overcome: "For this reason the cautious man, when it is time to become impetuous, does not know how to do it, whence he is ruined; although, if he could change his nature with the times and with the circumstances, he would not change in his fortune." Is our own fortune—good or bad fortune—in our control, at least potentially, if we can change our "nature" with fortune herself? Perhaps we should think of the advice encapsulated in the image in chapter 18 of the centaur Chiron, and exhibited in chapter 19 by Septimus Servius, of "using" the nature of man and the nature of the beast, with the beasts being the lion and the fox with their different natures. Would possessing such a composite "nature" overcome the problem of following a single nature?[5]

Rather than taking up the tantalizing possibility, Machiavelli dwells on the astonishing success of an ever-impetuous prince: Pope Julius II. "Pope Julius proceeded impetuously in all his affairs, and he found that the times and the circumstances so conformed to his way of proceeding that he always pulled out a happy ending." He then recounts a series of instances where the impetuous pope succeeded against all expectations. Machiavelli offered a similar discussion of Julius II earlier in *The Prince*, namely when discoursing on auxiliary arms in chapter 13, where he remarked that Julius, despite the fact that his actions "could not have been less considered," emerged unscathed "beyond all expectation" due to his "good fortune" (chap. 13, 81). Returning to chapter 25, Machiavelli concludes his account of the warrior pope: "Thus Julius brought about, by his impetuous movement, what another pope, with all human prudence, could never have brought about." Once again Machiavelli counts Julius lucky beyond all expectations. "And the brevity of his life did not allow him to experience the contrary," that is bad fortune: "For if there had come times in which it was necessary to proceed with caution, his ruin would have followed, for he would never have deviated from those ways toward which his nature inclined him." Unlike his predecessor Alexander VI, whom Machiavelli characterized in chapter 18 as being foxlike, Julius apparently knew only how to use the lion.

Machiavelli ends this chapter with an explicit conclusion and a troubling recommendation. "I conclude, therefore, that since fortune varies, and since men are obstinate in their ways, they are happy so long as together they agree, and when they disagree, they are unhappy." But then, as if on second thought, he makes a judgment about what can be done. "Yet, I judge the following: that it is better to be impetuous than cautious, for fortune is a lady, and it is necessary, if one wants to hold her down, to beat her and to dash her. And one sees that she lets herself be won more by these men, than by those who proceed coldly. For this reason, as a lady, she is always the friend of the young, because they are less cautious, more ferocious, and they command her with more audacity." Machiavelli's image of the lady Fortuna here is troubling, and has brought on him the charge of misogyny.[6] Be that as it may, how does this new image of combatting fortune relate to the simile of fortune as a river that can be controlled with embankments and dikes? To begin with, his earlier image of fortune as a river was part of his discussion of fortune's role in human affairs generally, and the embankments and dikes—laws and arms—necessary for combatting fortune seem to require a concerted political effort beyond the actions of a single prince. By contrast, this concluding advice about impetuously beating down fortune is part of his discussion of "particulars," that is the actions of particular princes. Perhaps both of the types of advice he offers are necessary, for a prince should immediately, perhaps even impetuously, seize the opportunity fortune presents to him, but must then turn to combatting fortune through laying good foundations in the form of new orders.

CHAPTER 26: AN EXHORTATION TO SEIZE ITALY, AND TO SET HER FREE FROM THE BARBARIANS

From almost the very beginning of *The Prince* the vulnerability of Italy to foreign invasion, as exemplified by the French invasion of 1494 and the subsequent wars on the peninsula, has never been far from Machiavelli's mind, and now he concludes his work with an exhortation to "seize" Italy and to set her free from "the barbarians." ("Her" because *Italia* is feminine in Italian.) Our author presents himself as an Italian patriot here, a presentation underscored by the fact that he ends the chapter, and the work, by quoting Petrarch's poem "Italia mia" urging Italian hearts to renew their ancient valor. The concluding chapter particularly echoes chapter 6 on new princes who found their principalities through their virtue and own arms, as we shall see, suggesting that he is calling on a prince to engage in an act of founding in Italy through "seizing" her, perhaps through an act of beating down fortune such as he described at the end of chapter 25.

The highly rhetorical and emotional tone of chapter 26 sets it apart from the rest of *The Prince*, which is largely coldly analytic in style. Various interpreters have noted the sudden change in style and have come to different conclusions about the relationship of the concluding chapter to the rest of the work. A traditional interpretation sees Machiavelli revealing himself to be an Italian patriot or nationalist, and also thereby revealing the "end," the unification of Italy, that would justify or excuse the "means" he advocates using to achieve that goal throughout the rest of his work. This reading of *The Prince* was particularly common in the age of nationalist movements during and following the French Revolution, and can be seen in the writings of various philosophers during that era, including Fichte and Hegel, and even more prominently during the struggle to unify Italy in the nineteenth century, with unification only finally achieved in 1870.[7] Some scholars have suggested that chapter 26 must have been written later than the rest of *The Prince*, for example a year or so later than the rest of the work during the brief period of 1514–15 when the Medici seemed poised to forge an independent state in northern Italy.[8] Finally, other interpreters admit that chapter 26 comes as something of a surprise, but conclude that the chapter makes a fitting finale to Machiavelli's small treatise by giving his unrespectable advice the respectable veneer of patriotism.[9]

Machiavelli begins the concluding chapter by looking back over what he has written and then looking forward to what might be possible for Italy:

> Having considered, therefore, all the things discussed above, while thinking to myself whether at present in Italy the times were running so as to honor a new prince, and whether there would be material that could give the opportunity to someone who was prudent and virtuous, so that by introducing form to the material, it would do honor to him and good to the collectivity of its inhabitants, it seems to me that so many things are coming together to the benefit of a new prince that I do not know what time for this has ever been more appropriate.

We already hear echoes of chapter 6 on the greatest new princes: the "material" is ready to be given "form" by someone with the requisite virtue and prudence. Machiavelli presents himself as being entirely optimistic that the "times" are such, or fortune is so disposed, that this new prince almost cannot fail. The "opportunity" he sees must be seized.

The new prince who seizes the opportunity to unite Italy should imitate Moses and the other exemplary new princes of chapter 6.

> And if, as I said, it was necessary, if one wanted to see the virtue of Moses, that the people of Israel should be enslaved in Egypt; and to recognize the greatness of the spirit of Cyrus, that the Persians should have been oppressed by the Medes; and for the excellence of Theseus, that the Athenians should have been dispersed; so at present, in order to recognize the virtue of an Italian spirit, it was necessary that Italy should be reduced to its present circumstances, and that she should be more enslaved than the Hebrews, more servile than the Persians, and more dispersed than the Athenians: without a head, without order, beaten, despoiled, torn, pillaged, and having suffered ruin of every sort.

Machiavelli's explicit reference to chapter 6 ("as I said") should lead us to compare what he writes here to what he wrote there. Two differences are notable, one subtle and the other obvious. The subtle difference is that here he takes the perspective of a spectator to the actions of Moses and his brethren: "it was necessary, if one wanted to *see* the virtue of Moses ...," "... to *recognize* the greatness of spirit of Cyrus ...," etc. By contrast, in chapter 6 he takes the perspective of the actor: "It was therefore necessary for Moses to find the people of Israel in Egypt, enslaved and oppressed ...," etc. (chap. 6, 56). Perhaps Machiavelli has descended from the mountain from which the prince surveys the people below into the plains where the people, here the oppressed Italians, look about for a prince to save them. The more obvious difference in his accounts is that, while he mentions Moses, Cyrus, and Theseus, he leaves out the other exemplary prince he cited in chapter 6: Romulus. Is the omission of Romulus an invitation for the new prince upon whom he calls to become a new Romulus in Italy? One other thing might be noted about this passage. Namely, whereas in chapter 24 in particular, but elsewhere as well, Machiavelli has strongly argued that the Italian princes who have lost their states ought not accuse fortune but instead recognize their own lack of virtue and arms, here he describes the ruin of Italy as the work of divine providence creating the opportunity for "an Italian spirit" to be recognized. Machiavelli's concluding exhortation is a kind of sermon.

Without naming him, Machiavelli claims that there was "a certain person" who seemed to have been "ordained by God for Italy's redemption," but who was "rejected by fortune." Who was this person? Various conjectures have been made, including Cesare Borgia, with the idea that Machiavelli is calling on a prince to imitate Borgia's attempt to create an independent state in northern Italy.[10] Or is this person a figment of Machiavelli's imagination, a nameless prince that allows the reader to fill in his or her own favorite prince to be imitated, perhaps a nameless substitute for the missing Romulus? In chapter 25 Machiavelli began by speaking of how the things of the world are governed by fortune and by God, only to drop any further mention of God, but now God is supposedly ordaining Italy's redemption and yet God's plans are resisted by fortune. With God's ordained prince having failed, Italy is left "as though lifeless" while awaiting someone to "heal her wounds" and "cure her of the sores with which she has been infested for so long. One sees how she prays to God that he send someone to redeem her from these cruelties and barbaric insolences. One sees her still completely ready and disposed to follow a banner, provided there be someone who takes it up." The language of healing wounds and curing sores and redemption suggests a prophet, presumably an armed prophet given what Machiavelli has said in chapter 6, but with powers reminiscent of Jesus as well.

Having described the ruinous condition of Italy and characterized it as a divinely ordained opportunity for a new prince, Machiavelli finally names a prince—or at least a princely family—who could take up the banner: the Medici. "Nor is there to be seen at present anyone in whom she could hope more than in your illustrious house, which, with its fortune and virtue favored by God and by the Church of which it is now the prince, can make itself the leader of this redemption." Since Machiavelli has dedicated his book to Lorenzo de' Medici, it is natural to assume that the new prince upon whom he calls to rescue Italy is Lorenzo. As we saw with the Dedicatory Letter, Machiavelli describes Lorenzo as possessing fortune, that is good fortune, though whether he also possesses virtue is still in question. But perhaps Machiavelli is addressing himself more to the head of the Medici family, Pope Leo X (Giovanni de' Medici), given that he remarks that he is now "prince" of the Church. Alternatively, given that he writes in chapter 15 that he has written his book for "anyone who understands it," perhaps his call on the Medici to redeem Italy is more a pretext than a statement of his expectation that they will do so or are capable of doing so, with Machiavelli meanwhile waiting for his book to fall into the hands of a new prince who has the virtue and fortune to carry out his project.

The redemption of Italy may seem to be an arduous undertaking, but Machiavelli makes it seem almost effortless. "Thus it will not be very difficult, if you keep in mind the actions and lives of the men named above. Although such men are rare and marvelous, nonetheless they were men, and each of them had a lesser opportunity than the present one, for their undertakings were not more just than this, nor easier, nor was God more a friend to them than to you." These "rare and marvelous" men are Moses, Cyrus, and Theseus, but far from being mere men they are mythical or semi-mythical figures. In chapter 6 they were presented as unreachable targets at whom we should nonetheless aim even if we know that we cannot fully imitate them, but now Machiavelli brings them down to earth and claims that the conditions in Italy present an even more favorable opportunity to a new prince than these exemplary princes enjoyed.

To buttress his claims about the ripeness of Italy for redemption, Machiavelli brings forth an ancient authority: "Here there is great justice: 'for war is just for those for whom it is necessary, and arms are pious where there is no hope save in arms.'" This is one of the very few mentions of justice in *The Prince*, but it seems from the quotation that it is less justice than necessity that justifies taking up arms in this cause. The quotation, which Machiavelli gives in Latin, comes from Livy in a speech he puts into the mouth of a Samnite captain addressing his fellow citizens and urging them to go to war with Rome.[11] Interestingly, the defeat of the Samnites put the Romans on course to unite almost the entire

Italian peninsula under their rule, the very project Machiavelli is urging his prince to accomplish by seizing Italy and uniting it. The quotation therefore has an ominous element, for not all the peoples of Italy will simply profit from its being united. Furthermore, the context of the quotation from Livy is revealing. For the Samnite captain who utters the speech has in fact cunningly fabricated the violation of peace into which he has drawn the Romans in order to provoke a fight, thereby creating the necessity (and thus supposed justice) which he claims justifies their going to war. Perhaps Machiavelli is hinting to his prince that he need not wait for just cause to begin this enterprise, but can instead likewise manufacture the necessity that will excuse it and give it a tincture of justice.[12]

Machiavelli is nonetheless silent here about winners and losers in the fight to unify Italy or the fabricated necessity that might justify doing so. Instead, he continues to downplay the difficulties involved in his proposed project: "Here there is a greatest readiness, and where there is great readiness there cannot be great difficulty, provided that your house takes up the institutions of those persons whom I have proposed for your aim." Machiavelli again addresses himself to the Medici, although he does not make it clear which "institutions" (*ordini*) he has in mind, but if "those persons" refers to Moses, Cyrus, and Theseus, then he must refer to the "new orders" (*ordini*) of establishing a new state. In chapter 6 he stated, "there is nothing more difficult to manage than to make oneself a leader who introduces new orders" (chap. 6, 56), but now he writes that "there cannot be great difficulty" in doing so. As proof that there is great readiness and thus no great difficulty he writes: "Beyond this, see here the extraordinary things, without precedent, conducted by God: the sea has opened; a cloud has shown you the way, the stone has poured forth water; here the manna has rained down." Of course, these extraordinary things are not "without precedent" if we consult the book of Exodus, where these miracles are related as occurring to the Hebrews during their years of wandering in the desert before reaching the promised land. Machiavelli thus once again likens the Italians to the Hebrews, awaiting their own armed prophet. "All things have come together for your greatness. The remainder you have to do yourselves. God does not want to do all things, so as not to take away our free will or any part of that glory that belongs to us." In chapter 25 Machiavelli explained that he judged that fortune allows us to be arbiter of about half of our actions "so that our free will may not be eliminated," and now he claims that God does so as well.

Continuing to urge the Medici to take up the banner, Machiavelli addresses a difficulty they may still recognize in accepting this divine mission, and here it is a difficulty of human and not divine making. Namely, it may seem that military valor is extinguished in Italy. "This arose from her former orders not being good ones, and from there not being anyone who knew how to find new ones." In chapter 12 Machiavelli addressed these ruinous military orders as being the result of the "sins" of princes. Here he promises redemption: "And nothing confers so much honor on a man who rises anew as do new laws and the new orders he invents." This claim should make us recall what he said in chapter 6 about the difficulties faced by new princes or new prophets in introducing "new orders," as well as his claim in chapter 15 that he himself was departing from the "orders" of others and thus introducing his own new ones. Returning to the language of "matter" and "form" he used earlier in this chapter, and still earlier in chapter 6, Machiavelli assures his prince that the time is ripe for these new laws and new orders: "And in Italy there is no want of material into which every form may be introduced; here there is great virtue in the limbs, provided she does not lack leaders." Everything has come from the weakness of the leaders, leading to the series of military losses experienced by the Italians.

Above all, Machiavelli tells his redeemer, you should provide yourself with "your own arms," which he terms the "true founda-tion of every undertaking." If he is vague about what institutions are needed for his project, Machiavelli offers relatively detailed advice about how to order these arms. If properly ordered and commanded by their princes, their "Italian virtue" will overcome the enemy, he claims with continued optimism. "And these are among those things which, when ordered anew, give reputation and greatness to a new prince."

Machiavelli concludes his exhortation by raising it to an even higher pitch:

This opportunity, therefore, should not be allowed to pass, so that Italy, after so much time, may see a redeemer for herself. Nor can I express with what love he would be received in all those provinces that have suffered from these foreign floods; with what thirst for revenge, with what obstinate faith, with what piety, with what tears. What gates would be closed to him? What peoples would deny him their obedience? What envy would oppose him? What Italian would deny him homage?

Does Machiavelli forget that he earlier wrote that new princes face great difficulties and dangers when establishing "new orders," including "envy" that has to be overcome? Moreover, although he claims that all of Italy will gladly open their gates and follow this prince, surely even if "all those provinces that have suffered from these foreign floods" might agree about the need to rid Italy of "barbarian domination," they would not all agree on which prince from one city or state or another should be the redeemer. But these difficulties are not Machiavelli's subject here. He therefore calls on the Medici to take up the enterprise "with that spirit and that hope with which just undertakings are taken up, so that under its insignia this fatherland may be ennobled, and under its auspices that saying of Petrarch may be realized," ending *The Prince* with Petrarch's rousing verses:

Virtue against fury
Will take up arms, and may the struggle be short;
since the ancient valor
in Italian hearts is not yet dead.[13]

Joining in Petrarch's enthusiasm, Machiavelli presents himself as an Italian patriot. As noted above, interpreters have therefore variously seen chapter 26 and his call to free Italy from the barbarians as revealing his ultimate intention of unifying Italy or as a rhetorical exercise that either adds an appealing varnish to his call for amoral actions in the service of princely glory or as a conclusion that simply does not accord with the previous twenty-five chapters.

Rather than attempt to resolve this question, perhaps we can conclude by noting how Machiavelli changes the thrust of Petrarch's poem by putting it in a different context. In his poem, Petrarch addresses himself to God and begs for mercy for Italy, torn apart by war and subject to foreign swords and a "deluge" (*diluvio*) that overflows Italy despite the natural barrier of the Alps because of her "sin." He then calls upon the deity to bring peace to Italy, offering the verses Machiavelli quotes. Finally, Petrarch concludes his poem by calling on his own song to go among the few who love the good, singing: "'Who will protect me? I go crying: Peace, peace, peace!'"[14] Much of the setting and imagery of Petrarch's poem are appropriated by Machiavelli: an Italy torn by war and outside invaders, imagery of a flood, etc. However, at least two differences are notable. First, if Petrarch addresses himself to God as the redeemer of Italy, Machiavelli calls upon a prince, perhaps a Medici prince, to undertake this redemption. Second, whereas Petrarch's poem is an appeal for peace—memorably ending with a triple exhortation "Peace, peace, peace!"—Machiavelli appropriates Petrarch to call for war.[15]

NOTES

1 For treatments of the background of *fortuna*, see esp. Flanagan 1972; Pitkin 1984, chap. 6; Parel 1992, chap. 4; Nederman 1999.

2 See Rahe 2007 for an argument that Machiavelli's view of nature is fundamentally Epicurean.

3 On Machiavelli's use of "belief" and "believing" in this context, see Tarcov 2013b, 576.

4 "Happy" and "unhappy"—*felice* and *infelice*—in this context meaning principally "fortunate" and "unfortunate."

5 In the *Discourses on Livy*, in a very similar discussion of how men fail to vary with the times due to their natural inclination or habit, Machiavelli remarks: "Hence it arises that a republic has greater life and has good fortune longer than a principality, for it can accommodate itself better than one prince to the diversity of times through the diversity of the citizens that are in it" (III.9, 240).

6 See, e.g., Pitkin 1984.

7 See Chabod 1964; Viroli 2010, 122ff., and Viroli 2013.

8 See Baron 1991.

9 See Strauss 1958, 62ff.

10 See, e.g., Baron 1991, 85.

11 Livy, *History of Rome* IX.1. Machiavelli quotes the same passage in the *Discourses on Livy* (III.12, 248).

12 See Hörnqvist 2004, 256–57.

13 Petrarch, "Italia mia," *Rime* no. 128 (Petrarch 1976). In the *Florentine Histories* Machiavelli relates that Stefano Porcari was also inspired by Petrarch's patriotic poetry: "This man desired, according to the custom of men who relish glory, to do or at least to try something worthy of memory; and he judged he could do nothing else than try to see if he could take his fatherland [i.e., Rome] from the hands of prelates and restore it to its ancient way of life, hoping by this, should he succeed, to be called the new founder and second father of that city. What made him hope for a prosperous end to his undertaking were the evil customs of the prelates and the discontent of the barons and the Roman people, but above all, what gave him hope were those lines of Petrarch in the canzone that begins 'Gentle spirit that rules those limbs,'... ." Machiavelli comments that "the intention of this man could be praised by anyone" (VI.29 [Machiavelli 1988, 263–64]). Porcari failed in his conspiracy and was tried and executed. The events took place in 1453. For an alternative reading of Machiavelli's use of Petrarch in *The Prince* and with reference to Porcari, see Viroli 2013, 125–26.

14 Petrarch 1976, 257–63.

15 See Hörnqvist 2004, 255–57.

11

MACHIAVELLI'S POLITICAL THOUGHT AND HIS LEGACY

Machiavelli is most widely known as the author of *The Prince*, but he wrote a number of other works, including works of political theory. This chapter has two purposes. First, I will examine the relationship between *The Prince* and Machiavelli's other writings, especially the *Discourses on Livy*, in order to contextualize his concerns in his short treatise within his thought as a whole. Without claiming to offer a comprehensive account of all the interpretations of *The Prince* and Machiavelli's political thought, I will sketch some of the more important interpretative approaches that have been and continue to be influential. Second, since Machiavelli's influence is inextricably bound up with the question of how his advice to princes in his short treatise is related to his other, seemingly more republican, works, I will discuss how various interpretations of his political thought have influenced later political thinkers and other writers, not to mention political actors. Finally, I will offer a few brief remarks at the end of the chapter on the legacy of *The Prince* more generally.

THE PRINCE AND MACHIAVELLI'S OTHER POLITICAL WRITINGS

Putting aside the large body of diplomatic and other correspondence, memoranda, and other writings we have from the time when he was in active government service from 1498 to 1512, much of which exhibits some of the sane concerns and contains some of the kernels evident in his later political writings, including *The Prince*, Machiavelli's political works were written after his fall from government service in 1512. As noted in Chapter 2 when discussing the composition of *The Prince*, Machiavelli began the work sometime in 1513 and seems to have completed it by the middle of 1515. He appears to have begun the other major political writing for which we now best know him, the *Discourses on Livy*, in 1515 and completed it by 1518 or 1519. At that point he took up his *Art of War*, which was published in 1521. In 1520 he was commissioned to write yet another major work, the *Florentine Histories*, which he finished in 1525. Finally, in addition to these major works on politics and related subjects, he composed his best-known comedy, *Mandragola*, around 1518. A full interpretation of Machiavelli's thought would require an extended engagement with at least *The Prince*, the *Discourses on Livy*, and the *Florentine Histories*, along with some attention to the *Art of War, Mandragola*, and other writings, as well as to his personal and diplomatic correspondence. Such an interpretation is beyond the scope of this guide, and I will confine myself to a brief sketch of various possibilities of how we might understand the relationship of *The Prince* to Machiavelli's other writings, and especially the *Discourses on Livy*.

The question of Machiavelli's intentions in writing *The Prince* has existed ever since he wrote the work. As noted in Chapter 1 above, Machiavelli himself makes two statements about his intentions, both in his letter of December 10, 1513, to Francesco Vettori in which he first announces that he is writing *The Prince*. First, he states that the work is his attempt to convert the nightly conversations he has with the ancient authors he reads into the full understanding that only comes from writing. Second, he also says there that he intends to present the work to the new prince of

Florence, Giuliano de' Medici, in hopes of regaining a government position.[1] From Machiavelli's own testimony, then, *The Prince* would appear to be simultaneously a work of political theory, on knowledge of politics for its own sake, and a work with a very practical and immediate purpose, namely to gain employment with the new lords of Florence. These two purposes may be in some tension, for if *The Prince* is a kind of job application then it would likely be tailored to that purpose and not simply contain all that Machiavelli has learned from his reading of the ancients or from his own experience with politics. Notably, the former servant of the Florentine Republic presents his work as being directed toward a princely audience and states that he will leave out any reasoning concerning republics. The potential gap between his two announced intentions therefore already raises the question of whether his pose as an adviser to princes fully captures his intentions in writing *The Prince*. In addition, in chapter 15 of *The Prince* Machiavelli states that his intention is "to write a thing that is useful for whoever understands it" (chap. 15, 87). While this statement casts doubt on whether his ultimate audience is in fact the dedicatee to the work, Lorenzo de' Medici, as we have seen, it begs the question of what we are supposed to understand from reading *The Prince* and how—and to whom—it will be useful. In sum, what Machiavelli himself directly states about *The Prince* perhaps raises as many questions about his intentions as it answers.

Nonetheless, if we approach *The Prince* from a more naive perspective and ask ourselves what leaps to the eye at first sight about the work, as I believe we should always do at least for starters, we can first probably agree that Machiavelli's short treatise is, at least on the surface, what it appears to be: a guide for princes, and especially new princes, on how to acquire and maintain political power. Certainly, *The Prince* has long been read in this way, especially during the first two centuries or so after its publication when Machiavelli was known primarily as the author of *The Prince*. If we attend to how Machiavelli frames the work, namely in its Dedicatory Letter to Lorenzo de' Medici and in its concluding chapter exhorting a prince to expel the barbarian foreigners from Italy, then we can probably also agree that *The Prince*, again at least on the surface, has the aim of encouraging a prince to unify

Italy. This reading of *The Prince* became particularly prominent in the period of nationalist movements following the French Revolution, and inspired the Italians struggling to achieve Machiavelli's goal of unifying Italy during the early and mid-nineteenth century, a goal only achieved in 1860, and also influenced political thinkers of that time such as Fichte and Hegel.[2]

These two surface readings of *The Prince* may or may not be seen as being related. First, if we privilege the appearance of *The Prince* as a guide on how to acquire and maintain political power and take note of the unscrupulous means Machiavelli often recommends for doing so, then we might read the work as a hard-nosed, if not amoral or even immoral, advice book for princes. Again, this view has long had its supporters, many of whom have seen Machiavelli as a "teacher of evil." As an example, we might point to Christopher Marlowe's *Jew of Malta* (1589/90), which I discussed at the very beginning of this guide, and note that the playwright's portrait of the sinister but clear-eyed Machiavel was commonplace in Elizabethan theater and other writings of the period.[3] Other prominent critics of Machiavelli in the next few centuries after he wrote *The Prince* similarly approached him as an immoralist, notably Innocent Gentillet, who wrote his *Anti-Machiavel* (1576) in the wake of the slaughter of his fellow Protestants in the St. Bartholomew Day's Massacre, suggesting that the French queen, Catherine de' Medici (daughter of none other than the dedicatee of *The Prince*, Lorenzo de' Medici) was influenced by Machiavelli.

Second, if we take both surface readings into account, then we have at least two routes open to us. First, we might argue that the concluding exhortation to unify Italy is so much garnish meant to obscure or soften the unscrupulous advice under the guise of a patriotic project, and therefore revert to the interpretation of *The Prince* as a hard-nosed guidebook for princes. Alternatively, we might take the concluding exhortation seriously and therefore see Machiavelli as suggesting that the "end" of unifying Italy justifies the "means" necessary for acquiring and maintaining the power in order to achieve that end. Again, such a view was prominent during the nineteenth century with its nationalist movements. In fact, versions of all of these interpretations of *The Prince* have been advanced since the appearance of the work and up to the present day, 500 years later.

If these different interpretations of *The Prince* and Machiavelli's intentions are generated by a relatively naive reading of the work, then matters are immediately complicated by the fact that Machiavelli also wrote a book devoted largely to republics, the *Discourses on Livy*. Similar complications arise if we take into account his *Florentine Histories*, which traces the history of Florence since its beginnings through the death of Lorenzo the Magnificent in 1492, focusing in particular on the internal politics of the Florentine Republic, and thus dealing delicately with the effectively princely rule of the city under the Medici from 1434 onward. To put the issue too bluntly, if we survey Machiavelli's political writings as a whole, *The Prince* is something of the odd man out.

In order to appreciate the complications for understanding *The Prince* posed by the *Discourses on the First Decade of Titus Livy* (the full title of the work), a summary of the work will be useful. As in *The Prince*, Machiavelli states in the dedication to the *Discourses on Livy* that his work contains all that he has learned about politics through his own experience and his continual reading, a claim that already raises issues about the relationship between the two works, for how can both works contain all Machiavelli knows given their different focuses? Unlike his work on principalities, however, the *Discourses on Livy* is dedicated not to a prince, but to two young men whom Machiavelli says deserve to be princes. Machiavelli explains that he has "gone outside the common usage of those who write, who are accustomed always to address their works to some prince and, blinded by ambition and avarice, praise him for all virtuous qualities when they should blame him for every part worthy of approach" (3). As noted in our discussion of the Dedicatory Letter to *The Prince*, Machiavelli almost seems to mock what he had done in *The Prince*, again making us wonder about his ultimate intentions in writing his short treatise. Furthermore, just as he proclaims his novelty in *The Prince* by stating that he will depart from the orders of others, although not until chapter 15, he straightaway opens the preface to Book I of the *Discourses on Livy* with a claim that he is the Christopher Columbus of his chosen field: "Although the envious nature of men has always made it no less dangerous to find new modes and orders than to seek unknown waters and lands ... nonetheless, driven by that natural desire that has always been in me to work, without any hesitation, for those things I believe will bring common benefit to everyone, I have decided to take a path as yet untrodden by anyone" (I Preface, 5). Since he also explains in this preface that his aim is to animate our desire to imitate the example of the ancients "in ordering republics, maintaining states, governing kingdoms, ordering the military and administering war, judging subjects, and increasing empire" (I Preface, 6), the primary puzzle in reading the *Discourses on Livy* is to square how Machiavelli's work can be simultaneously an exercise in appreciating the ancients and a novel political teaching, "a path as yet untrodden by anyone."

The *Discourses on Livy* takes the form of a commentary on the first ten books of the great history of the Roman Republic by Titus Livy, which cover the period from the founding of Rome to the eve of the republic's dominance of the Italian peninsula. Nonetheless, Machiavelli in fact ranges across the entire history of the Roman Republic, touches on the later history of the Roman Empire, extensively discusses other ancient republics and principalities such as Sparta and Athens, and offers a running comparison between ancient and modern practices concerning politics and warfare. The *Discourses on Livy* is in many ways primarily a book on republics, and certainly has been characterized as such. In this light it is revealing that Machiavelli not only speaks of tyrants in the work, which he never does in *The Prince*, but even calls "tyrants" some of the very same individuals he terms "princes" in *The Prince*, as has already been noted. Nonetheless, despite its more republican focus, Machiavelli in fact also discusses princes and offers them advice in the *Discourses on Livy*, including some of the same advice he gives in *The Prince*. Finally, just as Machiavelli appears to refer in *The Prince* to the *Discourses on Livy* when he remarks in chapter 2 that he will leave out any reasoning on republics since he has written on that subject elsewhere, in the *Discourses on Livy*, he twice specifically refers to *The Prince*, namely in II.1 (128) when he refers to his discussion of the Roman mode of conquering provinces in "our treatise of principalities" and in III.42 (302) when he explains that he will be silent on the subject of whether promises should be kept since he has discussed the matter at length in "our treatise of the prince." In addition, he refers less specifically to *The Prince* on several occasions, including in a discussion of auxiliary and mercenary arms (II.20) and in a discussion of fortresses (II.24). At minimum, then, even if it can be said that Machiavelli turned from writing on princes to discoursing on republics, the references to *The Prince* within the *Discourses on Livy* suggest that he did not simply leave behind his brief treatise on principalities or see the two works as having entirely different subjects or aims.

If we approach the *Discourses on Livy* with a more naive perspective and ask ourselves what leaps to the eye at first sight about the work, as we likewise did above with *The Prince*, then it comes to light as primarily a book on republics. Indeed, Machiavelli proclaims a preference for republics in the *Discourses on Livy*, something he of course never does in *The Prince*. For example, in a famous chapter "The Multitude Is Wiser and More Consistent Than a Prince" (I.58), Machiavelli traces the successes of republics to a greater respect for the law. Speaking in particular of the territorial increases seen in Rome and other republics, he avers that this "cannot arise from anything other than that governments of peoples are better than those of princes," although he goes on to point to a superiority of princes in certain regards: "If princes are superior to peoples in ordering laws, forming civil lives, and ordering new statutes and orders, peoples are so much superior in maintaining things ordered that without doubt they attain the glory of those who order them" (I.58, 115–18). We will come back to this claim. Likewise, in a discussion of the love of freedom and concern for the common good seen in various states, he writes:

> without doubt this common good is not observed if not in republics, since all that is for that purpose is executed ... . The contrary happens when there is a prince, in which case what suits him usually offends the city and what suits the city offends him. In this mode, as soon as a tyranny arises after a free way of life, the least evil that results for those cities is not to go ahead further nor to grow more in power or

riches, but usually—or rather always—it happens that they go backward. And if fate should make emerge there a virtuous tyrant, who by spirit and by virtue of arms expands his dominion, the result is of no utility to that republic, but is his own.

(II.2, 130)

Finally by way of example, in a discussion of how it is necessary to vary with the times in order to succeed, a principal issue in chapter 25 of *The Prince*, Machiavelli announces the superiority of republics: "Hence it arises that a republic has greater life and has good fortune longer than a principality, for it can accommodate itself better than one prince can to the diversity of times through the diversity of citizens that are in it" (III.9, 240).

To return then to the question of how we are to understand *The Prince* in light of the *Discourses on Livy* and to put the matter bluntly: how could Machiavelli simultaneously be the author of a book offering unscrupulous advice to princes and the author of a book promoting republicanism? Once again, this question has hovered over the interpretation of *The Prince*, and of Machiavelli's political theory as a whole, ever since the appearance of the two works.

INTERPRETATIONS OF *THE PRINCE* AND MACHIAVELLI'S OTHER POLITICAL WRITINGS

Broadly speaking, five solutions have been offered to the question of the relationship between *The Prince* and Machiavelli's other political writings, and especially the *Discourses on Livy*, all of which have long pedigrees and all of which still have their adherents.

First, readers have viewed *The Prince* as a cynical job application, a work aimed at doing precisely what the Dedicatory Letter suggests: gaining employment with the Medici. Such interpretations have therefore tended to view Machiavelli either as an equal opportunity adviser, willing to sell his services to princes and republics alike, or as a sincere republican willing to sell his soul to regain political office.

Second, other interpretations go to the opposite extreme suggested by the fact that Machiavelli was a patriotic servant of the

Florentine Republic, viewing *The Prince* as a satire on princes written by a disguised republican.

Third, some scholars have argued that Machiavelli simply changed his mind over what political solutions were viable at the time he was writing the two works, and they therefore concern themselves with the probable dates of the composition of *The Prince* and the *Discourses on Livy* and the changing political landscape when they were written.

Fourth, still other interpreters have suggested that Machiavelli views both princely and republican government as possible routes, perhaps more suitable in different circumstances, for achieving ultimate goals such as the security of the state or the unification of political power, including the unification of Italy.

Fifth, noting that some of the same concerns occupy Machiavelli in both works despite their apparently differing focuses on principalities and republics, a final group of interpreters have sought to distill a unified political teaching and intention on Machiavelli's part that explains both *The Prince* and the *Discourses on Livy* (and his other writings) and the relationship between them. For example, some of these interpreters have suggested that the modes of princely rule are necessary for founding or refounding a state, but that the ultimate goal is to establish a republic.

Very roughly speaking, I would say that scholarship on Machiavelli has tended to evolve away from the first alternatives and toward the latter alternatives sketched here. In other words, very few serious readers of *The Prince* now take the work to be a cynical job application, and more scholars are now offering interpretations that integrate *The Prince*, the *Discourses on Livy*, and Machiavelli's other political writings. (And I would consider myself as belonging to this last group.) Let us entertain each alternative in its turn.

The first approach is to take *The Prince* largely on its face as a book advising a prince how to acquire and maintain power and, given the Dedicatory Letter, as a work intended by Machiavelli to gain employment with the new Medici lords of Florence. Under this interpretation, then, Machiavelli is either a cynical author who will do anything to regain his political position or, in light of his service to the republic and his authorship of the *Discourses on*

Livy, he is an equal opportunity adviser to princes and republics alike. The charge of cynicism or opportunism by itself is not a very satisfying way of approaching *The Prince*, and certainly does not take into account the other motive he reveals in his letter to Vettori of converting his reading of the ancients and his own experience of politics into a fuller understanding of the art of politics. Indeed, although the characterization of *The Prince* as a job application persists as a common caricature of the work, no serious scholar simply maintains such a thesis. The more interesting and influential version of this first major approach is that Machiavelli is an equal opportunity adviser to princes and republics, a kind of neutral scientist or artist of political rule.[4] However, if it does not also collapse into a simply cynical reading of *The Prince*, this line of argument raises the question of what ends, if any, Machiavelli has in mind beyond the simple acquisition and maintenance of political power, and therefore essentially leads to the fourth or fifth interpretative approaches to be discussed below.

The second approach takes Machiavelli's republicanism seriously and therefore holds that *The Prince* is in actuality a satire of princely rule. Among the earliest exponents of this reading was Alberico Gentili (1552–1608), the Italian jurist who influenced the development of international law. Similarly, Sir Francis Bacon (1561–1626) offered an early appreciation of Machiavelli as a republican writer, although he did not go so far as to characterize *The Prince* as satirical. This approach became more common during the eighteenth century when Machiavelli became more widely known for being the author of the *Discourses on Livy* and when readers therefore made more serious attempts to reconcile his republican treatise with *The Prince*. Among the more prominent thinkers to advance such an interpretation was Jean-Jacques Rousseau, as has already been briefly noted above. In his chapter on monarchy in the *Social Contract* (1762), Rousseau ridicules the claim that kings will rule in their subjects' interest because it is in the monarch's own interest to do so, writing that kings "know perfectly well that this is not true." He then appeals to the Florentine for support: "This is what Machiavelli has so clearly proved. While pretending to teach lessons to kings, he taught great

ones to people. Machiavelli's *Prince* is the book of republicans."
To this striking statement Rousseau adds a note:

> Machiavelli was an honest man and a good citizen. But being attached to the house of the Medici, he was forced during the oppression of his fatherland to disguise his love of freedom. The choice of his execrable hero [i.e., Cesare Borgia] alone is enough to manifest his secret intention, and the conflict between the maxims of his book *The Prince* and those of his *Discourses on Titus Livy* and his *Florentine Histories* demonstrates that this profound political thinker has so far had only superficial or corrupt readers. The Court of Rome has severely prohibited his book. I should think so. It is this court that he most clearly depicts.[5]

By pointing to Machiavelli's supposed "execrable hero" as proof of his interpretation, Rousseau replies to his contemporary Montesquieu, whose contrary interpretation of *The Prince* in his *Spirit of the Laws* (1748) rests on a contrary inference from the very same evidence: "Machiavelli was full of his idol, Duke Valentino."[6] Another contemporary, Denis Diderot, joined Rousseau's side in the article "Machiavellianism" for the *Encyclopédie* (1751–72), the great bible of the Enlightenment. Posing the question of how the republican patriot could have written a book of advice to tyrants, Diderot concurs with the view advanced earlier by Sir Francis Bacon that Machiavelli's book presented a frank portrayal of the ways of tyrants rather than a guide for princes. Then, referring to Voltaire and his one-time patron Frederick the Great, the future absolutist monarch who cut his teeth by writing a refutation of *The Prince*, Diderot concludes his discussion by writing: "I have heard that a philosopher, who was questioned by a great prince on a refutation of Machiavellianism he had just published, replied 'Sire, I should think the first lesson Machiavelli taught his disciple was to refute his work.'"[7]

The reading of *The Prince* as a satire has enjoyed consistent, if intermittent, support from a variety of interpreters up to the present day. For example, a half century ago Garrett Mattingly reprised Rousseau's argument by suggesting that Machiavelli's choice of Cesare Borgia as a supposed model prince, along with his manifest republican sympathies as expressed in the *Discourses on Livy*, indicated that *The Prince* should be read as a satire rather than as a scientific guide for princes.[8] In a somewhat different vein, Mary Dietz finds in Machiavelli's advice to princes a trap that is meant to lure the unsuspecting prince into following advice that would undermine rather than maintain his state.[9] Finally, quite recently Erica Benner has put forward an interpretation of *The Prince* as a thoroughly ironic work, not so much as a satire of princes or a testament of concealed republicanism, but rather as a presentation of such terms as "fortune" and "virtue" which are actually subverted by Machiavelli in order to uphold a more traditional view of morality.[10] One obstacle faced by any version of the approach of seeing *The Prince* as some sort of satire is that Machiavelli makes similar arguments and offers similar advice in the *Discourses on Livy*, a work which interpreters following this approach nearly uniformly view as sincere.

Like the second interpretive approach to *The Prince*, the third approach sees the audiences or emphases of *The Prince* and the *Discourses on Livy* as sufficiently different to treat them as largely separate projects, but unlike the second approach does not read *The Prince* as a satire. In order to account for the differences in audience and emphasis, therefore, interpreters in this third camp tend to argue that Machiavelli changed his tack, or even his mind, due to changing circumstances or opportunities. Central to many of the interpretations in this vein, therefore, is the question of the dating of the two works. Contemporary scholars have generally come to agree that *The Prince* was composed between 1513 and 1515 and that the *Discourses on Livy* was written between 1515 and 1518 or 1519, but this was not always the consensus. One once-prominent hypothesis was that Machiavelli began the *Discourses on Livy* earlier than *The Prince*, and even perhaps as early as 1504–5, then dropped writing his work on republics when the Florentine Republic fell and he lost his government posts, turning to writing *The Prince* given the different circumstances in his own life and in Florence, and then took up the *Discourses on Livy* once again after failing to gain employment with the Medici with *The Prince*.[11] Under this interpretation, then, *The Prince* was effectively an opportunistic excursion by an essentially republican author. The great Renaissance scholar Hans Baron effectively overthrew this hypothesis, and, along with other scholars, began to lay down what has become the now generally accepted view concerning the dates of the composition of the works.[12] Under this interpretation, then, *The Prince* precedes Machiavelli's serious engagement with republicanism.

Scholars who have accepted the consensus regarding the dating of the composition of *The Prince* and the *Discourses on Livy*, but who see important divergences between the two works in terms of their aims and audiences, have therefore argued that changing circumstances in the political landscape led to Machiavelli's turn from writing for princes to writing about republics. Most prominent and influential on this score is Quentin Skinner and the school of scholars who have followed him. Skinner identifies the differences between the two works as stemming from a change in how fertile Italy was for principalities as opposed to republics at different times and from the fact that Machiavelli adapted his presentation in the two works to different traditional discourses on the topics.[13] One obstacle to this line of interpretation is that if we accept the dating of the completion of *The Prince* and the commencement of writing the *Discourses on Livy* as both occurring in or around 1515, we must be persuaded that political events—and Machiavelli's assessment of those events—must have changed dramatically in a very short period of time. At minimum, I would say, we have no compelling testimony from anything Machiavelli wrote that would lead us to think he identified any such shift in the political landscape. Perhaps it is more reasonable to suggest that Machiavelli turned to the *Discourses on Livy* after *The Prince* failed to gain him employment from the Medici, not from satire to sincere tract, but with a more or less different focus.[14] The question of what common aims he might have in the two works leads us to the fourth and fifth main interpretative approaches.

The fourth and fifth interpretative approaches I have identified see *The Prince* and the *Discourses on Livy* not so much as having distinctly different aims or audiences, unlike the first three approaches surveyed so far, but as constituting parts of a more or less unified political teaching. There is considerable overlap between these two approaches, but it is useful to distinguish them for the purposes of analysis. In this light, then, the fourth approach maintains that Machiavelli has the same or similar aims in both *The Prince* and the *Discourses on Livy*, for example the security or unity of the state, but that he generally approaches these aims from different directions in the two works. This approach might be characterized as "horizontal": two more or less equal routes that aim at the same end. By contrast, the fifth approach attempts to integrate the two works more thoroughly, for example arguing that the princely rule emphasized in *The Prince*, but not by any means absent from the *Discourses on Livy*, is viewed by Machiavelli as a necessary step toward a more fully republican form of state, such as emphasized in the *Discourses on Livy*, but also not entirely missing from *The Prince*. This approach might be termed "vertical": one route with different stages that aim at an ultimate end.

The fourth interpretive approach generally views *The Prince* and the *Discourses on Livy* as representing different means to the same ends, with these means being more available or apt in different circumstances. For example, various scholars have argued that Machiavelli saw princely and republican rule as being more appropriate or effective for differing political conditions, for instance suggesting that he saw princely rule as necessary in more corrupt times and republican rule as more possible in virtuous times.[15] Another set of scholars tend to embed such a reading of the texts within a broader consideration of Machiavelli's view on the relationship between politics and morals, including his famous discussion of "virtue" (*virtù*). One family of arguments within this approach might be characterized as being inspired by Benedetto Croce's statement that Machiavelli revealed "the necessity and autonomy of politics."[16] According to Croce, Machiavelli saw politics—whether as practiced by princes or republics—as constituting an autonomous realm with its own logic and set of standards distinct from traditional morality. A somewhat similar interpretation was put forward by Sheldon Wolin, who argues that Machiavelli consciously revived a version of ancient political thought and practice against the Christian and medieval worldview that preserved an autonomous realm for political action. According to Wolin, the autonomous realm of politics is characterized by the threat or use of violence required for the maintenance of the state, where such violence was to be restricted to that purpose, or what he terms an "economy of violence." Finally, Wolin contends that Machiavelli did not reject traditional morality so much as argue that political action had a different logic that sometimes necessitates actions that are immoral from the traditional perspective.[17] In another related but distinct argument, Isaiah Berlin sees Machiavelli as facing a choice between two different and opposed moral systems: a political morality associated with pagan virtues and a private morality associated with Christianity. Berlin argues that Machiavelli embraced political morality in part because of his assessment of Christian morality as being unsuitable to the demands of politics. According to Berlin, for Machiavelli the ultimate goal of politics is the security of the state, and he argues that although Machiavelli had a preference for republics as more likely to achieve this goal, he preferred a well-governed principality to a deficient republic in this regard.[18] In short, all of these influential interpretations see a unity of concerns between *The Prince* and the *Discourses on Livy* stemming from Machiavelli's vision of politics.

An alternative family of interpretations agrees that Machiavelli has a coherent theory which underlies *The Prince* and the *Discourses on Livy*, and his other writings, but does so by returning after a fashion to the traditional view of Machiavelli as an immoralist. The most influential exponent of this reading, Leo Strauss, famously began his *Thoughts on Machiavelli* by writing: "We shall not shock anyone, we shall merely expose ourselves to good-natured or at any rate harmless ridicule, if we profess ourselves inclined to the old-fashioned and simple opinion according to which Machiavelli was a teacher of evil."[19] Of course, Strauss did shock people and expose himself to considerable ridicule, and not of the good-natured or harmless sort, in making this profession. However, note that Strauss claims only that he is "inclined" to this old view, and insufficient attention has been paid to his qualification of the initial claim a few pages later: "We thus regard the simple opinion about Machiavelli as indeed decisively superior to the prevailing sophisticated views," namely that he is either a republican patriot or a "value free" political scientist, "though still insufficient."[20] According to Strauss and other interpreters in this tradition, Machiavelli's supposed patriotism or his project of unifying Italy are essentially rhetorical cover for Machiavelli himself and the prince or republic that would follow his teaching. The true aim is not the common good, but the acquisition of material goods for the many and especially of glory for the few. In this light, then, Machiavelli himself hoped to achieve glory by being a teacher of princes who themselves pursue glory. Furthermore, scholars in this tradition tend to argue that Machiavelli rejects traditional morality, and especially the legacy of Christianity, and see him less as trying to revive classical republicanism than as founding the modern state based on security and acquisition.[21] Finally, this interpretation has generated considerable debate over Machiavelli's thought and its relationship to later thinkers in the republican and liberal traditions, with some scholars arguing that his vision of the modern, acquisitive state makes him a forbearer of Hobbes, Locke, and liberal or liberal-republican thought,[22] and others resisting this argument by locating Machiavelli instead in the classical or civic republican tradition.[23]

Finally, the fifth interpretative approach I have identified attempts to integrate the princely focus of *The Prince* with the republican focus of the *Discourses on Livy* in one of at least two ways. First, some argue that *The Prince* is a more popular or republican work than first appears. Second, others suggest that Machiavelli sees princely rule as a necessary step in founding or refounding republics. In either case, however, they tend to see Machiavelli as ultimately a republican theorist. As with many of the other interpretations, these alternatives have a long pedigree. For example, at the very same time many writers during the sixteenth century, particularly on the Continent, were inveighing against Machiavelli as an immoralist, other authors, particularly in England, explicitly adopted Machiavelli as a republican theorist, reading *The Prince* in that light. Among these authors were James Harrington, whose *Commonwealth of Oceana* (1656) includes a number of critical engagements with Machiavelli, especially on the question of class conflict, Marchmont Nedham, who was effectively Oliver Cromwell's press agent and whose *The Excellencie of a Free-State* (published 1656) drew on Machiavelli for his argument for popular sovereignty, and Henry Neville (1620–1694), who translated Machiavelli's works.[24]

Under the first version of this fifth approach, scholars argue that Machiavelli essentially coaxes the reader of *The Prince* from being an autocratic ruler to being a more popular or even republican ruler. In this regard, they point to Machiavelli's advice in *The Prince* of how a prince should found on the people, and found on the people as opposed to on the "great," and of how a prince should arm his people rather than hire mercenary arms or protect himself in a fortress, and so on.[25] In many respects, this line of interpretation sees Machiavelli as doing something similar to what Aristotle did in his *Politics* by advising tyrants to moderate their rule for their own good, and it is interesting in this regard to note that Machiavelli's only reference to Aristotle in his works is when he refers in the *Discourses on Livy* (III.26) to Aristotle's discussion of tyranny.

Under the second version of this approach, scholars argue that Machiavelli saw princely and republican rule as both necessary for different purposes or at different stages within an ultimately republican framework. Pointing for example to Machiavelli's discussion in the *Discourses on Livy* of Romulus, Moses, Cyrus, and other founders who feature in *The Prince* as exemplary new princes, these scholars suggest that princely rule is necessary for founding and reordering republics, and that a far-sighted prince seeking glory would maximize his glory by founding or preparing the way for the founding of a republic since, according to Machiavelli, republics have longer lives. Similarly, they can point to a passage from the *Discourses on Livy* quoted above: "If princes are superior to peoples in ordering laws, forming civil lives, and ordering new statutes and orders, peoples are so much superior in maintaining things ordered that without doubt they attain the glory of those who order them" (I.58, 118).[26] Finally, these various versions of the fifth interpretative approach are often combined with the idea that Machiavelli's ultimate goal is the unification of Italy, hopefully as a republic.[27]

Finally, some scholars who might be characterized as blending these two alternatives within the broad fifth interpretative approach I have identified have gone yet further to argue that

Machiavelli is a democratic or populist thinker, or at least that his thought can be appropriated for more democratic or populist ends.[28] These scholars look to Machiavelli's analyses of class conflict in his works, including his discussions of the conflict between the two "humors" of the people and the great in *The Prince*. In this light, they also point to what is perhaps Machiavelli's most innovative argument in the *Discourses on Livy*, namely that the conflict between the patricians and plebeians in ancient Rome was the source of the republic's freedom and power (I.4), as well as his discussion of how the tribunate worked to check the ambitions of the patricians and incorporate a popular element into the government (e.g., I.5). Further, they can point to Machiavelli's extensive discussion in the *Florentine Histories* of the sources and outcomes of factional conflict in his native city (see esp. *Florentine Histories* III.1). One influential theorist, Antonio Gramsci, went yet further along this road in his Marxist appropriation of Machiavelli, arguing that, under the conditions of advanced capitalist societies, the "modern prince" is the revolutionary party working on behalf of the proletariat.[29] This appropriation of Machiavelli's thought leads us to his legacy as a thinker.

MACHIAVELLI'S LEGACY

What is Machiavelli's legacy as a thinker? At the outset of this guide to his best-known work, I noted that the adjective "Machiavellian" universally evokes a set of connotations of someone who maneuvers ruthlessly to acquire power, who argues that the ends justify the means, who adopts a realistic or even cynical stance toward politics and other human endeavors, and so on. To what extent the author of *The Prince* was himself a "Machiavellian" or taught such a doctrine is, of course, a matter of debate. But a thinker's legacy often outpaces or diverges from his or her own intentions, and Machiavelli is no exception.

In terms of intellectual history, Machiavelli is oftentimes claimed to be the first "modern" political thinker, whether because his thought marks a conscious break with the previous classical and medieval Christian traditions, or because of his influence on subsequent thinkers, or both. We have seen Machiavelli's declaration in chapter 15 of *The Prince*, "I shall depart from the orders of others" (chap.15, 87), and his similar claim in the *Discourses on Livy* that he is a kind of Columbus of the political world who has decided "to take a path as yet untrodden by anyone" (I Preface, 5). As a Renaissance thinker, Machiavelli is not alone in reconsidering traditional modes of thought, but he is perhaps unusually self-conscious about how his thought departs from that of his predecessors, or at least he is unusually bold in his claims about the degree of his departure.

In considering Machiavelli as a claimant to being the first "modern" political thinker, therefore, various interpreters have pointed to the supposedly thoroughly secular character of his thought and to its "realism" or even his supposedly "scientific" approach to politics and morals, as opposed to previous classical and Christian thinkers whom Machiavelli characterizes as focusing on "the imagination of the thing" rather than going to the "effectual truth." Relatedly, they have pointed to his emphasis on unleashing and channeling tendencies in human nature, above all the desire to acquire, that previous thinkers had condemned or considered the baser parts of our nature. Finally, they have Machiavelli as the first theorist of the modern state, both in the sense that he lived in a time when the modern state was coming into existence and in the sense that he was among the first to offer a political theory in which the emerging modern state was front and center. In all these respects, those who herald Machiavelli as the first modern political thinker point to his influence on later thinkers, for example likening his exhortation in chapter 25 of *The Prince* to use virtue to dam and dike fortune to Sir Francis Bacon's project of mastering nature for the benefit of mankind, or seeing his realism and even rather dim view of human nature reflected in Thomas Hobbes, or finding his emphasis on acquisition in John Locke. All of these claims of novelty on Machiavelli's part and of his influence on later thinkers are appealing, but are also of course contested. What we can say is that they are all among his possible legacies in political thought and intellectual history more broadly.

If we turn from high intellectual history, we should consider Machiavelli's legacies with regard to what might be called broad approaches to politics and morals: the theory of *raison d'état*, "realism" both in general and in relation to international relations, and the question of "dirty hands."

The theory of *raison d'état*, with the French term being more common than the English "reason of state," holds that the national interest of a state is the paramount goal, both in terms of internal and external politics. One can easily see how such a theory could be traced to Machiavelli, who writes in chapter 15 of *The Prince*: "For, if everything be well considered, something will be found that will appear a virtue, but will lead to his ruin if adopted; and something else that will appear a vice, if adopted, will result in his security and well-being" (chap. 15, 88). Machiavelli himself never uses that term, but it was first popularized by a compatriot about fifty years after his death, namely by the Giovanni Botero in his *Della ragion di stato* (1589), who simultaneously drew on and distanced himself from Machiavelli. Political thinkers and especially political actors over the centuries have appealed to the concept of *raison d'état* for pursuing policies in politics, diplomacy, economics, and so forth. Historians who have traced the history of *raison-d'état* approaches almost always point to Machiavelli as the founder or an important figure, as evidenced by the title of the classic study in the field by Friedrich Meinecke: *Machiavellism: The Doctrine of Raison d'État and Its Place in Modern History.* [30]

Closely related to the concept of *raison d'état* is "realism," both in the general sense of a "realist" approach to politics as opposed to an "idealist" approach and in the specific sense of "realism" in the practice and theory of international relations, and Machiavelli has been long associated with "realism" in both senses. We have already commented on the general sense of "realism" with regard to Machiavelli. As for the more specific sense concerned with international relations, theorists and practitioners of international relations have argued that concern with the national interest of a state is or should be the paramount consideration guiding policy. In terms of international relations theories, "realism" is one among several paradigms for understanding the actions of states and their leaders. Realist theorists such as Hans Morgenthau, writing in the wake of World War II, and Kenneth Waltz point to Machiavelli as an important influence. [31]

Finally, and also related to theories of *raison d'état* and realism, is Machiavelli's influence on the moral and political question of "dirty hands," that is, the idea that a politician (or anyone else) might have to get his or her hands "dirty" by violating moral standards for some great good. Once again, it is easy to see how Machiavelli might be associated with such a question, given that he counsels a prince "to learn to be able to be not good" (chap. 15, 87), whatever Machiavelli's ultimate view of traditional standards of morality. Once again, intellectual historians have traced the notion of "dirty hands" to Machiavelli, both in terms of justifications made for such departures from morality and, more broadly, in terms of related theories of justifying moral and political action in terms of acquisition, self-interest, etc.[32] In contemporary moral and political philosophy, perhaps the most influential analysis of "dirty hands" is by Michael Walzer, which has inspired a lively debate.[33]

NOTES

1 Machiavelli to Francesco Vettori, December 10, 1513, in Machiavelli 2004, 262–65.
2 For discussions of the reception of *The Prince* in the sixteenth through nineteenth centuries, see Baron 1961, 217–21; Anglo 2005; Kahn 2010.
3 See Raab 1965, Kahn 1994.
4 See Cassirer 1946; Butterfield 1962.
5 Rousseau, *Social Contract* III.6 and n. (Rousseau 2012, 218).
6 Montesquieu, *Spirit of the Laws* XXIX.19 (Montesquieu 1989 [1748], 618).
7 Diderot, "Machiavelisme," *Encyclopédie* IX (1765), quoted from the edition on the ARTFL *Encyclopédie* Project, http://artflsrv02.uchicago.edu/cgi-bin/philologic/getob ject.pl?c.8:2243.encyclopedie0513>, accessed June 26, 2015.
8 Mattingly 1958.
9 Dietz 1986.
10 Benner 2013. See also Benner 2009.
11 Chabod 1964. Chabod first put forward his thesis in 1926, and it remained highly influential, especially among Italian scholars, for the next half century and more.
12 Baron 1956 and Baron 1991.
13 Skinner 1978.
14 See, e.g., Baron 1991.
15 See Black 2013; Vivante 2013.
16 Croce 1925.
17 Wolin 1960. Wolin does not explicitly take up the question of the relationship between *The Prince* and the *Discourses on Livy*.
18 Berlin 1979 [1972].

19 Strauss 1958, 9.
20 Ibid., 12–13.
21 In addition to Strauss 1958, see esp. Orwin 1978; Mansfield 1996. Black (2013) offers a similar interpretation of Machiavelli's rejection of traditional and especially Christian morality and his concern with glory.
22 See Sullivan 2006; Rahe 2008.
23 Pocock 1975; Skinner 1990; Viroli 1998.
24 See Sullivan 2006; Rahe 2008.
25 See Hörnqvist 2004; Vatter 2013. Benner's (2013) interpretation of The Prince has a similar thrust in this regard.
26 See Lefort 2012 [2005], although his Hegelian-influenced interpretation of Machiavelli, which is provocative and often illuminating, is difficult to characterize.
27 Viroli 2013.
28 McCormick 2011; Vatter 2000, 2013.
29 Gramsci 1996 [1949].
30 Meinecke 1957 [1924]. See also Donaldson 1988.
31 Morgenthau 1948; Waltz 1959, 1979. For an analysis of Machiavelli's influence on realism in international relations theory, see Forde 1992, 1995.
32 See Parrish 2007.
33 Walzer 1973.

REFERENCES

EDITIONS AND TRANSLATIONS OF MACHIAVELLI'S WORKS

Machiavelli, Niccolò. 1971. *Tutte le opera*. Firenze: Sansoni.

Machiavelli, Niccolò. 1988. *Florentine Histories*. Trans. Laura F. Banfield and Harvey C. Mansfield, Jr. Princeton: Princeton University Press.

Machiavelli, Niccolò. 1996. *Discourses on Livy*. Trans. Harvey C. Mansfield and Nathan Tarcov. Chicago: University of Chicago Press.

Machiavelli, Niccolò. 2004. *Machiavelli and His Friends: Their Personal Correspondence*. Trans. and ed. James B. Atkinson and David Sices. De Kalb, IL: Northern Illinois University Press.

Machiavelli, Niccolò. 2005a. *The Prince*. Trans. and ed. William J. Connell. New York: St. Martin's.

Machiavelli, Niccolò. 2005b. *The Prince*. 2nd ed. Trans. and ed. Harvey C. Mansfield. Chicago: University of Chicago Press.

Machiavelli, Niccolò. 2013. *Il Principe*. Ed. Giorgio Inglese. Torino: Giulio Einaudi.

OTHER WORKS CITED

Anglo, Sydney. 2005. *Machiavelli—The First Century: Studies in Enthusiasm, Hostility, and Irrelevance*. Oxford: Oxford University Press.

Atkinson, James B. 2010. "Niccolò Machiavelli: A Portrait." In *The Cambridge Companion to Machiavelli*, ed. John M. Najemy. Cambridge: Cambridge University Press.

Baron, Hans. 1956. "*The Principe* and the Puzzle of the Date of the Discorsi." *Bibliothèque d'Humanisme et Renaissance* 18: 405–428.

Baron, Hans. 1961. "Machiavelli the Republican Citizen and the Author of *The Prince.*" *English Historical Review* 76: 217–253.

Baron, Hans. 1991. "*The Principe* and the Puzzle of the Date of Chapter 26." *Journal of Medieval and Renaissance Studies* 21: 83–102.

Benner, Erica. 2009. *Machiavelli's Ethics.* Princeton: Princeton University Press.

Benner, Erica. 2013. *Machiavelli's "Prince": A New Reading.* Oxford: Oxford University Press.

Berlin, Isaiah. 1979 [1972]. "The Originality of Machiavelli." In *Against the Current: Essays in the History of Ideas.* Princeton: Princeton University Press, pp. 25–79. Originally published in *Studies on Machiavelli*, ed. Myron P. Gilmore. Firenze: Sansone.

Black, Robert. 2011. "Notes on the Date and Genesis of Machiavelli's *De principatibus.*" In *Europe and Italy: Studies in Honour of Giorgio Chittolini.* Firenze: Firenze University Press, pp. 29–41.

Black, Robert. 2013. *Machiavelli.* London: Routledge.

Butterfield, Herbert. 1962. *The Statecraft of Machiavelli.* New York: Macmillan.

Cassirer, Ernst. 1946. *The Myth of the State.* New Haven: Yale University Press.

Chabod, Federico. 1964. *Scritti su Machiavelli.* Torino: Einaudi.

Connell, William J. 2011. "New Light on Machiavelli's Letter to Vettori, 10 December 1513." In *Europe and Italy: Studies in Honour of Giorgio Chittolini.* Firenze: Firenze University Press, pp. 93–127.

Connell, William J. 2013. "Dating *The Prince*: Beginnings and Endings." *Review of Politics* 75: 497–514.

Croce, Benedetto. 1925. *Elementi di politica.* Bari: Laterza.

de Alvarez, Leo Paul. 1999. *The Machiavellian Enterprise.* DeKalb, IL: Northern Illinois University Press.

Dietz, Mary G. 1986. "Trapping the *Prince*: Machiavelli and the Politics of Deception." *American Political Science Review* 80: 777–799.

Donaldson, Peter S. 1988. *Machiavelli and Mystery of State.* Cambridge: Cambridge University Press.

Flanagan, Thomas. 1972. "The Concept of *Fortuna* in Machiavelli." In *The Political Calculus*, ed. Anthony Parel. Toronto: University of Toronto Press, pp. 126–156.

Forde, Steven. 1992. "Varieties of Realism: Thucydides and Machiavelli." *Journal of Politics* 54: 372–393.

Forde, Steven. 1995. "International Realism and the Science of Politics: Thucydides, Machiavelli, and Neorealism." *International Studies Quarterly* 39: 141–160.

Gilbert, Felix. 1938. *Machiavelli's Prince and its Forerunners: the Prince as a Typical Book de Regimine Principum.* Durham, NC: Duke University Press.

Gramsci, Antonio. 1996 [1949]. *Note sul Machiavelli, sulla politica, e sul il stato moderno.* Rome: Editori Riuniti.

Hörnqvist, Mikael. 2004. *Machiavelli and Empire.* Cambridge: Cambridge University Press.

Kahn, Victoria. 1994. *Machiavellian Rhetoric: From the Counter-Reformation to Milton.* Princeton: Princeton University Press.

Kahn, Victoria. 2010. "Machiavelli's Afterlife and Reputation in the Eighteenth Century." In *The Cambridge Companion to Machiavelli*, ed. John M. Najemy. Cambridge: Cambridge University Press, pp. 239–255.

Kohl, B.G. and Witt, R.G. 1978. *The Earthly Republic: Italian Humanists on Government and Society.* Philadelphia: University of Pennsylvania Press.

Lefort, Claude. 2012 [2005]. *Machiavelli in the Making.* Trans. Michael B. Smith. Evanston, IL: Northwestern University Press. Originally published in a more expanded form as *Le travail de l'oeuvre: Machiavel.* Paris: Gallimard.

Mansfield, Harvey C. 1983. "On the Impersonality of the Modern State: A Comment on Machiavelli's Use of *Stato*." *American Political Science Review* 77: 849–857.

Mansfield, Harvey C. 1996. *Machiavelli's Virtue.* Chicago: University of Chicago Press.

Mattingly, Garrett. 1958. "Machiavelli's *Prince*: Political Science or Political Satire?" *American Scholar* 27: 482–491.

McCormick, John P. 2011. *Machiavellian Democracy.* Cambridge: Cambridge University Press.

Meinecke, Friedrich. 1957 [1924]. *Machiavellism: The Doctrine of Raison d'État and Its Place in Modern History.* Trans. Douglas Scott. New Haven: Yale University Press.

Montesquieu, Charles-Louis de Secondat, baron de. 1989 [1748]. *The Spirit of the Laws.* Trans. and ed. Anne M. Cohler, Basia Carolyn Miller, and Harold Samuel Stone. Cambridge: Cambridge University Press.

Morgenthau, Hans. 1948. *Politics among Nations: The Struggle for Power and Peace.* New York: Knopf.

Najemy, John M. 2013. "Machiavelli and Cesare Borgia: A Reconsideration of Chapter 7 of *The Prince*." *Review of Politics* 75: 539–556.

Nederman, Cary J. 1999. "Amazing Grace: Fortune, God, and Free Will in Machiavelli's Thought." *Journal of the History of Ideas* 60: 617–638.

Newell, Waller. 2013. *Tyranny: A New Interpretation.* Cambridge: Cambridge University Press.

Orwin, Clifford. 1978. "Machiavelli's Unchristian Charity." *American Political Science Review* 72: 1217–1228.

Parel, Anthony J. 1992. *The Machiavellian Cosmos.* New Haven: Yale University Press.

Parrish, John M. 2007. *Paradoxes of Political Ethics: From Dirty Hands to the Invisible Hand.* Cambridge: Cambridge University Press.

Petrarch, Francesco. 1976. *Petrarch's Lyric Poems: The Rime Sparse and Other Lyrics.* Trans. and ed. Robert M. Durling. Cambridge: Harvard University Press.

Pitkin, Hanna Fenichel. 1984. *Fortune is a Woman: Gender and Politics in the Thought of Niccolò Machiavelli.* Berkeley: University of California Press.

Pocock, J.G.A. 1975. *The Machiavellian Moment: Florentine Political Thought and the Atlantic Republican Tradition.* Princeton: Princeton University Press.

Raab, Felix. 1965. *The English Face of Machiavelli: A Changing Interpretation, 1500–1700.* London: Routledge.

Rahe, Paul A. 2007. "In the Shadow of Lucretius: The Epicurean Foundations of Machiavelli's Political Thought." *History of Political Thought* 28: 30–55.

Rahe, Paul A. 2008. *Against Throne and Altar: Machiavelli and Political Theory under the English Republic.* Cambridge: Cambridge University Press

Rousseau, Jean-Jacques. 2012. *The Major Political Writings of Jean-Jacques Rousseau: The Two Discourses and The Social Contract.* Trans. and ed. John T. Scott. Chicago: University of Chicago Press.

Scott, John T. 2014. "The Fortune of Machiavelli's Unarmed Prophet." Paper presented at the Association for Political Theory annual conference, October 16–18, 2014, Madison, WI.

Scott, John T. and Sullivan, Vickie B. 1994. "Patricide and the Plot of *The Prince*: Cesare Borgia and Machiavelli's Italy." *American Political Science Review* 88: 887–900.

Skinner, Quentin. 1978. *The Foundations of Modern Political Thought*, vol. 1: *The Renaissance.* Cambridge: Cambridge University Press.

Skinner, Quentin. 1990. "The Republican Ideal of Political Liberty." In *Machiavelli and Republicanism*, ed. Gisela Bock, Quentin Skinner and Maurizio Viroli. Cambridge: Cambridge University Press, pp. 293–309.

Stacey, Peter. 2007. *Roman Monarchy and the Renaissance Prince.* Cambridge: Cambridge University Press.

Strauss, Leo. 1958. *Thoughts on Machiavelli.* Chicago: University of Chicago Press.

Sullivan, Vickie B. 2006. *Machiavelli, Hobbes, and the Formation of a Liberal Republicanism in England.* Cambridge: Cambridge University Press.

Sullivan, Vickie B. 2013. "Alexander the Great as 'Lord of Asia' and Rome as His Successor in Machiavelli's *Prince*." *Review of Politics* 75: 515–537.

Tarcov, Nathan. 2000. "Machiavelli and the Foundations of Modernity: A Reading of Chapter III of *The Prince*." In *Educating the Prince*, ed. Mark Blitz and William Kristol. Lanham, MD: Rowman & Littlefield, pp. 30–44.

Tarcov, Nathan. 2013a. "Machiavelli in *The Prince*: His Way of Life in Question." In *Political Philosophy Cross-Examined*, ed. Thomas L. Pangle and J. Harvey Lomax. New York: Palgrave Macmillan, pp. 101–118.

Tarcov, Nathan. 2013b. "Belief and Opinion in Machiavelli's *Prince*." *Review of Politics* 75: 573–586.

Vatter, Miguel. 2000. *Between Form and Event: Machiavelli's Theory of Political Freedom.* Dordrecht: Kluwer Academic Publishers.

Vatter, Miguel. 2013. *Machiavelli's "The Prince."* London: Bloomsbury.

Viroli, Maurizio. 1998. *Machiavelli.* Oxford: Oxford University Press.

Viroli, Maurizio. 2007. "Machiavelli's Realism." *Constellations* 14: 466–482.

Viroli, Maurizio. 2010. *Machiavelli's God.* Princeton: Princeton University Press.

Viroli, Maurizio. 2013. *Redeeming "The Prince": The Meaning of Machiavelli's Masterpiece.* Princeton: Princeton University Press.

Vivante, Corrado. 2013. *Machiavelli: An Intellectual Biography.* Trans. Simon MacMichael. Princeton: Princeton University Press.

Waltz, Kenneth N. 1959. *Man, the State, and War.* New York: Columbia University Press.

Waltz, Kenneth N. 1979. *Theory of International Politics*. New York: McGraw Hill.

Walzer, Michael 1973. "Political Action: The Problem of Dirty Hands." *Philosophy & Public Affairs* 2: 160–180.

Warner, John M. and Scott, John T. 2011. "Sin City: Augustine and Machiavelli's Reordering of Rome." *Journal of Politics* 73: 857–871.

Wolin, Sheldon S. 1960. *Politics and Vision: Continuity and Innovation in Western Political Thought*. Princeton: Princeton University Press.

INDEX

Achilles 145, 166, 177
Aeneas 168
Agathocles 103–11, 114, 140, 155–56, 158, 167, 172
Alexander the Great 63–69, 85, 142, 145, 166, 212, 221
Alexander VI, Pope (Rodrigo Borgia) 5, 8, 59, 61, 83, 87–90, 93–98, 107–8, 123–26, 132, 137, 180, 228
Alvarez, Leo Paul de 127
Anglo, Sydney 259
Antiochus III 212, 221
Antoninus Caracalla 193, 195–96
Aquinas, Thomas 129
Aristotle 46–47, 51, 54, 77, 129, 146, 151, 156, 162–64, 178, 202–3, 205, 218, 255
Art of War 13, 16, 130, 240
Athens 70, 80, 244
Atkinson, James B. 16
Augustine 122, 151

Bacon, Francis 248–49, 257
Baron, Hans 21, 100, 237–38, 251, 259
Benner, Erica xv, xviii, 39, 99–100, 127, 250, 259–60

Berlin, Isaiah 152, 202, 253, 259
Black, Robert 16, 21, 259–60
Bodin, Jean 44
Borgia, Cesare xiii, 7–8, 62, 74, 85–100, 103, 107–9, 115, 124–26, 130, 134, 137, 139–40, 142, 146–47, 167, 196, 226, 232, 249
Buondelmonti, Zanobi 13, 16, 34
Butterfield, Herbert 72, 259

Caesar, Julius 39, 69, 133, 145, 165–66, 173, 204
Carthage 70–71, 134, 168
Cassirer, Ernst 259
Chabod, Federico 237, 259
Charles V, Holy Roman Emperor 15
Charles VIII, King of France 4, 53, 59, 123, 131, 226
Chiron 178–79, 203, 227
Christianity 36, 54, 57–58, 78, 97, 99, 108–9, 122, 127, 153, 167, 182, 199–200, 203, 211–12, 223, 252–54, 256–57, 260
Cicero 39, 54, 129, 147, 178–179, 202–203

Clement VII, Pope (Giulio de' Medici) 13–14, 19
Colonna family 15, 90, 124–25
Commodus 193–95, 200–1
Connell, William J. xvii, 16, 21, 99, 106, 146, 218
Corsini, Marietta 8
Croce, Benedetto 202, 252, 259
Cromwell, Oliver 254
cruelty 71, 92, 105–10, 155–56, 167–76, 184–86, 191–96, 201–2, 211–12
Cyaxares 80
Cyrus 74–84, 105, 145–49, 151, 166, 174–76, 200, 207, 231, 233–34, 255

da Vinci, Leonardo 7
Dante (Alighieri, Dante) 3, 17, 36
Darius I 85
Darius III 63, 66–67
David 136, 140–42, 147, 153
Decennale 13
Diderot, Denis 249, 259
Dido 168–169
Dietz, Mary G. 204, 250, 259
Discourses on Livy xii–xiii, xvi–xvii, 2, 13, 16, 23, 25, 34–35, 39, 46–48, 56, 58, 69, 72, 79–84, 99, 102, 104, 111, 114, 119, 122, 126–27, 132, 137, 146–47, 171–75, 186–87, 199, 201–4, 218, 237–57, 259
Donaldson, Peter S. 260

evil 103, 108–9, 123, 153–54, 167, 181–82, 203, 215; Machiavelli as teacher of xi–xiii, 16, 154, 242, 253

Fabius Maximus 173–74
faith 62, 105, 108, 116, 155, 176–82, 184, 203, 207, 209, 212, 214–15, 218, 222
Ferdinand II, King of Aragon and Spain 59, 137, 164, 184, 211–12, 226
Ferrara, Dukes of 48–49
Flanagan, Thomas 237
Florentine Histories 14, 57, 72, 204, 218, 238, 240, 243, 249, 256

Forde, Steven 260
Forlì, Countess of (Caterina Sforza) xvii, 211
fortune (fortuna) xv, 32–35, 41, 43, 72–79, 84–88, 90–91, 94–98, 100–6, 111, 113, 117, 121, 124, 126, 130, 137, 141–42, 171, 181, 200, 204, 209, 219–37, 250, 257
France 4, 7, 9, 44–45, 53, 55–57, 59, 63, 65–68, 89–90, 94, 126, 131, 137, 141–42, 189–91, 202, 225–26
French Revolution 230, 242

Germany 9, 118, 225–26
Gilbert, Felix 39, 202
Gracchi (Tiberius and Gaius) 115
Gramsci, Antonio 256, 260
Guicciardini, Francesco 15

Hannibal 71, 147, 171–76, 221
Harrington, James 254
Herodian 204
Hiero II of Syracuse 47, 84, 99, 103, 114, 139–40
Hörnqvist, Mikael 72, 201, 238, 260

Inglese, Giorgio xvii

Julius II, Pope (Giuliano della Rovere) 8–9, 48–49, 53, 89, 95–97, 100, 124–25, 136–38, 164–165, 180, 228

Kahn, Victoria 259
Kohl, B.G. 39

Lefort, Claude 40, 72, 127, 184, 203, 260
Leo X, Pope (Giovanni de' Medici) 10, 14, 98, 125–126, 233
liberality 145–46, 155–56, 159, 162–66, 173, 185, 202
Liverotto the Fermano (or de Fermo) 107–8, 140
Louis XII, King of France 52–54, 59–63, 89, 127, 164, 202, 226

Lucretius 3

McCormick, John P. 260
Machiavelli, Bernardo 2
Machiavellian xi–xii, 60, 215, 256
Machiavellianism 249
Mandragola 13, 240
Mansfield, Harvey C. xvii, 72, 202, 260
Marcus Aurelius 191, 193–95, 198, 200–1, 204
Marlowe, Christopher xi–xii, 154, 242
Mattingly, Garrett 249, 259
Maximilian I, Holy Roman Emperor 8–9, 216–18
Maximinus 191, 193, 195–96, 200, 204
Medici, Giuliano de' 3, 12, 17–20, 241
Medici, Lorenzo de' (the Magnificent) 3–4, 218, 243
Medici, Lorenzo de' (the Younger) 14, 18–22, 26–39, 61, 72, 76, 86, 98, 126, 133, 150, 214–15, 219, 222, 232–33, 241–42
Medici, Piero de' 4
Meinecke, Friedrich 21, 258, 260
mercenary arms 7–8, 86, 89–90, 99, 130–36, 138–42, 146, 191, 207–8, 225–26, 255
mercy (*pietà*) 109, 146, 167, 173
Milan 42, 52–54, 86, 90, 134
mirror–of–princes genre 24, 39, 47, 129, 151, 202, 214
modes (*modi*) 40–43, 48, 69–73, 80–81, 101–6, 127, 174–75, 201, 210, 245, 247
Montesquieu, Charles–Louis de Secondat, baron de 98, 100, 249, 259
Morgenthau, Hans 258, 260
Moses 74–84, 97, 104, 122, 140, 146, 148, 207, 231–34, 255

Nabis the Spartan 114, 127, 144, 187
Najemy, John M. 99–100
Nederman, Cary J. 237

Nedham, Marchmont 254
Newell, Waller 99
Niso, Agostino 20

Orco, Remirro de 8, 92, 115, 167, 196
Orsini family 90, 124–25
Orwin, Clifford 202, 260

Parel, Anthony J. 237
Parrish, John M. 260
parsimony 162–166
Peace of Westphalia of 1648 44
Pertinax 193–95, 197, 200, 204
Petrarch, Francesco 3, 10, 24, 39, 229, 236–38
Philip II of Macedon 136, 142, 221
Philip V of Macedon 221–22
Pisa 7, 71–72, 129, 134–35, 138, 208
Pitkin, Hanna Fenichel 237
Plato 54, 129, 151–53, 178, 202
Plutarch 80, 145
Pocock, J.G.A. 260
Polybius 99, 145
Priest Luca (Luca Rinaldi, bishop of Trieste) 216–18
Prince (*principe*) 22–24, 42, 45, 49
Protestant Reformation 16, 44, 120
prudence 58, 61–62, 111, 141–42, 158, 161–162, 169, 205–18, 220, 223, 227–28, 230
Pyrrhus 68–69

Raab, Felix 259
Rahe, Paul A. 237, 260
republics xii–xii, xvi–xvii, 2–15, 25–26, 41–43, 46–48, 57–58, 67–69, 71–72, 102, 110–12, 133–34, 142, 151–52, 243–56
Romagna 7, 15, 59, 61–62, 89–92, 95–98, 109, 124, 137, 167, 196
Romulus 74–84, 99, 103, 146, 148, 202–3, 207, 231–32, 255

Rouen, Cardinal (Georges d'Amboise) 61–62, 96, 126
Rousseau, Jean-Jacques xii–xiii, 98–99, 100, 248–49, 259
Rucellai, Cosimo 13, 34

Saul 140–41
Savonarola, Girolamo 4–5, 80, 83, 99, 132, 140, 223
Scala, Bartolomeo 2
Scali, Giorgio 115
Scipio Africanus (Publius Cornelius Scipio Africanus) 145–47, 166, 171–76, 200, 203
Scott, John T. 99–100, 127, 203
Septimus Severus 193, 195–196, 198, 200–1, 204, 212, 227
Severus Alexander 193–95, 200
Sforza, Francesco 42–43, 53, 86, 134, 143
Sforza, Ludovico 52–53
Shakespeare, William 44
Skinner, Quentin 39, 251, 259–60
Soderini, Piero 9–10
Sparta 70, 114, 129, 134, 144, 187, 244
Stacey, Peter 39
Strauss, Leo 253
Sullivan, Vickie B. 72, 100, 127, 260

Tacitus 147
Tarcov, Nathan xvii, 39, 72, 97, 100, 127, 237
Temple of Delphi 30
Theseus 74–84, 146, 148, 207, 231, 233–34
Thucydides 153
Titus Quinctius Flamininus 221
Turks 56–57, 65, 138, 199, 222
tyrant, tyranny xii, 5, 47, 65, 84–85, 103, 114, 153, 202, 244–46, 249, 255

Vatter, Miguel xvi, 72, 127, 260
Vettori, Francesco 8, 10–12, 16–21, 23–24, 36, 39, 240, 248, 259
Viroli, Maurizio 99, 202, 237–38, 260
virtue; virtù 76, 105–6, 252; and fortune 76, 111, 219–38; and vice 106–7, 148–204
Vitelli, Paolo 134
Vivante, Corrado 16, 72, 259

Waltz, Kenneth N. 258, 260
Walzer, Michael 259
Warner, John M. 99, 203
Witt, R.G. 39
Wolin, Sheldon 202, 252–53, 259

Xenophon 80, 84, 145–47, 149, 151, 166, 174–76, 200, 203